Financial Data Science With Python

Financial Data Science With Python

An Integrated Approach to Analysis, Modeling, and Machine Learning

Haojun Chen

BEP

BUSINESS EXPERT PRESS

Leader in applied, concise business books

Financial Data Science With Python:
An Integrated Approach to Analysis, Modeling, and Machine Learning

First published in 2025 by
Business Expert Press, LLC
222 East 46th Street, New York, NY 10017
www.businessexpertpress.com

ISBN-13: 978-1-63742-825-2 (paperback)
ISBN-13: 978-1-63742-826-9 (e-book)

Business Expert Press Finance and Financial Management Collection

First edition: 2025

10 9 8 7 6 5 4 3 2 1

EU SAFETY REPRESENTATIVE
Mare Nostrum Group B.V.
Mauritskade 21D
1091 GC Amsterdam
The Netherlands
gpsr@mare-nostrum.co.uk

Description

In today's finance industry, data-driven decision making is essential. *Financial Data Science with Python: An Integrated Approach to Analysis, Modeling, and Machine Learning* **bridges the gap between traditional finance and modern data science, offering a comprehensive guide for students, analysts, and professionals.**

This book equips readers with the tools to analyze complex financial data, build predictive models, and apply machine learning techniques to real-world financial challenges.

Beginning with foundational Python concepts, the author covers essential topics such as data structures, object-oriented programming, and key libraries, including NumPy and Pandas. Grounded in quantitative principles, the book progresses into advanced areas, including financial statistics, simulation techniques, time series analysis, financial market forecasting, and machine learning methods for finance. Practical techniques such as regression, classification, and clustering are explored within a financial context, demonstrating their application through Python programming.

A key feature is the hands-on approach. Through real-world examples, projects, and exercises, readers will apply Python to tasks like risk assessment, market forecasting, and financial pattern recognition. All code examples are provided in Jupyter Notebooks, enhancing interactivity.

Whether you're a student building foundational skills, a financial analyst enhancing technical expertise, or a professional staying competitive in a data-driven industry, this book offers the knowledge and tools to succeed in financial data science.

Contents

Preface

Welcome to *Financial Data Science with Python: An Integrated Approach to Analysis, Modeling, and Machine Learning*. This textbook is designed for finance and business students with little background in Python and computer science, aiming to bridge the gap between current financial practices and data science applications.

In today's data-driven world, the ability to analyze large data sets and extract meaningful insights is essential for financial professionals. Python has emerged as a powerful tool in this domain, offering extensive libraries and frameworks tailored for data analysis, financial modeling, and machine learning. This book provides a comprehensive introduction to Python, starting from the basic Python programming and gradually advancing to more complex real-life applications. It aims to equip readers with a strong foundation in both Python programming and financial data science.

Throughout this book, we emphasize hands-on learning through practical examples and real-life projects. By working through these examples, readers will gain a deeper understanding of how to apply Python to solve common financial problems, perform data analysis, and build predictive models. Each chapter is designed to build on the previous ones, progressively introducing new concepts and techniques in a clear and structured manner.

Key Features of This Book

Comprehensive coverage: We cover a wide range of topics, from basic Python programming to advanced data science and machine learning techniques, ensuring that readers develop a well-rounded skill set.

Practical examples: Each chapter includes numerous examples and exercises that demonstrate how to apply the concepts discussed to real-world financial data.

Real-life projects: The advanced topics section includes project demon-
strations on market volatility modeling, financial time series analysis, machine learning approaches for price prediction, clustering
analysis on stocks, and high-dimensional data analysis.

Finance-focused: The book is specifically tailored to financial applications, making the skills and techniques learned directly applicable
to the finance industry.

Integrated data science techniques: The book incorporates a variety of
data science techniques, showing how they can be applied to solve
real-world finance problems. This integration helps readers understand the practical relevance and application of data science in the
finance sector.

Accessible code examples: All code examples are available online in
Jupyter Notebook format, allowing students to easily reproduce all
the programming projects on their own computers.

As the field of financial data science is constantly evolving, this book also
encourages continuous learning and exploration. We provide additional
resources and references for further reading, helping readers stay updated
with the latest developments and advancements in the field. Whether you
are looking to deepen your knowledge or expand your skill set, you will
find valuable guidance and insights throughout this book.

Dr. Haojun Chen

Guide for Readers

Code Reference

To enhance your learning experience, this book is accompanied by a Jupyter Notebook file containing all the code examples referenced in the text. Each code cell in the notebook is carefully linked to the corresponding section of the book, allowing you to practice and explore the code while following along with the explanations.

All Jupyter Notebook files essential for navigating the text can be accessed at: www.kaggle.com/work/collections/15295681 or pan.baidu.com/s/1AudNMCwyaTIVMq1Ts-RQAg?pwd=x5ij. These files contain the source code necessary for reinforcing key concepts and experimenting with hands-on examples.

Throughout the book, you will notice a symbol like this: à. This symbol is followed by a reference to a specific code cell in the Jupyter Notebook. Here's how to interpret it:

- Example reference: → C2NB 2.1.2b
  This indicates that the code for the discussed concept is located in the Jupyter Notebook for Chapter 2 (C2), under Section 2.1.2, and specifically in code cell "b."

Steps to use the Notebook

1. Locate the Notebook file:
   Download the Jupyter Notebook file corresponding to the book. Each chapter has its own notebook file, named to match the chapter (e.g., Chapter_2_Notebook.ipynb).
2. Navigate to the specified code cell:
3. Run and experiment with the code:
   Execute the code in the notebook cell to see how it works. Feel free to modify the code and experiment to deepen your understanding.
4. Relate the code to the text:

Structure of the Book

Chapters 1 to 4 of this book are designed for readers who are new to Python. If you are an experienced programmer, you may choose to skip these introductory chapters and move directly to the more advanced topics covered in later chapters.

End-of-Chapter Exercises

At the end of most chapters, you will find exercises designed to test and reinforce your understanding of the material. These exercises are suitable for both readers and instructors to facilitate learning and review. For instructors, solutions to the exercises are available upon request. If you are an instructor using this book in your course, feel free to contact us for access to the solution files.

External Python Packages

Some chapters in this book make use of external Python packages that may require installation in your Python environment. All such packages are listed in the appendix, along with references to their official documentation, ensuring that you have the resources needed to install and understand these tools.

CHAPTER 1

Introduction to Python Programming

1.1 Why Python for Finance?

Python has become the go-to language for financial data analysis due to its numerous advantages:

- Ease of learning and use: Python's straightforward syntax resembles plain English, making it accessible even to those who are new to programming. This simplicity allows users to focus on solving financial problems rather than getting bogged down by complex syntax (Downey 2015).
- Extensive libraries: Python offers a rich ecosystem of libraries such as NumPy, Pandas, and Matplotlib, specifically designed for data manipulation, analysis, and visualization. These libraries streamline complex financial calculations and data handling (McKinney 2018).
- Versatility: Beyond data analysis, Python can be used for web development, automation, machine learning, and more, making it a versatile tool in the finance industry (Grus 2019).
- Community support: Python has a large and active community. This means that plenty of resources, tutorials, and forums are available to help you overcome any challenges you might encounter.
- **CFA Institute and Python**: The CFA Institute, a global association of investment professionals, is known for its rigorous Chartered Financial Analyst (CFA) program, which sets the standard for financial expertise and ethics.

Recognizing the importance of Python in modern finance, the CFA Institute has incorporated Python into its learning modules. This inclusion underscores the growing relevance of Python skills for financial professionals. The CFA Python module covers various aspects of Python programming, data analysis, and financial modeling, providing a comprehensive introduction to this essential tool. By integrating Python into their curriculum, the CFA Institute ensures that finance professionals are equipped with the skills necessary to thrive in today's data-driven financial landscape.

1.1.1 Real-World Applications

Python's strengths in finance stem from its versatility, powerful libraries, and ease of integration with various financial tools and platforms. Let's dive deeper into these strengths and explore some real-world applications where Python shines in the finance industry:

- Data analysis and visualization: Python excels at handling large data sets and performing complex calculations. Libraries, such as Pandas and NumPy, allow for efficient data manipulation, while Matplotlib and Seaborn enable the creation of detailed and insightful visualizations. These tools help financial analysts to spot trends, identify patterns, and make data-driven decisions (Hunter 2007).
- Algorithmic trading: Python is widely used to develop, test, and implement trading strategies. The availability of backtesting libraries, such as Backtrader and Zipline, allows traders to test their strategies on historical data before deploying them in live markets. Python's ability to interface with trading platforms and APIs(Application Programming Interfaces) enables seamless execution of trades based on predefined algorithms (Jansen 2020).
- Risk management: Financial institutions use Python to build models that assess and manage risk. By leveraging machine learning libraries like scikit-learn and TensorFlow, Python

can help predict potential risks and mitigate them effectively. This is crucial for maintaining the stability and profitability of financial portfolios (Bengio et al. 2013).

- Automation of financial tasks: Python's simplicity and flexibility make it ideal for automating repetitive financial tasks. Whether it's data entry, report generation, or even more complex tasks like reconciling transactions, Python can handle it all. Automation not only saves time but also reduces the likelihood of human errors (Lutz 2013).
- Integration with financial systems: Python can easily integrate with other financial systems and databases. Using libraries such as SQLAlchemy for database operations or requests for interacting with web APIs, Python can pull in data from various sources, process it, and store or display it as needed (Yves 2019).

To illustrate Python's practical applications in finance, here are a few examples from the industry:

- Investment banks: Major investment banks use Python for quantitative research and analysis. They develop complex financial models to predict market trends, optimize portfolios, and assess risk. Python's robustness and scalability make it suitable for handling the vast amounts of data generated by financial markets (Hilpisch 2014; Hilpisch 2020).
- Hedge funds: Hedge funds employ Python to develop algorithmic trading strategies. By backtesting these strategies with historical data, they can refine their approaches to maximize returns. Python's integration with trading platforms allows for real-time execution of trades based on sophisticated algorithms (Chan 2013).
- Financial technology (FinTech) companies: FinTech startups use Python to build innovative financial products and services. From payment processing systems to robo-advisors, Python's versatility supports the rapid development and deployment of new technologies that disrupt traditional finance (Day et al. 2018).

- Insurance companies: Python is used in the insurance industry for risk assessment and fraud detection. Machine learning models developed in Python can analyze customer data to predict the likelihood of claims and identify potentially fraudulent activities (Maniraj et al. 2019).
- Corporate finance: Companies use Python for financial reporting, budgeting, and forecasting. Python's ability to handle complex calculations and generate detailed reports makes it invaluable for corporate finance departments (Lewis and Young 2019).

1.2 Setting up Your Python Environment

Before we dive into coding, it's essential to set up a Python environment. But what exactly is a Python environment, and why do you need one?

A Python environment is your digital workspace where you can write, run, and manage your Python code. Think of it as your coding toolbox where all your tools and resources are neatly organized. A well-configured Python environment ensures that your code runs smoothly and that you have access to the necessary libraries and tools for your projects.

Setting up your Python environment involves installing Python itself, as well as any additional tools or libraries you'll need. In this section, we'll guide you through the installation and environment setup process using the Anaconda Distribution. We recommend **Anaconda*** because it's free, open-source, and simplifies compatibility issues, making it ideal for beginners.

What Does It Mean to "Install Python"?

Installing Python on your computer means you are getting the Python interpreter. Python is an interpreted language, which means that Python code is executed line by line by the Python interpreter. The interpreter reads your Python scripts, interprets the commands, and executes them directly. This allows for quick testing and debugging of code. In contrast,

---

* **Anaconda Distribution:** www.anaconda.com/download/success.

languages like C or Java use compilers. The compiler checks for errors in the entire code before converting it into an executable file.

What Is a Python Version?

A Python version refers to a specific iteration of the Python programming language. Python evolves over time, with new versions introducing features, improvements, and sometimes changes that might not be compatible with older versions. Each version is identified by a unique number, such as Python 2.7, Python 3.6, Python 3.9, and, for this book, the latest version, Python 3.12.

Why Focus on Python 3.12?

In this book, we focus on Python 3.12 for several reasons:

- Latest features: Python 3.12 includes the newest features and improvements that make coding easier and more efficient. These updates often include performance enhancements and new libraries that are beneficial for financial data analysis.
- Community support: As the latest version, Python 3.12 has strong community support. This means you can easily find resources, tutorials, and help online.
- Security updates: Newer versions of Python receive security updates that protect your system and code from vulnerabilities.

What to Be Aware of When Using Other Versions

While this book is based on Python 3.12, you might encounter different versions in various environments. Here are a few things to keep in mind:

- Compatibility: Some libraries or features used in Python 3.12 may not be available in older versions. This can lead to compatibility issues when running code.

- Syntax differences: Python 2 and Python 3 have some syntax differences. For instance, print is a statement in Python 2 (print "Hello, World!") but a function in Python 3 (print ("Hello, World!")). Always ensure you are following the correct syntax for your version.
- **Updating:** If you are using an older version of Python, consider updating to the latest version to take full advantage of new features and improvements.

Step-by-Step Guide for Setting up Your Python Environment

a) Open Anaconda Navigator: Launch the Anaconda Navigator from your system's application list. Note: After your initial installation, Anaconda will create a root environment for you. Beginners are advised not to modify this environment before getting familiar with the applications.
b) Create a New Python Environment:
c) Click on "Environments" in the left-side menu, as indicated by red arrows in Figure 1.1.

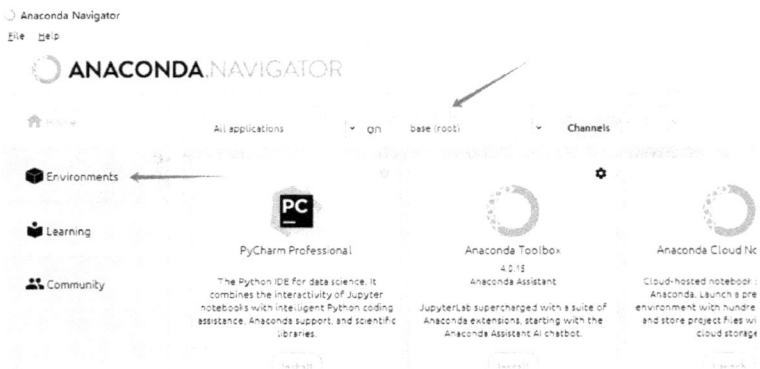

Figure 1.1 Screenshot of the Anaconda Navigator interface

d) Click "Create" at the bottom middle bar.
e) Enter a name for the environment and select Python 3.12.X from the dropdown menu, as shown in Figure 1.2.

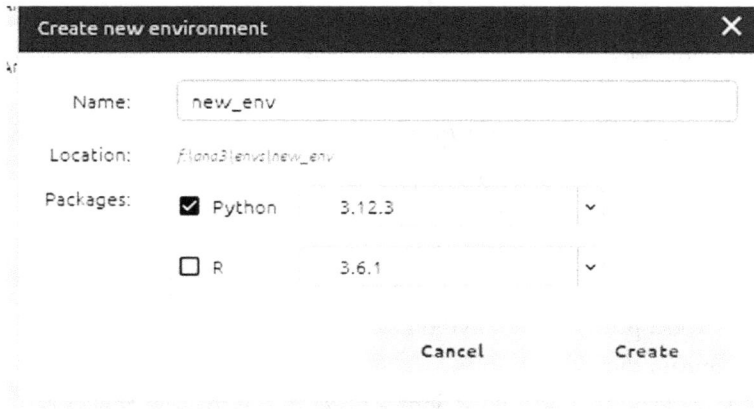

Figure 1.2 Screenshot of the Anaconda Navigator interface for creating new environment

    f) Click "Create" and wait for the computer to process your request. Once completed, you should see your new environment listed in the middle menu.

    g) Install Jupyter Notebook: Return to the Home menu, where the newly created environment should be available in the dropdown menu. Find Jupyter Notebook in the application list and click *Install*. Once the installation is complete, you should see the *Launch* button for Jupyter Notebook.

1.2.1 Using Jupyter Notebook as Your Python IDE

Integrated development environments (IDEs) are coding tools and software applications that provide comprehensive support for programmers. Jupyter Notebook is a dynamic, interactive platform that facilitates the writing and execution of Python code with ease.

Creating and Running Your First Jupyter Notebook

Step 1: Open a new notebook
- Launch Jupyter Notebook: Open Anaconda Navigator and launch Jupyter Notebook.
- Once Jupyter Notebook is open, you'll see the dashboard.

- Navigate to the directory where you want to create your notebook.
- Create a New Python 3 Notebook: Click on the *New* button on the right and select *Python 3* from the dropdown menu. This will create a new notebook.

Step 2: Write your first code

- Type your first Python code:
- In the first cell of your new notebook, type the following code: print ("Hello, Python for Financial Data Analysis!").

Step 3: Run the cell

- Execute the code: Press Shift + Enter to run the cell. You should see the output below the cell.

Different Types of Cells in Jupyter Notebook

a) Code cells

Purpose: Code cells are used to write and execute programming code. They support various programming languages, with Python being the most commonly used.

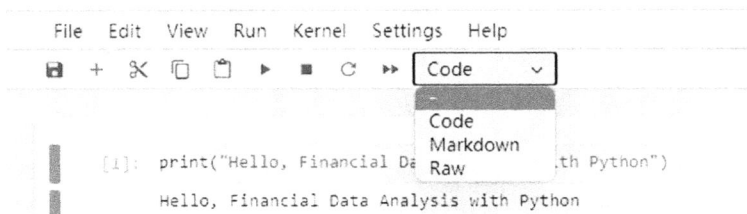

Figure 1.3 Screenshot of Jupyter Notebook interface for changing cell type

b) Markdown cells

Purpose: Markdown cells are used for writing rich text using Markdown and Latex, a lightweight markup language. These cells are ideal for adding narrative, explanations, instructions, and documentation to your notebook. The following is an example of writing a mathematical formula in a Markdown cell.

```
1  The Black-Scheles formula for call option using Latex:
2  $$C = S_0 N(d-1) - X e^(-rT) N(d_2) $$
```

Figure 1.4a Screenshot of markdown code for BS formula

The above Markdown cell will display as:

The Black-Scheles formula for call option using Latex:

$$C - S_0 N(d - 1) - Xe^{-rT} N(d_2)$$

Figure 1.4b Screenshot of markdown code output for displaying BS formula

c) Raw cells

Purpose: Raw cells allow you to include content that should not be processed by the notebook's renderer. This content is included as-is, and it is useful when you need to include code or text that you don't want Jupyter to interpret.

1.3 Basic Syntax and Commands

The basic syntax of Python is very simple. The language was designed to be a human-readable programming language. We will look at some basics as an appetizer.

- Variables and data type

```
1  age = 25   # integer
2  height = 5.9   # float
3  name = "John"   # string
4  is_student = True   # boolean
```

Figure 1.5 Jupyter Notebook screenshot for showing examples of variable and data type in Python

- Comments: Comments are text meant for human readers and are ignored by the Python interpreter.

```
1  # This is a single-line comment
2
3  # you can
4  # use the shortcut Ctrl + /
5  # to comment out multiple lines of code
```

Figure 1.6 Jupyter Notebook screenshot for showing examples of comments in Python

- Indentation: Indentation (tab space, indicated by red arrows) is a crucial aspect of Python syntax. It is used to define the scope of loops, functions, conditional statements, and other code blocks. In Python, indentation is not just for readability—it is a part of the syntax and must be used correctly for the code to run. In most cases, indentation is automatically handled by the IDE (e.g., Jupyter Notebook) for programmers.

```
1  r = 1.1
2  if r > 0:
3      print("positive return")
4  elif r < 0:
5      print("negative return")
6  else:
7      print ("no return")
positive return
```

Figure 1.7 Jupyter Notebook screenshot for showing examples of indentation in Python

- Operators: There are arithmetic, comparison, logical, and assignment operators in Python.

```
1  # Arithmetic operators
2  sum = 5 + 3
3  difference = 5 - 3
4  product = 5 * 3
5  quotient = 5 / 3
6
7  # Comparison operators
8  is_equal = (5 == 3)
9  is_greater = (5 > 3)
10
11 # Logical operators
12 is_true = (5 > 3) and (3 < 5)
13
14 # Assignment operators
15 x = 5
16 x += 3  # x is now 8
```

Figure 1.8 Jupyter Notebook screenshot for showing examples of arithmetic, comparison, logical, and assignment operators in Python

- Line continuation: The backslash (\) is used as a line continuation character. This allows you to break a long line of code into multiple lines for better readability.

```
1  # Without
2  answer = 1 + 2 + 3 + 4 + 5 + 6 + 7 + 8 + 9 + 10
3
4  # With line continuation
5  answer = 1 + 2 + 3 + 4 + 5 + 6 + \
6          7 + 8 + 9 + 10
```

Figure 1.9 Jupyter Notebook screenshot for showing line continuation in Python

Python Commands

A Python command is an instruction given to the Python interpreter to perform a specific task. Commands can include a variety of actions such as:

- Arithmetic commands: Perform basic mathematical operations.
- Comparison commands: Compare values and return a Boolean result.
- Example: 5 > 3 (greater than)
- Logical commands: Perform logical operations and return a Boolean result.
- Example: True and False (logical AND)
- Assignment commands: Assign values to variables.
- Example: x = 10 (assignment)
- Control flow commands: Control the flow of the program.
- Example: if, else, for, while
- Function calls: Execute functions to perform specific tasks.
- Example: print ("Hello, World!")
- Data structure manipulation: Commands to manipulate lists, dictionaries, sets, and tuples.
- Example: my_list.append(5)
- Import commands: Import modules or specific functions from modules.
- Example: import math or from math import sqrt
- Input/output commands: Handle user input and output.
- Example: input ("Enter your name: ")
- Exception handling: Handle errors and exceptions.

Don't worry if you are new to Python programming. We will learn more about the programming language by putting it into practical applications. Hopefully, by the end of this book, you will become an expert in both Python programming and financial data science!

Conclusion

In this chapter, we introduced the basics of Python programming and its significant role in financial data analysis. We discussed why Python is highly favored in finance due to its ease of learning, extensive libraries, and strong community support. We guided you through setting up your Python environment using Anaconda and demonstrated the use of Jupyter Notebook for coding. We also covered Python's basic syntax, including variables, data types, comments, indentation, and operators. Real-world applications of Python in finance were explored, such as data analysis, algorithmic trading, risk management, and automation. By the end of this chapter, you should have a solid foundation in Python programming, ready to tackle more advanced topics in financial data science.

CHAPTER 2

Python Programming Fundamentals

Python is known for its simplicity and readability (Lutz 2013), making it an excellent choice for beginners and experienced programmers alike. Compared to languages like C and Java, Python's syntax is more concise and easier to learn. For example, in Python, you don't need to declare the type of a variable explicitly (Downey 2015), and there are fewer lines of code to achieve the same functionality. This efficiency and ease of learning make Python an ideal language for financial data analysis (McKinney 2018), where the focus is often on solving problems quickly and effectively.

2.1 Data Types and Variables

2.1.1 Understanding Variables as Pointers in Python

In Python, data is stored in variables, but it's important to understand that a variable doesn't directly hold the data itself. Instead, a variable holds a reference to a data object. This means that when we say "data is stored in variables," we are really saying that the variable acts like a label or a name that points to the location in memory where the actual data object is kept. In essence, variables in Python serve as references to the data, not containers of the data itself.

2.1.2 Variable Creation

In Python, creating a variable is as simple as assigning a value to a name. Python will automatically determine the data type based on the value assigned. → C2NB 2.1.2a

We just created two variables, stock_name and stock_price, by assigning values to them. Now, we'll delete these variables using the del keyword. Once the variables are deleted, they are removed from the namespace (for now, think of it as a record of effective reference). If we try to access these deleted variables, a NameError will be raised. → C2NB 2.1.2b

2.2.1 Numbers, Strings, and Booleans

Numbers

Python supports different types of numbers, including integers (int), floating-point numbers (float), and complex numbers (complex). Each type serves a specific purpose and has unique characteristics, particularly regarding memory management.

- **Integer (int)**: int objects represent whole numbers. In Python 3, integers have arbitrary precision, meaning they can grow as large as the available memory allows, unlike the fixed-precision integers in languages like C. Python's memory management system automatically allocates more memory for larger integers as needed. Additionally, Python uses *integer caching* for small integers (typically between –5 and 256), allowing for quick reuse of these numbers.
- **Floating-point (float)**: float objects represent real numbers with fractional parts. Floats in Python are fixed-size objects, typically occupying 24 bytes on most systems (8 bytes for the value itself and 16 bytes for the object overhead). Memory allocation for floats is straightforward and does not vary based on the size of the number.
- **Complex (complex)**: complex objects represent complex numbers, consisting of real and imaginary parts. Each complex object in Python is also a fixed-size object, usually occupying 32 bytes (16 bytes for the two float values and 16 bytes for the object overhead).

Here are some examples: →C2NB 2.2.1a

Strings.   Strings are sequences of characters enclosed in single or double quotes. They are used to represent text data. In Python 3, strings (str type) are sequences of Unicode code points. This means you can use characters from any language (including Chinese characters) directly in your Python code. The internal representation of strings in Python 3 can vary (UTF-16 or UTF-32) based on the characters in the string and the platform. This is optimized for memory efficiency and performance. →C2NB 2.2.1b

In Python, both single quotes (') and double quotes (") can be used to create string literals. However, there are differences and specific use cases:

- Single quotes inside double-quoted strings: If your string contains a single quote (apostrophe), you can enclose the string in double quotes to avoid the need for escaping the single quote.
- Double quotes inside single-quoted strings: If your string contains double quotes, you can enclose the string in single quotes to avoid the need for escaping the double quotes, which is optimized for efficiency.
- Escaping quotes: If you need to use both single and double quotes within a string, you can escape the quotes using a backslash (\).
- Triple quotes for multiline strings: For multiline strings, Python uses triple quotes (either ''' or """). This is useful for long strings that span multiple lines, such as documentation strings (docstrings) or when you want to preserve the formatting of the text.

Here are some examples: →C2NB 2.2.1c

F-Strings: Formatted String Literals

F-strings (available since Python 3.6), also known as **formatted string literals,** provide a fast, concise, and readable way to format strings. They allow you to embed expressions inside string literals, using curly braces {} and evaluate them at runtime. Here are some examples: →C2NB 2.2.1d

Booleans.   Booleans represent one of two possible values: True or False. These values are commonly used in conditional statements to control the flow of a program. Boolean values can be combined using the logical operators and," "or," and "not" to perform more complex logical operations. →C2NB 2.2.1e

2.2.2 Type Conversion

Sometimes you need to convert data from one type to another. Python provides built-in functions for type conversion. →C2NB 2.2.2a

In the code example above, float(), int(), str(), and bool() are built-in functions used to convert inputs into specific data types. Built-in functions in Python are readily available and can be used without importing any additional modules. They are part of Python's standard library and offer a wide range of functionality. We will explore Python functions in more detail shortly.

Dynamically Typed Versus Statically Typed Languages

In Python, variables can be converted into different types because the language is dynamically typed. In dynamically typed languages, the type of a variable is checked during runtime, meaning you don't have to declare the type of a variable when you write your code. The interpreter assigns the type automatically based on the variable's value. Examples of dynamically typed languages include Python and JavaScript. In statically typed languages, the type of a variable is determined at compile-time, meaning you must declare the type of each variable before you use it. This allows the compiler to check for type errors before the program runs.

2.3 Control Structures: Conditionals and Loops

The default flow of execution in Python refers to the order in which statements are executed. Python executes code sequentially from the top of the script to the bottom, one line at a time. This linear execution continues unless altered by control structures (e.g., loops, conditionals) or function calls.

2.3.1 If Statements

The if statement allows conditional execution of a block of code. Following the initial if statement, elif statements can be added to check multiple conditions. Finally, the else statement provides a way to handle cases where none of the preceding conditions are met. Both the elif and else statements are optional.

→C2NB 2.3.1a

2.3.2 For and While Loops

For loop in Python is used to iterate over a sequence (such as a list, tuple, dictionary, set, or string) or other iterable objects. The for loop allows you to execute a block of code repeatedly for each item in the sequence.
→C2NB 2.3.2a; C2NB 2.3.2b; C2NB 2.3.2c

We will look into the list object and the range function in the next chapter. For now, it is sufficient to understand that range is a type of iterable object that can be used with the for statement to generate a loop.

While loops repeat as long as a condition is true. →C2NB 2.3.2d

Infinite Loops

An infinite loop occurs when a loop continues to execute indefinitely because the loop's terminating condition is never met or there is no terminating condition. This can happen in both while loops and for loops, though it is more common in while loops. Infinite loops can consume significant amounts of CPU and memory, potentially slowing down or crashing the system. Despite their potential downsides, infinite loops can be useful in certain scenarios where the loop's execution is intended to be controlled by external factors rather than a predefined condition.

2.4 Functions and Modules

In Python, a function is a reusable block of code designed to perform a specific task. Functions help organize code into manageable and logical sections, making it easier to read, maintain, and debug.

2.4.1 Defining and Calling Functions

In Python, functions are defined using the def keyword. The def keyword is followed by the function name, a set of parentheses containing any parameters, and a colon. The body of the function follows, indented (highlighted by the red rectangle below) to denote the code block that belongs to the function.

Python beginners should be aware that the indentation indicates the block of code that belongs to the function. Indentation is usually handled by the IDE (Integrated Development Environment) automatically, but occasionally it may require manual adjustment. Without proper indentation, the Python interpreter will not be able to determine which part of the code belongs to the function.

The example code cell below defines a function that prints a message to the user with a name specified as the input of the function. The code within the function is not executed until the function is called.

→C2NB 2.4.1a

Default Parameters in a Function

In Python, you can define functions with default parameters. Default parameters allow you to specify default values for one or more parameters when defining a function. If the caller does not provide a value for a parameter with a default value, the function uses the default value. Parameters with default values must be placed after parameters without default values in the function definition. →C2NB 2.4.1b

Function Scope

In Python, the concept of scope determines the visibility and lifetime of variables. The scope of a variable refers to the region of the program where the variable is defined and can be accessed. Variables defined inside a function have a different scope compared to those defined outside a function.

Types of Scope

Local scope: Variables defined inside a function are in the local scope.

These variables are only accessible within that function and are created when the function is called and destroyed when the function exits. →C2NB 2.4.1c

Global scope: Variables defined outside any function are in the global scope.

These variables are accessible throughout the entire program, inside and outside of functions.
→C2NB 2.4.1d

2.4.2 Importing and Using Modules

A module in Python is a file containing Python code, which can include variables, functions, classes, and runnable code. A package is a collection of modules. Modules help in organizing code by logically grouping related functionalities, making code easier to manage and reuse. There are two types of Python modules based on their sources.

- Standard library modules:
  Python comes with a large standard library of modules that provide functionalities for various tasks such as file (Input/Output), system calls, web programming, and more. These modules are available to programmers without additional installation.

- Third-party modules:
  You can also use third-party modules, which are packages developed by the Python community. A Python package is a collection of modules organized in directories. These modules and packages can be downloaded and installed into your Python environment through Anaconda or the built-in package manager pip. The following content will demonstrate the necessary steps.

Installing New Modules Through Anaconda

1. Open Anaconda Navigator
2. Click on "Environments" in the left-side menu

3. Select the Python environment to which the new modules will be installed

4. On the right-side menu click update index to renew the package list

5. Select or search for the Python packages on the right-side menu, as highlighted in Figure 2.1.

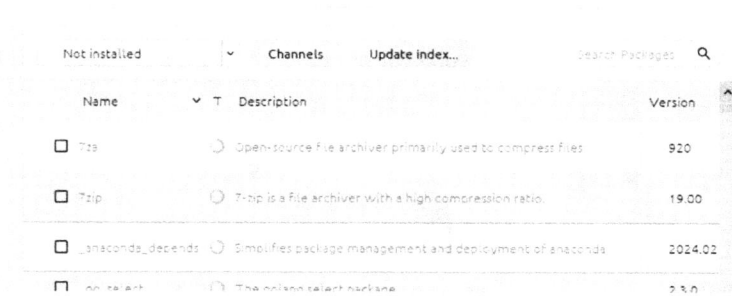

Figure 2.1 *Screenshot of Anaconda interface screenshot for installing new packages*

Installing New Modules Through pip

1. Select "Open Terminal" from your Python environment
2. To install a package, enter command: pip install package_name
3. To upgrade a package: pip install –upgrade package_name
4. To install a specific version of package:
5. pip install package_name==version (e.g., 2.2.1)
6. To uninstall a package: pip uninstall package_name

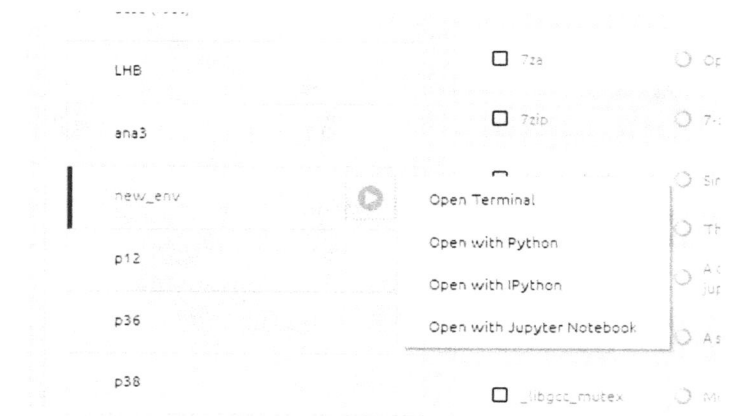

Figure 2.2 *Screen of Anaconda interface screenshot for accessing terminal*

Importing and Using Modules in Python

When you use the import statement, Python searches for the specified module in its module search path and loads it into memory. The module's code is executed once, and any top-level statements in the module are run. Python provides several ways to import modules:

- Import the entire module using the import statement. This method makes all functions, classes, and variables in the module available with the module's name as a prefix. All members of the module are accessed using the dot (.) notation. For example, math.sqrt.
- Use the "import module_name as alias" statement to the module with an alias. For example, import pandas as pd.
- Use the combination of from and import keywords: This method only imports a specific attribute from the module.
- Use from module_name import * statement to import all attributes from the module (not recommended).

The following code cell demonstrates all the modules importing commands →C2NB 2.4.2a

How Python Finds Modules

When you import a module, Python looks for it in the following sequence:

   a. Built-in Modules:
   b. First, Python checks if the module is a built-in module.
   c. sys.path Directories:
   d. Python then searches through the list of directories specified in sys.path. This list includes:
   e. The directory containing the input script (or the current directory if no script is specified).
   f. The list of directories specified in the PYTHONPATH environment variable (if set).
   g. Installation-dependent default directories (such as the site-packages directory).

2.5 Python Exceptions

When writing Python code, errors, or "exceptions," can occur due to unexpected or invalid operations, such as dividing by zero, trying to access an undefined variable, or attempting to open a file that doesn't exist. Exceptions can cause your program to crash if they aren't handled properly.

Common exceptions include:

- ZeroDivisionError: Trying to divide a number by zero.
- ValueError: Passing an invalid value to a function.
- TypeError: Using incompatible data types in an operation.
- FileNotFoundError: Attempting to open a file that doesn't exist.

2.5.1 Exception Handling With try and Except Blocks

To handle exceptions, Python provides the try and except blocks. When you wrap code inside a try block, Python will execute the code. If an exception occurs, it will jump to the corresponding except block to handle it instead of crashing the program. Here's the basic syntax:

```
try:
    # Code that may raise an exception
    risky_operation()
except ExceptionType:
    # Code that runs if an exception occurs
    handle_the_exception()
```

Here is an example for handling an exception caused by division by zero: →C2NB 2.5.1a

Conclusion

In this chapter, we explored essential Python programming concepts crucial for financial data analysis. We started by understanding fundamental data types such as numbers, strings, and booleans and learned how to manipulate them efficiently. We then delved into control structures, including conditionals and loops, which are vital for implementing logic and iterating over data sets. Finally, we covered functions and modules, essential for organizing code and leveraging external libraries in our analysis.

By mastering these fundamentals, you now possess the necessary tools to begin writing Python code for financial data analysis tasks. In the subsequent chapters, we will build upon these foundations to explore more advanced techniques and applications in Python.

Exercises

1. Data types and variables:
   a) Create variables of different data types (integer, float, string, and boolean) and print their values.
   b) Convert a string to an integer and a float to a string, and print the results.

2. Control structures:
   a) Write an if statement that prints different messages based on the value of a variable.
   b) Create a for loop that prints the numbers from 1 to 10.

3. Write a while loop that prints the numbers from 10 to 1.

4. Functions and modules:
   a) Define a function that takes two numbers as arguments and returns their sum. Call the function with different arguments and print the results.

5. Import the random module and use it to generate a random number between 1 and 100. Print the result.

CHAPTER 3

Data Structures in Python

Python provides a variety of data structures to help you organize and manage your data efficiently (Lutz 2013). In this chapter, we will explore three fundamental data structures: lists, tuples, and dictionaries. These structures allow you to store collections of data, making it easier to perform various operations and manipulations.

3.1 Lists

Lists are ordered, mutable collections of items. In Python, an ordered list refers to a collection of items where the order in which elements are added is preserved. This means that the first element added to the list remains the first element, the second element remains the second, and so on.

Mutable versus immutable objects: A mutable list refers to a list whose elements can be changed after the list has been created. This includes adding, removing, or modifying elements within the list. The term *mutable* means that the object can be altered in place, without creating a new object. Conversely, an immutable object means that the state of the object cannot be changed once it has been created.

3.1.1 Creating List Objects

In Python, you can create a new list using square brackets [ ], and elements within the list are separated by commas. Lists can contain elements of various data types, including integers, floats, strings, and even other lists and objects. →C3NB 3.1.1a

3.1.2 Accessing List Elements

You can access elements by their index. Python list indexing is zero-based, meaning the first element of the list is at index 0, the second element is at index 1, and so on. →C3NB 3.1.2a

Negative indices can be used to access elements from the end of the list. The last element is at index –1, the second-to-last at –2, and so on. →C3NB 3.1.2b

Python lists can be sliced using a range of indices. The slicing syntax is list[start:stop], where start is the index of the first element to include and stop is the index of the first element to exclude. Notice that the slicing operation returns a new list object. →C3NB 3.1.2c

If the start position is omitted, it defaults to 0. If the stop position is omitted, it defaults to the length of the list. →C3NB 3.1.2d

You can also specify a step in slicing, which determines the increment between each index for slicing. The syntax is list[start:stop:step]. →C3NB 3.1.2e

3.1.3 Altering List Elements

Lists are mutable, so you can change their elements.
→C3NB 3.1.3a

In the above example, dot notation is used to access the list object's embedded methods such as sort() and reverse(). Similar to user-created functions, each of these methods has its own parameters.

Adding Elements

You can add elements to the list using methods like append(), insert(), and extend().
→C3NB 3.1.3b

Removing Elements

You can remove elements using remove(), pop(), or del().
→C3NB 3.1.3c

Notice that in the above code examples, all the embedded methods alter the caller instead of producing a new list.

Python provides several built-in functions and methods to operate on lists. You should be familiar with the most commonly used ones demonstrated below. The official source provides a more comprehensive introduction: https://docs.python.org/3/library/stdtypes.html#sequence-types-list-tuple-range.

3.2 Tuples

Tuples are ordered, immutable collections of items. Once a tuple is created, its elements cannot be changed, added, or removed. This immutability makes tuples a reliable choice for storing data that should not be modified. Tuples are defined using parentheses () and can contain elements of different types, including other tuples.

3.2.1 Creating Tuple Objects

You can create a tuple by placing comma-separated values inside parentheses. →C3NB 3.2.1a

Using the Tuple() Constructor

You can also create a tuple using the tuple() constructor, which is useful for converting other iterable types (such as lists, strings, or sets) into tuples. →C3NB 3.2.1b

3.2.2 Accessing Tuple Elements

Indexing and Slicing

Accessing tuple elements through indexing and slicing operations are identical to those of lists.

→C3NB 3.2.2a

3.2.3 Altering Tuple Elements (Concatenation, Exclusion)

Since tuples are immutable, you cannot change, add, or remove elements directly. However, you can create new tuples by concatenation or exclusion. →C3NB 3.2.3a

Concatenation

You can concatenate two or more tuples to create a new tuple. →C3NB 3.2.3b

Exclusion

To exclude elements, you can create a new tuple by slicing and concatenating the parts you want to keep. →C3NB 3.2.3c

Using Tuples for Functions With Multiple Return Values

In Python, tuples are often used to return multiple values from a function. This feature allows a function to return more than one value in a single return statement, which can then be easily unpacked into multiple variables. This is a common and efficient way to handle multiple return values. →C3NB 3.2.3d

3.3 Dictionaries

Dictionaries are one of the most powerful and flexible data structures in Python. Imagine a dictionary as a real-world dictionary where you look up a word (key) to find its definition (value). In Python, dictionaries allow you to store and retrieve data using keys, which makes them incredibly efficient for certain types of lookups. A dictionary is essentially a collection of key-value pairs, where each key is unique and maps to a value.

3.3.1 Creating Dictionary Objects

Creating a dictionary in Python is simple and intuitive. You can create a dictionary by enclosing a comma-separated list of key-value pairs in curly braces { }. →C3NB 3.3.1a

In the above code cell, portfolio is a dictionary where the keys are stock ticker symbols and the values are the stock prices.

You can also create an empty dictionary and add key-value pairs later: →C3NB 3.3.1b

Python dictionary cannot have duplicate keys. Each key in a dictionary must be unique. If you try to create a dictionary with duplicate keys, the latter value for the duplicate key will overwrite the former value. →C3NB 3.3.1c

3.3.2 Accessing Dictionary Elements

Accessing elements in a dictionary is straightforward. You use the key to retrieve the corresponding value. This operation is both simple and fast, thanks to the way dictionaries are implemented in Python: →C3NB 3.3.2a

You can use built-in methods to get the collections of keys and values. →C3NB 3.3.2b

3.3.3 Altering Dictionary Elements (Modifying, Adding, Removing)

Dictionaries in Python are mutable, which means you can modify them after they are created. Here's how you can modify, add, and remove elements in a dictionary:

Modifying Elements

To modify an element in a dictionary, you simply assign a new value to an existing key: →C3NB 3.3.3a

The update() method takes either another dictionary or an iterable of key-value pairs (like a list of tuples) as an argument and merges it into the original dictionary. →C3NB 3.3.3b

Adding Elements

Adding a new element to a dictionary is as easy as assigning a value to a new key: →C3NB 3.3.3c

Removing Elements

You can remove elements from a dictionary using the del statement or the pop() method: →C3NB 3.3.3d

The popitem() method removes and returns the last key-value pair added to the dictionary. This method is useful for implementing LIFO (last in, first out) order removal: →C3NB 3.3.3e

The clear() method removes all elements from the dictionary, leaving it empty: →C3NB 3.3.3f

Memory Management in Python.   Python uses automatic memory management and garbage collection to handle memory allocation and deallocation. When you call the clear() method on a dictionary, it removes references to the key-value pairs stored in the dictionary. Once there are no more references to these objects, Python's garbage collector will eventually reclaim the memory (Python Software Foundation 2023), freeing it up for other uses. However, if there are other references to the objects stored in the dictionary elsewhere in your program, those objects will not be immediately deallocated, as Python's garbage collector only collects objects that are no longer referenced by any part of the program.

3.4 Sets

Sets are an essential data structure in Python that allow you to store unique elements in an unordered collection. Think of a set as a collection of distinct items, like a bag of marbles where duplicates are not allowed. Sets are useful for membership testing and eliminating duplicate entries, making them a powerful tool for data manipulation.

3.4.1 Creating Set Objects

Creating a set in Python is straightforward. You can create a set by enclosing a comma-separated list of elements in curly braces { } or by using the set() constructor. →C3NB 3.4.1a

Note that a set cannot contain duplicate elements. If you attempt to create a set with duplicates, only unique elements will be stored. →C3NB 3.4.1b

3.4.2 Accessing Set Elements

While you can't access elements in a set by index (since they are unordered), you can check for the presence of an element using the in keyword: → C3NB 3.4.2a

You can also iterate over the elements of a set using a loop: →C3NB 3.4.2b

3.4.3 Altering Set Elements (Modifying, Adding, Removing)

Sets in Python are mutable, allowing you to modify them after creation. Here's how you can modify, add, and remove elements:

Modifying Elements

To modify a set, you generally add or remove elements since you cannot change an element in place. You can add and remove an element to a set using the add(), remove(), discard(), and pop() methods:

→C3NB 3.4.3a

Notice that the remove() method raises an error if the element is not found while the discard() method does not raise an error.

The pop() method removes and returns an arbitrary element from the set: →C3NB 3.4.3b

The clear() methods are also available among sets: →C3NB 3.4.3c

3.4.4 Set Operations

Sets support several operations that allow you to combine and compare collections of unique elements. Two of the most common operations are union and difference.

Union

The union of two sets combines all unique elements from both sets. In Python, you can perform a union using the union() method or the | operator. →C3NB 3.4.4a

Difference (- Operator)

The difference operation allows you to find elements that are in one set but not in another. In Python, you can use the difference () method or the - operator to achieve this. →C3NB 3.4.4b

Intersection

You can find common elements between two sets using the intersection() method or the & operator.
     →C3NB 3.4.4c

Symmetric Difference

This operation gives you elements that are in either set but not in both, which can be achieved using the symmetric_difference() method or the ^ operator. →C3NB 3.4.4d

3.5 Built-in Methods for Iterables

In Python, an iterable is an object capable of returning its members one at a time, allowing it to be looped over in a for loop. In this chapter, we have covered the three most important iterables in Python.

Python provides several built-in methods that can be applied to iterable or list-like objects. Here are some common ones:

- len(): Returns the number of items in an iterable.
- sum(): Returns the sum of all elements in an iterable.
- max(): Returns the largest item in an iterable.
- min(): Returns the smallest item in an iterable.
- sorted(): Returns a new sorted list from the elements of any iterable.
- map(): Applies a function to all items in an iterable and returns a map object.
- filter(): Constructs an iterator from elements of an iterable for which a function returns true.

- zip(): Aggregates elements from two o or more iterables (lists, tuples, etc.).

Here are some code examples: →C3NB 3.5a

TypeError

Applying certain methods to an iterable can raise exceptions depending on the data type of its elements. For instance, using the sum() method on a list containing string elements will indeed raise a TypeError because strings cannot be summed in the same way numerical values can. It's important to handle such exceptions appropriately or ensure that the data passed to these methods is of the expected type to avoid errors during program execution. →C3NB 3.5b

Conclusion

In this chapter, we explored fundamental data structures in Python—lists, tuples, and dictionaries. We learned how lists provide mutable collections, tuples offer immutable sequences, and dictionaries facilitate efficient key-value pair storage. Understanding these structures equips us with powerful tools for organizing and manipulating data in financial analysis and beyond.

Exercises

1. Task: Create a list of stock prices called stock_prices containing the following values: 150.75, 298.20, 2728.80, and 3450.00. Then, print the list.
2. Task: Using the stock_prices list from Task 1, access and print the third element. Then, change the second element to 300.00 and print the modified list.
3. Task: Create a tuple called company_names containing the following values: 'Apple,' 'Microsoft,' 'Google,' and 'Amazon.' Print the first and last elements of the tuple.

4. Task: Create another tuple called more_companies containing the values 'Facebook' and 'Tesla.' Concatenate company_names and more_companies to form a new tuple called all_companies. Then, create a new tuple some_companies that excludes 'Google' and print it.

5. Task: Create a dictionary called stock_prices_dict with the company names as keys and their corresponding stock prices as values. Access and print the stock price of 'Google.'

6. Task: Using the stock_prices_dict from Exercise 5, update the stock price of 'Apple' to 155.00 and add a new entry for 'Tesla' with a stock price of 625.00. Then, remove 'Amazon' from the dictionary and print the modified dictionary.

CHAPTER 4

Objects and Classes in Python

4.1 Introduction to OOP

Python is an object-oriented programming (OOP) language, which means that it is designed to support and encourage the use of OOP principles. OOP is a programming paradigm that uses objects and classes to structure and organize code in a way that models real-world entities and their interactions.

4.1.1 The Basic Structure of OOP

Classes and Objects

- Class: The blueprint for creating objects. It defines a set of attributes (data) and methods (functions) that the created objects will have.
- Object: An instance of a class. When you create an object from a class, you are essentially creating a specific example of that class with its own set of data (attributes).

4.1.2 The Basic Principle of OOP

- Encapsulation: Bundling the data (attributes) and methods (functions) that operate on the data into a single unit, that is, a class. It also involves restricting access to certain components to protect the internal state of an object.

- Inheritance: It allows a class (subclass) to inherit attributes and methods from another class (superclass). This promotes code reusability and the creation of a class hierarchy.
- Polymorphism: It allows different classes to be treated as instances of the same class through a common interface. It enables the same operation to behave differently in different classes.

We will see how Python fully supports the OOP structures and principles in a mini project where we develop a class for modeling investment asset. →C4NB 4.1.2a

In the above code block, a class named "Asset" has been created. Notice that the order of indentation is crucial here. The largest rectangle highlights the indentation covering the scope of the class, and the two smaller rectangles cover the scope of the two class methods. The basic syntax for creating a class in Python is simple:

- Arrow 1: This line defines a new class called Asset. The class name should be capitalized by convention.
- Arrow 2: The __init__ method is a special method in Python that initializes a new instance of the class. It is called a constructor.
- Arrow 3: Additional parameters can be added in the parameter list. Here, the value of the additional parameter (name) is passed to become an attribute for the class's instance (self).
- Arrow 4: This defines a class method get_value. The method has the self parameter as the basic input. The method returns the value of the instance's attribute referred as *self.__value* to the caller.

The Self Parameter

In Python, self is a conventionally used parameter name in instance methods of a class. It refers to the instance of the class itself. When defining a class, self is explicitly passed as the first parameter to all instance methods, including the __init__ method (the constructor). Inside the class, self helps differentiate between local variables (within a method) and instance variables (belonging to the class instance). Without self, Python would treat variables as local to the method scope. In the __init__ method, self refers to the newly created instance of the class. It is used to initialize instance variables when the object is instantiated. When calling a method on an instance (e.g., obj.method()), Python automatically passes the instance (obj) as the first argument (self) to the method.

4.2 Class Instances

Once the class is defined, you can create instances (objects) of the class by using the name of as the constructor: →C4NB 4.2a

Public Attributes

In the above code example, the attribute name is directly accessible using dot notation. In Python, attributes (variables) are public by default. This means they can be accessed and modified directly from outside the class using dot notation. Public attributes are suitable for data that you are comfortable exposing and allowing to be modified directly by the user.

However, in some cases, users should not be allowed to modify certain attributes. For example, the market value of an asset should not be changed by traders, as it should be determined by the recent transaction data.

Private Attributes

Private attributes are intended to be accessed only within the class itself. In Python, you can define a private attribute by prefixing its name with double underscores (__). This triggers name mangling, which changes the attribute name in a way that makes it harder (but not impossible) to access from outside the class. Private attributes are useful for encapsulating internal data that you do not want to expose directly.

The code cell example below demonstrates a new version of the Asset class where users can read the value attribute through the get_value()

method (see the read circled output) but cannot access it directly using the dot notation. →C4NB 4.2b

4.3 Class Inheritance

Inheritance is a fundamental concept in OOP that allows a class (called a subclass or derived class) to inherit attributes and methods from another class (called a superclass or base class). This promotes code reuse and establishes a natural hierarchy between classes. Using the Asset class as an example, a subclass describing a particular asset such as a stock or bond represents a plausible natural extension.

Basic Syntax of Inheritance

To create a subclass in Python, you simply define a new class and specify the base class in parentheses:

```
class BaseClass:
    <Base class definition>
class SubClass(BaseClass):
    <Subclass definition>
```

→C4NB 4.3a

In the above code example (C4NB 4.3a), two subclasses, Stock and Bond, are declared as inheriting from the Asset class. The super() function in Python is a built-in function used to call a method from the parent class. In most cases, you will use super() without any arguments in modern Python code, which implicitly refers to the immediate parent class and the current instance. In the above example, super().__init__(name) calls the constructor of the base class and passes the parameter name. As a result, the for value for the attribute name is assigned.

Polymorphism in Action

Polymorphism is a fundamental concept in OOP that allows objects of different classes to be treated as objects of a common superclass. This is particularly useful when you want to write generic code that can work with objects of various types, provided they share a common interface or superclass.

With polymorphism, we can write code that works with instances of the Asset class and its subclasses (Stock and Bond) interchangeably. This allows us to call the get_value() method on any object that is an instance of Asset, regardless of whether it is a Stock or a Bond.

4.4 Examining Built-in Classes

Python provides many built-in classes such as int, str, list, and dict. Each of these classes comes with its own set of attributes and methods that define their behavior. Understanding the interfaces provided by these built-in classes is crucial for effective programming.

Using Built-in Functions to Examine Classes

The following built-in functions are commonly used to examine the properties and methods of a class:

- type(): Returns the type of an object.
- dir(): Lists the attributes and methods of an object.
- help(): Provides detailed information about an object, including its methods and attributes →C4NB 4.4a

4.5 Examining External Classes

Classes can be imported from external modules and packages. Once a class is imported, you can create an instance of the imported class in the current programming session. The three built-in functions—type(), dir(), and help()—for getting a quick look at a class can also be used on the imported class. In the example code below, an external class named array is imported from the NumPy package. →C4NB 4.5a

Conclusion

This chapter has introduced you to the essential concepts of OOP in Python, focusing on classes and objects. You've learned how classes serve as blueprints for creating objects, encapsulating data and behavior. Through examples, we explored class instantiation, attribute management with encapsulation, and the use of inheritance for code reuse and specialization.

Moving Forward

The knowledge gained here provides a solid foundation for advancing through the rest of this textbook. While we've covered fundamental topics, there are more advanced aspects of Python classes that we haven't explored due to scope limitations. For those looking to enhance their Python programming skills, consider studying:

1. Special methods (magic methods): Customize object behavior using methods like __str__ and __repr__ (Downey 2015).
2. Property decorators: Control attribute access with @property, @<attribute_name>.setter, and @<attribute_name>.deleter (Martelli et al. 2017).
3. Method Resolution Order (MRO): Understand how Python resolves method calls in complex class hierarchies (e.g., Python Software Foundation n.d.).
4. Abstract Base Classes (ABCs): Define interfaces and enforce method implementations using the abc module (Ramalho 2015).
5. Class variables versus instance variables: Learn about shared class variables and instance-specific variables (Grus 2019).

Mastering these advanced topics will further strengthen your Python programming skills and prepare you for more complex programming challenges.

Exercises

1. Stock portfolio management
   a) Create a class Stock with attributes symbol, price, and quantity.
   b) Implement methods to calculate the total value of the stock (price * quantity) and update the price of a stock.

c) Create instances of Stock representing different stocks in a portfolio. Calculate and print the total value of the portfolio.

2. Annuity calculation

Part 1: Define the Base Class

a) Define a base class SimpleAnnuity with attributes, principal: Initial principal amount, annual_payment: Fixed annual payment amount, years: Number of years over which payments are made.

b) Implement a method calculate_present_value() in SimpleAnnuity, the method should take discount_rate as a parameter for calculating the present value (PV) of the annuity, which equals the sum of the PV of all future payments.

Part 2: Create a Subclass

a) Create a subclass IncreasingAnnuity that inherits from SimpleAnnuity.

b) Add an attribute increase_rate to represent the annual increase percentage in payments.

c) Override the calculate_present_value() method in IncreasingAnnuity to compute the PV of the increasing annuity.

Part 3: Test your Code

a) Calculate the PV of an increasing annuity with an initial payment of $100, increasing by 10 percent annually over the next 10 years. The discount rate is assumed to be fixed at 5 percent.

CHAPTER 5

NumPy for Financial Computation

5.1 Introduction to NumPy

NumPy, or Numerical Python, is essential for financial computations due to its efficiency in handling large data sets and performing complex operations. NumPy needs to be installed separately using package managers (see Appendix).

Checking the Version of NumPy →C5NB 5.1a

Introduction to Array

An array is a data structure that stores elements of the same data type (homogeneous) in a contiguous block of memory. NumPy arrays are homogeneous, efficient containers for numerical data. They support vectorized operations, crucial for financial calculations.

Comparing NumPy Arrays With Lists

There are some similarities between NumPy arrays and lists in terms of accessing elements, but they are fundamentally different Python objects. Generally speaking, NumPy arrays are specialized data structures optimized for numerical computations, while lists are general-purpose containers that provide flexibility with heterogeneous data types and dynamic resizing capabilities. The choice between arrays and lists depends on the specific requirements of the application, particularly regarding performance and the nature of data manipulation needed.

5.2 Creating and Manipulating Arrays

Creating Arrays

NumPy array can be created by passing a list object to the NumPy's array function as shown in the code cell below. →C5NB 5.2a

Explanation: In this code cell, three homogeneous arrays with increasing dimensions from 1 to 3 are created using NumPy. In NumPy, multidimensional arrays can be represented as nested arrays. For example, a two-dimensional array is constructed by nesting two one-dimensional arrays. The shape of a NumPy array is determined by counting the number of elements in each dimension, starting from the outermost level. For instance, array2 has a shape of (2, 3) and array3 has a shape of (3, 3, 2). It's important to note that heterogeneous arrays can also be created, but they should not be used for computational purposes.

Reshaping Arrays

NumPy arrays can be reshaped by using the reshape method →C5NB 5.2b

Explanation: Reshaping a NumPy array is akin to rearranging bricks; you need to consider both the total number of elements and the structure of your new arrangement. For instance, array1 can be reshaped into a two-dimensional array with a single row or column, depending on how you want to structure it.

Accessing Elements and Slicing

Unlike lists, arrays allow for accessing elements through indexing and slicing across multiple dimensions. As always, the order of the index is from outer to inner of the nested arrays. For a two-dimensional array, this means (row_index, columns_index). →C5NB 5.2c

5.3 Mathematical Operations With NumPy

NumPy provides optimized functions for mathematical operations, essential for financial computations.

5.3.1 Basic Arithmetic Operations

Vectorized Operations

NumPy arrays support vectorization, which allows mathematical operations to be applied element-wise without the need for explicit looping. This means that operations like addition, subtraction, multiplication, and division can be performed directly on entire arrays, rather than on individual elements one at a time. This leads to significant performance improvements compared to traditional Python lists. →C5NB 5.3.1a

Broadcasting

NumPy arrays also support broadcasting, which is a powerful mechanism that allows arrays of different shapes to be combined in arithmetic operations. When operating on arrays with different shapes, NumPy "broadcasts" the arrays to make their shapes compatible. For example, you can add a scalar (single value) to an entire array, and NumPy will automatically extend the scalar to match the shape of the array. →C5NB 5.3.1b

Aggregation Functions

NumPy arrays support aggregation operations, such as np.sum(), np.mean(), np.min(), np.max(), and np.std(), which allow you to compute summary statistics across array elements. These functions are optimized for performance and can handle large data sets efficiently. →C5NB 5.3.1c

Example: Calculating Weighted Returns

The code cell below demonstrates how to use NumPy array to calculate weighted returns. →C5NB 5.3.1d

5.4 Using NumPy for Financial Calculations

NumPy facilitates various financial calculations, from basic metrics to complex financial modeling. Here, we demonstrate some of the commonly used financial computing functionality provided by numpy-financial.*

---

* All the financial functions in NumPy are deprecated and moved to a new package called numpy-financial.

5.4.1 Financial Functions in NumPy

Net Present Value (NPV)

The net present value (NPV) function evaluates the present value (pv) of a series of cash flows, considering a specified discount rate. It helps determine the profitability of an investment or project by accounting for the time value of money. The formula for NPV is as follows:

$$NPV = \sum_{t=1}^{n} \frac{C_t}{(1+d)^t}$$

where C_t = investment income at time t, d = discount rate, n = total periods.

A positive NPV indicates that the projected earnings (or savings) exceed the anticipated costs, making the investment potentially profitable. The code cell below calculates the NPV of a bond that pays 10 USD annually for the next five years and returns a principal of 100 USD at the end of the period when the discount rate is 5 percent. →C5NB 5.4.1a

Explanation: The npv function from NPF requires discount_rate and cashflows as inputs for the calculation. The value at index position 0 represents the initial cash outflow, typically denoting the acquisition cost or initial investment. Regarding the bond example, positive NPV indicates that the investment is expected to generate value and is considered financially attractive under the given assumptions and discount rate.

Calculate IRR

The internal rate of return (IRR) is another financial metric used to evaluate the profitability of an investment. It represents the discount rate that makes the NPV of all future incomes equal to the current acquisition price of an investment. In simpler terms, IRR is the discount rate d such that $\sum_{t=1}^{n} \frac{C_t}{(1+d)^t} = p_0$, where p_0 is the current acquisition cost of the investment.

NumPy provides a convenient function for computing the IRR. →C5NB 5.4.1b

Explanation: The IRR function from NPF takes cash flows as its input. When the calculated IRR exceeds the discount rate used for comparison, it indicates that the investment opportunity potentially adds value.

Future Value (FV)

The FV of an investment at a future date represents the end-period interest-compounded value of the investment. It is calculated based on periodic, constant payments and a fixed interest rate. This metric is invaluable for forecasting investment growth and setting savings goals. The code cell demonstrates the calculation of FV for retirement funds that require a monthly payment of 1,000 USD for 20 years (with a fixed interest rate of 5%). →C5NB 5.4.1c

Explanation: Notice that for this example, periods are counted monthly, so the annual interest rate needs to be divided by 12. The fv function of numpy_financial(npf) requires inputs such as the period interest rate, total number of periods, monthly payment (pmt), and the present value of the investment. By default, payments are assumed to be made at the beginning of each period, hence pv is set as negative (e.g., –1,000). If payments are made at the end of each period, specify an additional argument when = 'end' in the fv function. It's important to note that pmt is negative because it represents cash outflows from the perspective of the account holder.

Payment (PMT)

The Payment function calculates the periodic payment required, given a fixed interest rate, to fully amortize a loan or periodic deposit required to achieve a future account balance given the initial deposit. It helps in budgeting and financial planning by determining regular payments. The code cell below calculates: (1) the monthly mortgage payment for a 1 million USD loan to be paid off in 20 years and (2) the monthly savings required to retire with 1 million USD in 30 years. In both questions, the interest rate or investment return is fixed at 5 percent. →C5NB 5.4.1d

Explanation: The pmt function requires three main inputs: rate, nper, and pv. The rate represents the annual interest rate, nper denotes the total number of periods, and pv stands for *present value*, which is the initial principal amount of the investment or loan. Additionally, there are two optional inputs: fv and when (specifying whether payments are made at the beginning or end of each period). By default, fv is set to 0 and when to 'end.' The signs of the inputs (pv, fv, and pmt) indicate cash inflows (positive) or outflows (negative) respectively.

Conclusion

In this chapter, we have explored the fundamental capabilities of NumPy for financial computations. NumPy's efficiency in handling large data sets and performing complex mathematical operations makes it indispensable for financial analysis. We began with an introduction to NumPy, highlighting its installation process and the importance of checking its version. Understanding NumPy arrays, their homogeneous nature, and their efficiency in mathematical operations distinguishes them from Python lists. We explored creating, reshaping, and accessing elements in arrays, emphasizing their role in financial modeling and analysis.

Mathematical operations in NumPy, including basic arithmetic, vectorized operations, broadcasting, and aggregation functions, were discussed with practical examples. The chapter also introduced financial functions in NumPy, such as NPV, IRR, FV, and PMT, illustrating their application in evaluating investments, forecasting returns, and financial planning.

Exercises

The following questions are based on simulated financial data generated in the accompanying workbook (FDSP_Chapter5_Notebook.ipynb).

1. Portfolio analysis using stock prices data
    a) Calculate the mean daily return for each stock.
    b) Compute the daily return volatility (standard deviation) for each stock.
    c) Identify the stock with the highest and lowest volatility.
2. Net present value (NPV) calculation

a) Compute the NPV of the cash flows provided (cash_flows) using a discount rate of 5 percent.

b) Interpret the result in terms of project profitability.

3. Internal rate of return (IRR) calculation

a) Calculate the IRR for the investment scenario (cash_flows_irr) provided.

b) Discuss the implications of a positive IRR value.

4. Future value (FV) calculation

a) Determine the FV of monthly contributions (monthly_contributions) made over 20 years with an annual interest rate of 5 percent.

b) Discuss how this calculation can be useful in financial planning.

5. Mortgage payment calculation

a) Calculate the monthly mortgage payment required to fully amortize a loan amount of 500,000 USD over 30 years with an annual interest rate of 4 percent.

b) Discuss the impact of adjusting the interest rate or loan duration on monthly payments.

CHAPTER 6

Financial Data Processing With Pandas

6.1 Introduction to Pandas

Pandas[*] is a powerful Python library for data manipulation and analysis, particularly well-suited for handling structured data such as financial dat sets. It offers two primary data structures: Series (a one-dimensional labeled array) and DataFrame (a two-dimensional labeled data structure with columns of potentially different types). Pandas is actively developed, with updates often introducing significant changes to methods covered in this chapter. We will focus on the essential functionalities for processing financial data, crucial for exploring the financial analytics topics covered in the rest of this textbook. The first step is to ensure that Pandas is properly installed and imported into your workbook. →C6NB 6.1a

6.2 Introduction to Series

A series in Pandas is a one-dimensional array-like object that can hold various data types (heterogenous) such as integers, floats, and strings. It consists of a sequence of index values and an associated array of data.

Series Structure Diagram:

```
Index    ::    Values
  0      |     value0
  1      |     value1
  2      |     value2
```

The Roles of Indexes of Pandas Data Object

- **Labeling and identification:** Indexes provide labels or positions that uniquely identify each element (or row in the case of DataFrames) in the Series or DataFrame.

---

[*] See appendix for instruction of installing Pandas to your Python environment.

- **Fast access:** They facilitate rapid data retrieval via label-based indexing (loc) or position-based indexing (iloc).
- **Alignment:** Indexes ensure seamless data alignment during operations involving different Series or between Series and DataFrames.
- **Immutable nature:** Indexes are typically immutable, meaning they cannot be altered once assigned to a Series or DataFrame.
- **Diverse types:** Indexes can encompass various types (integer, string, datetime, etc.) depending on the associated data.

The key in understanding the data structure of Pandas Series hinges on grasping its index, which denotes the position or label of each value in the series. While indexes in Pandas efficiently organize and access data, they differ from pointers in traditional programming terms. Instead, they serve as labels and metadata that enhance data manipulation capabilities within Pandas.

6.2.1 Creating and Accessing Pandas Series

There are three important parameters for the constructor of a Pandas Series: data, index, and dtype. The following code cells demonstrate different ways of creating a Series object.

Creating a Series from a List or Array → C6NB 6.2.1a

Notice that when a list or list-like object is passed to the constructor without specifying an index, Pandas will use the default integer index starting from 0 (highlighted in rectangle). Pandas data objects also have a dtype attribute (highlighted in oval), which stands for datatype. Here, the dtype is set to float by Pandas based on the homogeneous data.

Specifying the Index and Data Type

You can also specify your own custom index when creating a Series. This is useful when the data has meaningful labels associated with each value. → C6NB 6.2.1b

Note that specifications for the index and dtype are passed to the constructor. The index of a Pandas Series object can be accessed as an attribute using dot notation.

6.2.2 Data Type Specification in Pandas

The dtype specification helps Pandas to manage memory more efficiently and perform operations accurately based on the expected data type.

- **Automatic inference:** By default, when you create a Pandas object (Series or DataFrame) without explicitly specifying a dtype, Pandas will infer the data type based on the input data.
- **Explicit specification:** Using dtype Parameter, you can explicitly specify the data type when creating a Pandas object. This is particularly useful when you want to ensure consistency or optimize memory usage.

Common Data Types in Pandas

- **Numeric data types:** int64, float64, int32, float32, and so on. specify integer and floating-point numbers with different levels of precision.
- **DateTime data types:** datetime64 and timedelta64 handle dates and times with various resolutions.
- **Categorical data types:** This optimizes storage and enables efficient operations on categorical data with a fixed set of possible values.
- **Object data types:** This accommodates mixed data types or strings when the data cannot be easily categorized.

6.2.3 Accessing Series

Each data point in a Series object is referenced by an index label. We will focus on the most efficient ways of accessing these data points.

Using Label/Index

Elements in a Pandas Series can be accessed via their index labels or integer positions using the .at or .iat attributes. The label is enclosed in square brackets [ ]. → C6NB 6.2.3a

Notice: .at provides rapid access to series values by referencing the index label, while .iat uses the default integer index position. Both methods yield identical results.

Slicing. Similar to slicing operations with lists and arrays introduced in previous chapters, elements of a series object can be accessed using the .loc or .iloc attributes. The input slice is enclosed in square brackets [ ]. → C6NB 6.2.3b

Notice: When slicing with the .loc attribute, both the starting and ending positions are inclusive, compared to exclusive on the right with the .iloc attribute. Additionally, it's important to note that slicing operations return a sub-Series object rather than just values.

List of Labels

The .loc and .iloc attributes also allow retrieving sub-Series by passing a list of labels or integer positions, respectively. → C6NB 6.2.3c

Notice: When using the .loc or .iloc attributes, labels are enclosed within square brackets [ ], creating list objects that are passed to the attribute calls(the outer [ ]). This method allows for selecting elements that are not contiguous, unlike slicing.

Boolean Array

When a boolean array of the same size as the series is passed to the .loc attribute, Pandas retrieves only the elements corresponding to the default index positions highlighted by the True values. → C6NB 6.2.3d

6.2.4 Reassigning or Adding Entries to a Series

Reassigning Entries

To change an existing entry in a Series, you simply refer to its label (index) and assign it a new value. Here's an example: →C6NB 6.2.4a

In this example, the value associated with 'AAPL' (ticker of Apple Inc.) is updated from 150 to 155.

Adding New Entries

Adding a new entry to a Series is just as easy as reassigning an existing one. If the label you assign a value to doesn't exist, it will be added to the Series: → C6NB 6.2.4b

As shown above, the stock price for Microsoft (MSFT) was added to the Series.

6.3 Introduction to DataFrame

Pandas DataFrame is a powerful data structure for handling labeled data in Python. It is designed to handle two-dimensional data, similar to a spreadsheet or SQL table, with labeled axes (rows and columns).

DataFrame Structure Diagram

	Column1	Column2	...	ColumnP
Index1	$Value_{11}$	$Value_{21}$	...	$Value_{1p}$
Index2	$Value_{21}$	$Value_{22}$	...	$Value_{2p}$
.....	...	...	...	...
IndexN	$Value_{N1}$	$Value_{N2}$	...	$Value_{Np}$

Compared to a Pandas Series, a DataFrame has two dimensions of index attributes: the row index and the column labels. Each data element is indexed accordingly. In typical settings, each row often represents an observation or sample, while each column represents a feature. For example, in a DataFrame of historical prices, each row contains the open, high, low, and close prices for a trading day.

6.3.1 Creating DataFrame

There are many ways to construct a DataFrame object. In practice, Data-Frame object is not constructed by manual inputs of data as a part of your code but rather by using Pandas's data import interfaces.

From a Dictionary

The most straightforward approach to creating a DataFrame is by passing a dictionary object to the pd.DataFrame constructor. → C6NB 6.3.1a

Notice: In a dataFrame created from a dictionary, the keys of the dictionary become the column labels, and the elements of the lists associated with these keys become the column values. The default integer indexes are assigned to the rows of the dataFrame.

Setting Row, Column, and Data Type

When using the DataFrame constructor, the index and columns can be specified by passing list-like objects of appropriate size consistent with the shape of the data. Additionally, the dtype setting is similar to that used for Series. → C6NB 6.3.1b

Notice: When using the DataFrame constructor, you can specify the index and columns by passing array objects of appropriate size consistent with the shape of the data. The dtype parameter, similar to its usage in Series, allows you to set the data type of the DataFrame's elements. In Jupyter Notebook, the display may truncate the output for better presentation. This differs from how the DataFrame is displayed in a native Python interpreter or an IPython console.

Import From a File

Pandas provide methods for creating a new DataFrame by importing from a data file. The commonly used file types include:

- **Excel (.xlsx, .xls)**: Microsoft Excel files are spreadsheet documents containing data organized into rows and columns. They can store multiple sheets within a single file.
- **Comma-separated values (CSV)**: CSV files are plain text files where each line represents a row of data, and values are separated by commas (or other delimiters). CSV files are widely used for storing tabular data.
- **JavaScript Object Notation (JSON)**: JSON files store data in a structured format using key-value pairs. They are commonly used for transmitting data between a server and web application but can also be used for structured data storage.

- **QL Database**: Data stored in relational databases (like SQLite, MySQL, PostgreSQL) that can be queried and imported into Pandas DataFrames using SQL queries or ORM libraries like SQLAlchemy.
- **Parquet**: Columnar storage format that provides efficient storage and retrieval of data, often used in big data processing frameworks like Apache Spark.
- **Feather**: Fast, lightweight binary columnar serialization format that is language agnostic and can be used to exchange data between Python and R efficiently.

The code cell below shows some examples of creating DataFrames by importing from local data files. →C6NB 6.3.1c

Notice: The file path is the only required argument for importing data. When creating a new DataFrame from files, Pandas infers data types and uses the first row as headers for column labels. However, Pandas does not automatically identify which column should be used as the index unless specified by the user. For Excel and CSV files, you can specify the index column by passing the label to the index_col parameter. If df_excel is created without setting an index column, a default index is provided.

It's important to note that when importing from specialized data files such as Excel and Parquet, additional dependencies may be required for Python to execute these commands.

Save to a file: To store the data of DataFrame or Series in a file, simply use the associated object methods provided by Pandas. It is important to note that only the data is saved not the object. It is, however, possible to "save" and "load" the entire object to and from a file by pickling and unpickling the object (unpickled using pd.read_pickle) as shown in the code cell below. → C6NB 6.3.1d

6.3.2 Accessing DataFrame

Accessing data in Pandas DataFrames involves retrieving specific rows, columns, or individual elements for analysis or manipulation. Here are the primary methods for accessing data.

Accessing Columns

Columns in a DataFrame can be accessed using their labels as attributes or by indexing with square brackets [ ]. →C6NB 6.3.2a

Notice that accessing a single column attribute results in a Series object, while accessing multiple columns, including a list with just one column, results in a DataFrame object.

Accessing Rows

Rows in a DataFrame can be accessed using .loc[] and .iloc[] accessors with the row label and integer index position, respectively. →C6NB 6.3.2b

Accessors With Indexes and Slices

The accessors at, iat, loc, and iloc, introduced with Series, provide similar functionality in DataFrames, with the distinction that they require speci-fying both row and column indexes. →C6NB 6.3.2c

Notice: Index addresses or slices passed to the accessors are specified from row to column. An empty input on either side of the slice operator : indicates *include all* in that corresponding direction. If the : operator is completely omitted, Pandas interprets it as including all rows or columns.

6.3.3 Modifying Series and DataFrame

Changing Index and Column Labels

Index and column labels should be chosen wisely to improve the read-ability and presentative quality of the DataFrame. Index and Column labels of a DataFrame can be changed by direct reassignment or using the rename method. →C6NB 6.3.3a

```
1  #changing the index and column labels
2  df_copy = df.copy() #create a duplicated object
3  df_copy.columns = ['open','high','low','close'] #replace the old column labels with lowercase ones
4  df_copy.rename(index=['2023-01-03':'2023/01/03',\
5            columns =["date":"trade_date","close":"close_price",inplace=True)
6  print(df_copy)

            open   high    low   close_price
Date
2023-01-01  100.0  102.2  99.5      101.8
2023-01-02  101.5  103.0  100.2     102.5
2023/01/03  99.8   100.5  98.5       99.9
```

Notice: in this code example, a copy of the original DataFrame (df_copy) is created. This copy is another DataFrame object with identical attributes to the original one but a different identity. This means that any changes applied to df_copy will not affect the original DataFrame.

The set_index method, when used with the inplace=True option, instructs the function to change the calling object (df_copy). Without this setting, the method will only return an object with "date" as the index without modifying df_copy. The inplace option is available for many methods associated with Pandas data objects, allowing you to modify the object directly.

Additionally, note that the rename method accepts index and columns as optional inputs. It changes the labels specified in the dictionary passed to it.

Changing Data Entries

Pandas data objects (Series and DataFrame) are capable of holding data of any type. Changing data entries in a Series or DataFrame involves accessing specific elements by their index label or integer position and assigning new values. If the new value is not compatible with the current dtype setting of the data object, Pandas may issue a warning message or (in future versions) raise an error. →C6NB 6.3.3b

Removing and Adding Data Entries

Pandas data objects are equipped with a drop method for removing items (for Series) and rows/columns (for DataFrame).

Dropping Entries From a Series →C6NB 6.3.3c

Notice: Here, the string entry added in the previous code cell is removed using the drop method, which requires the index or indexes (passed as a list) of items to be dropped. It's important to note that without setting inplace=True, the method does not modify the calling object (series_custom_index). Instead, it completes the dropping operation and returns a new Series.

Furthermore, after adding a string entry to the series, Pandas infers the dtype as object. Even after removing the string entry, the dtype remains object. This detail is insignificant for small-scale projects but can lead to significant performance issues in projects requiring high-performance computing. To convert the Series back to a homogeneous type, you can use the astype method associated with Pandas data objects. However, since the astype method for Series does not support inplace option, you need to reassign the Series (series_custom_index) to apply the dtype change.

Dropping Entries From a DataFrame

It's not possible to drop just one entry from a DataFrame unless it has a shape of one-by-one. The drop method, when used with a DataFrame object, applies to entire rows or columns. →C6NB 6.3.3d

Adding Entries to DataFrame

It is not possible to just one entry to a DataFrame. The new entry must be associated with a new column or row. →C6NB 6.3.3e

Notice: When adding new rows and columns to a DataFrame, it's crucial to ensure that the new data array matches the existing DataFrame's size. For instance, if a DataFrame has a shape of 3 rows by 2 columns, any array used to assign a new column should contain three elements corresponding to each row. This ensures consistency in data alignment and prevents errors during assignment operations.

Adding New Rows and Columns With Concat (Pandas.concat)

In practice, it's uncommon to add entries to an existing DataFrame one at a time. More often, we need to append a new set of data to the existing one. Pandas provides a flexible and efficient method for these tasks. The concat method can be used to join multiple Series or DataFrame objects into one. When concatenating DataFrames, the axis parameter is required. Setting axis=0 joins the DataFrames vertically (row-wise), while axis=1 joins them horizontally (column-wise). Data objects are passed to the function as a list, and the order in the list determines the concatenation order. This method is flexible because it allows for misalignment, meaning the data objects can have different index and column labels. →C6NB 6.3.3f

Notice: Here, a new DataFrame is created with two additional observations, and a single-column DataFrame introduces a new feature named "Sentiment" with observations for the most recent two trade days. It's important to note that although the order of columns (marked by arrows) in the new DataFrame may differ from the existing one, the concat function automatically aligns the data. When concatenating column-wise, the operation executes without raising an error, and the data is aligned based on the index values. Missing data cells are automatically assigned NaN values.[†]

6.4 Operations With Series and DataFrame

Similar to NumPy arrays, Pandas' data objects support various operations from applying functions to mathematical operations across rows or columns.

Element-Wise Operations

Series objects (including rows and columns of a DataFrame) support element-wise operations similar to NumPy arrays. Operations like addition (+), subtraction (–), multiplication (*), and division (/) can be performed directly on Series. Notice that these operations will result in a new Pandas data object. →C6NB 6.4a

Broadcasting

Operations between a scalar value and a Series or DataFrame are broadcasted across all elements of the Series: →C6NB 6.4b

Aggregation Methods

Pandas Series and DataFrame have built-in methods for common aggregations such as sum(), mean(), min(), max(), and so on. For DataFrame,

---

[†] NaN stands for "Not a Number." In both Pandas and NumPy, NaN is a special floating-point value that represents undefined or missing data. Other similar entries include None and pd.NA. It serves as a marker to indicate that a particular value is not available or could not be represented as a standard numerical value.

the functions are applied to each column, and the results are returned as a Series. →C6NB 6.4c

Element-Wise Operations: 'Apply' and 'Map'

Pandas DataFrame and Series are equipped with the .apply and .map functions to apply functions to each element, row, or column of the object. →C6NB 6.4d

Notice: The apply method by default applies to each column of the DataFrame. The return data structure is inferred based on the input function. In the first call, the np.sqrt function, which returns an array object, causes the apply function to return a DataFrame object. In the second call, the sum function returns a single value, so the apply function returns a Series of results for each row (axis=0) of the DataFrame.

The result is more straightforward with the map function, which applies a function to each cell of the data object. The data within each cell must be valid input for the function being applied. →C6NB 6.4e

The Update Function

The update function in Pandas DataFrame is used to modify a DataFrame with the non-NA values from another DataFrame or Series. It updates the current DataFrame in place, aligning rows and columns by their index labels. → C6NB 6.4f

Notice: Only values with matching indices in the target DataFrame col_new are updated, as highlighted in rectangles. The update function also provides a filter_function parameter that allows the program to determine whether to process the update. A function that returns either True or False, indicating the decision, should be passed as an argument.

6.5 Data Cleaning and Filtering

Data cleaning and filtering are critical processes in data analysis, essential for preparing data for further analysis by addressing issues such as missing values, incorrect data types, outliers, and unwanted data. These processes lay the foundation for more advanced data science applications discussed in later chapters. Here, we will focus on basic operations commonly performed in data science projects.

Handling missing and invalid data: Missing and invalid data should be handled by marking them as NaN values in Series and DataFrames. Invalid data includes entries of incorrect types, duplicates, outliers, and data that does not meet specified requirements.

Converting Data Using to_numeric Function (Pandas.to_numeric)

Pandas' to_numeric function allows for the forced conversion of data arrays into numerical values. Entries that cannot be converted can be marked as NaN. The function can be applied to each column of a DataFrame to perform full-data conversion. →C6NB 6.5a

Notice: The original Series includes a string '1.11' and the integer 100. The string can be converted to float, while the integer is already in numerical form. By default, the to_numeric function raises an error for entries that cannot be converted, unless errors='coerce' is set.

Marking Invalid Entries

To perform a more specific screening of each data element, we can customize a screen function and then pass it to the apply or map function. In the code cell below, a function for checking each data whether it is a number between 0 and 200. → C6NB 6.5b

Dropping NA Entries

The dropna function associated with Series or DataFrame objects can be used to drop invalid observations. By default, the function drops all rows with any NA entries (None, np.NaN, pd.NA, pd.NaT). → C6NB 6.5c

Conditional Filtering

When passing a boolean array to the accessor, DataFrame will perform conditional filtering by removing rows matching the False values in the array. This feature allows us to filter out observations that are not meeting the condition. → C6NB 6.5d

Conclusion

As we conclude this chapter on Pandas, it's important to recognize that Pandas is a vast library with extensive capabilities for data manipulation and analysis.

Throughout this chapter, we have explored fundamental concepts such as creating and accessing Series and DataFrames, performing operations, and cleaning and filtering data.

Pandas offers multiple approaches to achieve the same analytical goals, allowing flexibility in data handling based on specific needs. To deepen your understanding and proficiency with Pandas, we encourage you to refer to the package's official manual and explore its rich documentation (Pandas Documentation 2023). This will empower you to leverage Pandas effectively in your data science endeavors, gaining insights and making informed decisions from your data sets.

Exercises

Use the simulated data set provided in the chapter workbook (FDSP_Chapter6_Notebook.ipynb) to finish the following exercise:

1. Combine quarter1_sales and quarter2_sales into a single DataFrame annual_salesrepresenting sales data for the entire year.
2. Calculate the total sales for each quarter and store them in variables total_q1_sales.
3. Create a DataFrame high_sales_months containing only the months where salesexceeded $175,000.
4. Add a new column Profit to annual_sales calculated as 20 percent of the 'Sales' column.
5. Increase the sales for the month of February in quarter1_sales by 10 percent and update annual_sales accordingly.
6. Introduce NaN values in quarter2_sales for the month of June. Use .fillna() to replace the NaN value with the average sales of the remaining months in quarter2_sales.

CHAPTER 7

Principle of Statistics for Financial Data Science

7.1 Introduction to Financial Statistics

For financial professionals, statistics serves as a powerful tool to extract valuable information efficiently and accurately from the vast ocean of financial data. Financial data differs significantly from other types due to its distinctive characteristics:

- Temporal dependency: Financial data often exhibits time-dependent relationships, where past values influence future outcomes. For instance, today's stock prices are influenced by historical prices and market trends (Tsay 2005).
- Non-normality: Financial data frequently deviates from a normal distribution, often showing fat tails and skewness. This departure from normality complicates traditional statistical analyses that assume data follows a Gaussian distribution (McLeay and Omar 2000).
- Volatility and heteroscedasticity: Financial data can demonstrate varying levels of volatility (e.g., stock returns) and heteroscedasticity (unequal variance over time), challenging assumptions of constant variance in statistical models (Engle 1982).
- Outliers and extreme events: Financial markets are susceptible to outliers and extreme events (e.g., market crashes), which can significantly impact statistical conclusions and risk assessments (Danielsson 2011).

Given these unique characteristics, several areas of statistics are particularly crucial in financial analysis:

- Time series analysis: Due to temporal dependency, methods for analyzing and forecasting based on historical patterns are essential in financial data analysis (Hamilton 1994).
- Nonparametric statistics: To address non-normality and volatility, nonparametric methods provide robust alternatives to parametric tests, ensuring reliable inference without strict distributional assumptions (Hollander and Wolfe 1999).
- Machine learning: for addressing the dynamic nature of financial activities and effectively capturing nonlinear relationships and interactions among variables (Bishop 2006).

In this chapter, we will explore fundamental statistical principles essential for understanding these advanced topics. Our approach diverges from traditional statistics teachings, which often emphasize mathematical and analytical methods. Instead, we will focus on practical implications and programming implementations.

Introduction to Computer Simulation

If you are not familiar with probability distributions, you can think of the data simulation as results obtained from repeatedly drawing random samples from a virtual population of data. Our goal is to estimate population parameters such as the center and dispersion, as well as relationships with other populations. Once the virtual population is generated, we can obtain the true answers we seek using various statistical methods. This allows us to validate these methods by comparing our estimates with the true population parameters.

To start, we will generate the necessary data for this chapter. The following code cell simulates monthly return on equity (ROE) data for two hypothetical companies. → C7NB 7.1a

Explain: The ROE rates of the two companies are generated from two different normal distributions. Specifically, the population average ROE rate of company A is intentionally lower than that of company B, and its rates exhibit greater volatility. This disparity is represented by the range of uniform distributions used to generate parameters for these normal distributions. The randomness in these population parameters mimics real-world scenarios where the true population parameters are unknown.

A random seed is initialized at the beginning of the code cell to enable readers to reproduce the results. It's important to note that because the parameters are randomly generated, without the random seed setting, each time the code cell is executed, a different set of population parameters and observations will likely appear.

The simulation data may represent a hypothetical scenario involving time series sample data from two competing companies. A research analyst could be tasked with evaluating which company is a better investment. From our perspective, we already know that company A is considered an inferior investment (unless investors are risk-seeking). However, in real life, the true population parameters remain unknown. Therefore, the analyst may need to infer the answer from the sample observations and statistics.

7.2 Probability Distributions

In the previous code cell example, we demonstrated how to generate observations from uniform and normal distributions. Several other commonly used distributions in finance deserve our attention. We will conduct a brief review and show their simulation methods in Python.

7.2.1 *Review of Common Probability Distribution in Finance*

Uniform Distribution

The uniform distribution describes a set of outcomes where each value in a specified interval is equally probable.
Parameters: a—lower bound of the interval (inclusive); b—upper bound of the interval (inclusive).

Mean: $(a+b)/2$
Variance: $(b-a)^2/12$

Binomial Distribution

The binomial distribution models the number of successes in a fixed number of independent Bernoulli trials, which is relevant in finance for modeling scenarios involving binary.

Parameters: n—number of trials; p—probability of success in each trail.

Mean: np
Variance: $np\,(1{-}p)$

Lognormal Distribution

The lognormal distribution is often used in finance to model asset prices or returns, which are naturally nonnegative and can have a skewed distribution.

Parameters: μ —mean of the underlying normal distribution after taking the natural logarithm;
σ—controls the spread or shape of the distribution.
Mean: $e^{\mu+\sigma^2/2}$
Variance: $(e^{\sigma^2}-1)\,e^{2\mu+\sigma^2}$

Chi-Square Distribution (χ^2)

The chi-square distribution is a special case of the gamma distribution. It is widely used in statistics, particularly in hypothesis testing and confidence interval construction.

Parameters: k—degrees of freedom, which determine the shape of the distribution.

Mean: $\mu = k$
Variance: $\sigma^2 = 2k$

F Distribution

The F distribution is a continuous probability distribution that arises in the context of analysis of variance and regression analysis.

Parameters: d_1—degrees of freedom of the numerator; d_2—degrees of freedom of the numerator.

Mean: $\mu = d_2/(d_2-2)$ for $d_1 > 2$

Variance: $\sigma^2 = \dfrac{2d_2^2(d_1+d_2-2)}{d_1(d_2-2)^2(d_2-4)}$ for $d_2 > 4$

Student's t-Distribution. The *t*-distribution (Student's *t*-distribution) is a continuous probability distribution that is symmetric and bell-shaped like the normal distribution but has heavier tails, making it suitable for smaller sample sizes where the population standard deviation (std) is unknown and must be estimated from the sample.

Parameters: v—degrees of freedom, which determine the shape of the distribution. As v increases, the *t*-distribution approaches the normal distribution.

Mean: $\mu = 0$

Variance: $\sigma^2 = \dfrac{v}{v-2}$ *for* $v > 2$

7.2.2 Probability Distributions Using Python

Probability distributions describe the likelihood of different outcomes in a random event. There are several key concepts used to understand and work with these distributions, including the probability density function (PDF), probability mass function (PMF), cumulative distribution function (CDF), and inverse CDF. Each of these serves a specific purpose in probability theory, depending on the type of data (continuous or discrete) you're dealing with.

- PDF: For continuous random variables, the PDF gives the relative likelihood of observing a specific value. It indicates the probability density over a range of values, allowing for the calculation of probabilities for intervals.
- PMF: For discrete random variables, the PMF gives the probability that a random variable takes on a specific value. It lists all possible values and their associated probabilities.

- CDF: The CDF gives the probability that a random variable takes on a value less than or equal to a specified value. It provides a cumulative view of the probability distribution, summing up probabilities as you move along the possible values.
- Inverse CDF (percent point function): The inverse CDF gives the value for which the CDF equals a specified probability. It is useful for finding critical values or quantiles corresponding to a given probability.

The following code cell demonstrates how to generate random samples and compute the PDF for continuous distributions and PMF for discrete distributions, as well as CDF and inverse CDF. → C7NB 7.2.2a; C7NB 7.2.2b

Explanation: These probability functions are readily available in numerous programming languages and statistical packages. Memorizing the exact formulas for each distribution is not necessary. In practical applications, it's important to familiarize yourself with how to call these functions, what they return, and their real-life applications.

7.3 Descriptive Statistics

Descriptive statistics are numerical measures used to describe the basic features of a sample data set. They summarize and simplify large amounts of data into meaningful patterns, providing insights into central tendencies, variability, and other distribution characteristics.

In finance, descriptive statistics are essential for understanding and interpreting market behaviors, investment performance, and risk levels. Here are some day-to-day examples of descriptive statistics:

- Dow Jones Industrial Average or S&P 500 Index provides daily averages of stock prices, reflecting overall market performance.
- Stock beta indicates the variability of stock returns or the sensitivity of a stock's returns to market movements.
- Statistics like GDP growth rate, unemployment rate, or inflation rate summarize economic trends and conditions.

- Daily closing prices, opening prices, and trading volumes of stocks or commodities provide insights into market activities and investor sentiment.
- Market-wide or portfolio-based averages of financial ratios such as PE (Price-to-Earnings), PS (Price-to-Sales), and PB (Price-to-Book) also fall under the category of descriptive statistics and are often utilized in financial research literature.

7.3.1 Review of Common Descriptive Statistics

Sample Mean

Definition: The arithmetic average of a set of numbers. It represents the central tendency of the data.

Formular: $\bar{x} = \dfrac{\sum_n x_i}{n}$

Example application: Calculating the average return of a stock portfolio over a period to assess performance.

Sample Median

Definition: The middle value in a sorted list of numbers. It divides the data into two equal halves. Median is an alternative to mean when the influence of outliers needs to be reduced.

Formula: For an odd number of observations, it is the middle value. For an even number, it is the average of the two middle values.

Example application: Assessing the central value of a data set like income distributions or asset prices to understand typical values.

Sample Standard Deviation (std)

Definition: Measures the amount of variation or dispersion of a set of values from the mean.

Formula: $S^2 = \dfrac{\sum_n (x_i - \bar{x})^2}{n-1}$

Example application: Assessing the risk and volatility of an investment portfolio or stock returns. Higher std indicates higher risk.

Sample Skewness

Definition: It measures the asymmetry of the sample; positive skewness means the data is skewed to the right, with most data clustered on the left but outliers on the right.

Formula: $g_1 = \dfrac{n \sum_n \left(\dfrac{x_i - \bar{x}}{s} \right)^3}{(n-1)(n-2)} \approx \dfrac{\sum_n \left(\dfrac{x_i - \bar{x}}{s} \right)^3}{n}$ for large n

Example application: Some investors prefer assets exhibiting positively skewed returns because the occasional large positive returns can significantly contribute to overall portfolio growth, potentially outweighing smaller losses.

Sample Kurtosis

Kurtosis measures the *peakedness* or *tailedness* of a data distribution compared to a normal distribution.

- Mesokurtic: A distribution with kurtosis equal to 3 is considered mesokurtic, indicating it has similar tail behavior to a normal distribution.
- Leptokurtic: A distribution with kurtosis greater than 3 is leptokurtic. It has fatter tails and a sharper peak than a normal distribution, suggesting more extreme values occur more frequently.
- Platykurtic: A distribution with kurtosis less than 3 is platykurtic. It has thinner tails and a flatter peak than a normal distribution, indicating fewer extreme values compared to a normal distribution.

Formula:

$$g_2 = \frac{n(n-1)}{(n-1)(n-2)(n-3)}\left(\frac{\sum_n x_i - \bar{x}}{s}\right)^4 - \frac{3(n-1)^2}{(n-2)(n-3)} = \frac{n(n-1)}{(n-1)(n-2)(n-3)}\left(\frac{\sum_n x_i - \bar{x}}{s}\right)^4$$

for large n

Example application: Investors and analysts gauge the risk associated with investments by identifying the likelihood of extreme events beyond what std alone indicates.

7.3.2 Calculating Descriptive Statistics

Going back to our simulation data set, we can calculate the descriptive statistics of data associated a DataFrame using the object's agg method, which applies a list of operations along a specified axis of the object. → C7NB 7.3.2a

Explain: By default, the agg method applies operations column-wise. The operations are specified in a list passed to the agg function. Each string in the list represents the name of an operation function that is applied individually to each column of the DataFrame. Here, we have included the most commonly known descriptive statistics which are often used to provide a quick summary of the data.

Comparing the results of descriptive statistics with the true population parameters generated during simulation, we observe that both the sample mean and median exceed the population mean, with the median closer to the true population mean value for both companies. The sample stds also deviate from the population stds for both companies, with one overestimating and the other underestimating. These findings suggest that our descriptive statistics are not effectively estimating the population parameters.

To understand the reasons behind these results, we need to delve into the nature of statistical estimators.

7.4 Statistical Estimators

The descriptive statistics calculated from sample data can serve as estimators of population parameters. For instance, the sample mean estimates the population mean, and the sample std estimates the population std. In practice, since population parameters are typically unknown, it is crucial to grasp the function and limitations of the statistics being employed.

Randomness

It is important to understand the randomness of statistical estimators. By definition, a random sample implies that any statistic calculated based on observations from that sample will also be random. This means that if another random sample is drawn from the population, a different realization of the statistic should appear. This important statistical principle leads to the following metrics for assessing statistical estimators.

Accuracy (Unbiasness)

Bias refers to the systematic error or deviation of an estimator from the true population parameter. A biased estimator consistently overestimates or underestimates the true value it is intended to estimate.

A biased estimator does not necessarily imply it is inferior to unbiased ones. As we will see in later chapters, in some cases, it is preferred to accept some degree of bias in return for a more reliable estimator. For example, an error within one decimal point may be irrelevant for a portfolio manager with a long holding horizon but could be crucial for high-frequency traders.

Preciseness (Reliability)

The preciseness of an estimator refers to its ability to provide estimates that are tightly clustered around the true population parameter or value it aims to estimate. In statistical terms, preciseness is related to the variability or spread of the estimator's sampling distribution. Put simply, a precise estimator is reliable because it consistently produces close estimations across repeated samples.

It is important to note that a precise estimator is not necessarily unbiased. While we generally prefer both unbiased and precise estimators, in the reality of data science, we often need to strike a balance between these two characteristics when selecting the best estimator for our projects. We will explore more examples of this trade-off in later chapters.

Consistency

Consistency refers to the property of an estimator that converges to the true parameter value as the sample size increases indefinitely. A consistent estimator produces estimates that become increasingly accurate with larger sample sizes.

By definition, unbiasedness and consistency do not imply each other. In other words, an unbiased estimator can lack consistency, and a consistent estimator can be biased. In practice, however, this distinction can be trivial as the more important question is how quickly the sample statistics converge to their true values, which is termed the asymptotic behavior of the estimator.

Selecting Estimators

The choice of estimators heavily depends on the objectives of our data science project. Generally speaking, since unbiasedness and consistency are related to the precision, and preciseness adds to the reliability of an estimator, we should prefer estimators that exhibit at least one trait of unbiasedness or consistency, and ideally both for optimal reliability. Importantly, a consistent estimator generally becomes more precise and reliable as more samples become available. This characteristic is valuable for financial learning systems where new samples are continuously added to the training process.

7.4.1 Evaluating Estimators

The precision and reliability of an estimator can be assessed through analytical or simulation-based methods. However, the mathematical analysis of the asymptotic behavior of statistical estimators can be challenging for estimators based on nonlinear functions (e.g., percentiles). Here, we focus on simulation, which provides robust results without requiring advanced mathematical expertise from the data scientist. The only requirement is that the simulation mirrors real-world scenarios accurately.

The basic idea of evaluating a statistical estimator is straightforward: through iterative simulation processes that generate samples, we obtain realizations of the statistical estimators. This allows us to observe the distribution of these estimators based on the samples.

The following code cell iterates the sampling of ROE rates data for companies A and B 500 times. In each iteration, a realization of estimators is obtained based on a simulated ROE data sample. → C7NB 7.4.1a

7.4.2 Eye-Balling Analysis

Whenever sample data becomes available, it is good practice for data scientists to conduct a visual inspection or eyeballing analysis of the data before applying complex quantitative tools. This approach is akin to driving a car with autopilot: while you can rely on it, it's essential to keep your hands on the wheel and stay attentive.

As we will show more visual inspection techniques in later chapters, here, we will focus on the checking frequency distribution. **A frequency plot** shows how often different values or ranges appear in a data set, using bars to display counts or frequencies of outcomes. It helps visualize the distribution and pattern of data values. →C7NB 7.4.2a

Explain: The code generates three frequency plots (see Figure 7.1 below) depicting the distributions of sample mean, sample median, and sample std. Each plot overlays the frequency distributions for companies A and B on the same scales.

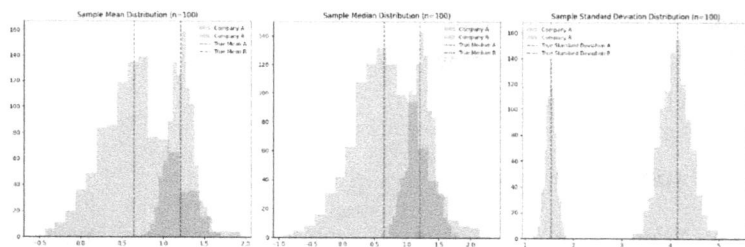

Figure 7.1 Jupyter Notebook screenshot of frequency plots with Python

The frequency plots indicate that company B exhibits a higher mean ROE than company A, with less volatility. While we already know this as the correct outcome, the hypothetical analyst, with only one realization of actual sample, faces uncertainty as true parameter values (represented by dashed lines) are unknown.

Examining the distributions, we can see that both sample mean and sample median observations appear to center around the true population mean, with the median showing greater concentration. However, a noteworthy detail is that the true population average (depicted by the blue dashed line) does not align with the mode (peak) of the sample median distribution. This discrepancy suggests a small bias when using the sample median as an estimator for the population mean, despite mathematical proof that the sample median is an unbiased estimator of population mean for symmetric distributions like the normal distribution. Thus, while theoretically the sample median should center around the population mean, the discrete nature of the statistics introduces bias.

Another observation from the plots is that the sample std consistently underestimates the population std, evident by the distribution center being leftward of the true population value. This observation contradicts mathematical analysis, which states that the expected value of sample std (with $n-1$ correction) equals the population std.

7.4.3 Asymptotic Analysis

An often-overlooked aspect of statistical estimators is their asymptotic behavior as sample size increases. With advancements in computer techniques, we can now easily explore this crucial aspect to gain deeper insights into the practical value of statistical estimators.

We will reuse the previous code cell to generate another set of frequency plots (see Figure 7.2 below), where the sample size in each iteration increases from 10 to 100. →C7NB 7.4.3a

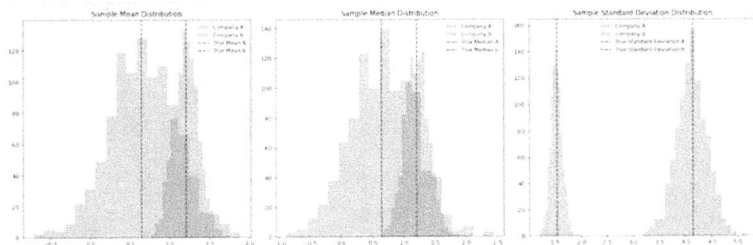

Figure 7.2 Jupyter Notebook screenshot for another frequency plots with Python with iteration sample size = 100

The asymptotic behavior of our statistical estimator can be inferred by comparing two sets of plots based on different sample sizes.

It is shown that the dispersion of the distributions has significantly decreased, except for the sample median. This suggests that the sample mean and sample std exhibit consistent estimator behavior. The sample median continues to show a small bias as an estimator for the population mean, but the bias in the sample std has reduced.

Overall, the simulation results suggest that the sample median lacks the virtue of being a consistent estimator but performs better in small samples compared to its sample mean counterpart. Both the sample mean and sample std become more accurate and reliable as statistical estimators as the sample size increases.

Complex Estimators

The results of the simulation study have provided insightful knowledge about three commonly used estimators. In practice, data scientists often need to adopt ad hoc estimators in various professional settings. For instance, securities analysts frequently utilize financial indicators such as beta, Sharpe ratio, and RSI in their work. To better manage the uncertainty inherent in these indicators, securities analysts may adopt the data science approach demonstrated earlier to gain in-depth knowledge about these indicators.

The probability model used to generate simulated observations becomes the most crucial element in validating such studies. In practice, this step often involves specialists who understand the nuances of financial mechanisms underlying the data. As a data scientist, your role is to translate these specialists' insights into a simulation system that accurately mimics real-world scenarios.

7.5 Hypothesis Testing

Eyeballing analyses such as frequency distribution plots provide initial insights into the central tendency and spread of data. For a more rigorous examination of evidence, hypothesis testing is essential.

Hypothesis testing is a fundamental statistical method in finance used to make decisions or draw conclusions about population parameters based on sample data. It begins with formulating a hypothesis about the population parameter and then using sample data to evaluate the validity of this hypothesis. Let's delve into the key components and terms associated with hypothesis testing in finance.

Major Steps

Step 1: Formulating hypotheses:

- In hypothesis testing, the null hypothesis (H_0) states there is no effect or difference in the population parameter. It's the default assumption.
  Example: H_0: $u = u_0$
- The alternative hypothesis (H_1) suggests there is an effect or difference and can be formatted in three different ways:

1. **Two-tailed test:**
   - Tests if the parameter is different (either higher or lower) from the H_0 value.
     Example: H_a: $u \neq u_0$
   - Used when we are interested in any significant difference, regardless of direction.

2. **One-tailed test (right-tailed):**
   - Tests if the parameter is greater than the H_0 value.
     Example: H_a: $u > u_0$
   - Used when we are only interested in detecting an increase.

3. **One-tailed test (left-tailed):**
   - Tests if the parameter is less than the H_0 value.
     Example: H_a: $u < u_0$
   - Used when we are only interested in detecting a decrease.

Step 2: Choosing a test statistic and significance level (α):

- The test statistic is calculated based on the sample data, and therefore it is a random variable. Its probability distribution is often inferred based on assumptions about the data or the sampling process.

- The significance level (α) is a threshold value for comparing the likelihood of realizing the test statistic. If the likelihood is smaller than α, then the evidence is considered significant for rejecting the H_0.

Step 3: Collecting data, calculating the test statistic, and reaching a conclusion:

- Sample data is collected, the test statistic is computed, and then translated into a p-value, which represents the likelihood of its occurrence if the H_0 is true. If the p-value is less than α, then the H_0 is rejected.

Test Statistic

The test statistic is a statistical measure we use for examining the evidence and deciding whether they are strong enough to reject the H_0. When choosing a test statistic, there are several considerations:

a) Calculability: The test statistic must be calculable from the data. This means it should be straightforward to compute using the available sample data without requiring impractical or overly complex computations.

b) Reliability (volatility): The test statistic should be a reliable measure with low volatility. A reliable test statistic provides consistent results across different samples drawn from the same population. High variability in the test statistic can lead to incorrect conclusions, increasing the risk of type I or type II errors.

c) Statistical properties with the population parameter: The test statistic should have known statistical properties under the H_0 and the alternative hypothesis. This includes understanding its distribution under these hypotheses. For example, the t-statistic in a t-test follows a t-distribution under the H_0. These properties allow us to determine critical values and p-values for hypothesis testing.

d) Sensitivity: The test statistic should be sensitive to the effects it is intended to detect. This means it should have the ability to reflect the true differences or relationships present in the data. A sensitive test statistic increases the power of the test, enabling the detection of true effects even when they are small.

e) Robustness: The test statistic should be robust to violations of the assumptions underlying the statistical test. For instance, some test statistics may be more resilient to deviations from normality or homogeneity of variances, making them more reliable in real-world scenarios where these assumptions might not hold perfectly.

f) Interpretability: The test statistic should be easily interpretable. Researchers and practitioners should understand what the value of the test statistic represents and how it relates to the hypotheses being tested. Clear interpretability facilitates better decision making and communication of results.

The p-Value

The p-value is the probability of obtaining test results at least as extreme as the observed results, assuming that the H_0 is true. It quantifies the evidence against the H_0: the smaller the p-value, the stronger the evidence to reject the H_0.

To calculate the p-value, the probability map of the test statistics under the H_0 is utilized to compute the value of $P(T \geq t \mid H_0$ is true), where T is the random variable representing the test statistic and ttt is its realization based on the sample. For test statistics involving the sum or mean of samples, the central limit theorem (CLT) plays a crucial role.

The CLT states that, given a sufficiently large sample size, the distribution of the sample mean will approximate a normal distribution, regardless of the population's distribution, provided the population has a finite variance (Weiss 2016). This theorem allows us to make inferences about the population mean using the sample mean and std.

When the sample size is small or the population distribution is not normal, the t-distribution is used instead of the normal distribution. The t-distribution, which accounts for additional variability due to small sample sizes, is characterized by heavier tails compared to the normal distribution. It is important to know that when the sample size is too small or the original distribution of the underlying population is too far from normality, the distribution of the test statistics can be far from normality, making the t-distribution not a good approximation.

7.5.1 One-Sample and Two-Sample t-Test

The t-test family is commonly used for testing central tendencies and dispersion of population parameters. The one-sample t-test tests a single parameter, while the two-sample t-test compares a parameter, usually the population means, between two populations. All these tests use t values as the test statistics, hence the term t-test. The t-test is specifically designed for situations where the sample size is too small (less than 35) for the CLT to ensure the normality of the test statistics. However, if the original distribution of the data deviates significantly from normality, the t-test family should not be used.

In the following code cell, we demonstrate the implementation of one-sample and two-sample t-tests on the population means using our ROE data. First, we test the hypothesis that the population mean ROE is positive for company A, and then we test the hypothesis that the mean population ROE is larger for company B compared to company A. →C7NB 7.5.1a

Explanation: Here, we utilize the stats module from the scipy package. There are two versions of the two-sample t-test available. One is called the "independent" two-sample t-test, and the other is called the "related" (or "paired") two-sample t-test. The associated scipy.stats functions are ttest_ind and ttest_rel, respectively. We adopt the related version of the two-sample t-test (ttest_rel) because we assume the observations are obtained at the same time. In other scenarios, where the sampling processes between the two populations are independent of each other, the independent version of the two-sample t-test (ttest_ind) should be used. The reason for having different versions is that the population dispersion of the t-statistic should be smaller when the observations are related.

The one-sample t-test result indicates that the H_0 is rejected in favor of the alternative hypothesis of a positive ROE for company A, which we know is the correct answer. For the two-sample t-test, the invalidity of the result (not rejecting the null) is known to us but not to the hypothetical analyst conducting the hypothesis testing.

Type I and Type II Errors and Power of Hypothesis Testing

- Type I error (false positive): This occurs when the H_0 is rejected when it is actually true. It is commonly referred to as the α of the test. The significance level represents the maximum type I error rate the test designer is willing to accept. A higher α level increases the likelihood of rejecting the H_0 but also raises the risk of a type I error.
- Type II error (false negative): This occurs when the H_0 is not rejected when it is actually false. It is commonly referred to as the β of the test.
- Power: The power of a hypothesis test is the probability that the test correctly rejects a false H_0, calculated as $1-\beta$.

7.5.2 Power Analysis

In our ROE data example, as simulation participants, we can calculate the exact true values of β and the power of our hypothesis tests because we have a complete map of the population. However, in practice, the distribution and parameters of the population are unknown, which is why statistics are needed. Without complete knowledge of the population, we can either use our prior knowledge to make a good assumption about the true population parameters or estimate the values based on the sample. The supporting idea for the latter is that the sample is the best representation of the population, allowing us to use sample estimators as replacements for the population parameters. Be aware that this idea is only valid when strictly random sampling is applied and the sample size is large enough to control for uncertainty.

For traditional parametric tests, such as the t-test family, the probability distribution of the test statistics is assumed to be normal, so we only need to estimate the population mean and variance from the sample for estimating the population distribution. Some statistical packages have programmed this solution into their functions. In the code cell below, we demonstrate the usage of solver functions from the stats module of the statsmodels package. →C7NB 7.5.2a

Explanation: There are two methods associated with a TTestPower object: power and solve_power. The former provides a quick answer for the power of a test given the inputs of effect size, sample size (nobs), alpha, and direction of the alternative hypothesis ("larger," "smaller," or "two-sided"). The latter solves for any of the aforementioned inputs when the rest are provided. In this example, we use the solve_power method to determine the sample size required to achieve a power level of at least 0.8.

Here, we analyze the relationship between power and sample size using our one-sample t-test and the paired two-sample t-test. We calculate power using the effect size derived from the sample mean. In this case, the effect size is calculated as the sample mean minus the hypothesized mean (which is 0), divided by the sample std. We also calculate the power using the true effect size, defined as the true mean minus the hypothesized mean, divided by the population std.

The results suggest that the power of tests generally increases with sample size. However, the power calculated based on the sample can be inaccurate, especially when the underlying distribution has a large variance (e.g., company A). The results show that to ensure the test has more than an 80 percent chance of rejecting the H_0 when it is false, the sample size needs to be at least 256 and 274 for the one-sample t-test and the paired two-sample t-test, respectively.

7.5.3 Testing the Relationship

In finance, understanding the relationships between different financial variables is crucial for making informed decisions. For example, investors often analyze the correlation between the returns of different stocks in their portfolio. A positive correlation suggests that the stocks tend to move together, which might increase portfolio risk. Conversely, a negative correlation can provide diversification benefits, reducing overall risk.

Turning to our ROE data, we aim to develop a hypothesis test to examine whether there is a significant dependency between the two companies.

Formulating Hypothesis

- Null Hypothesis (H$_0$): There is no correlation between the ROE of company A and company B (ρ=0).
- Alternative hypothesis (H$_a$): There is a significant correlation between the ROE of company A and company B (ρ≠0).

Perform Hypothesis Testing

We use Pearson correlation coefficient (γ) as the test statistics:

$$\gamma = \frac{\sum_n (x_i - \bar{x})(y_i - \bar{y})}{\sqrt{\sum_n (x_i - \bar{x})^2 \sum_n (y_i - \bar{y})^2}}$$

The code for performing the test on Python is shown below: →C7NB 7.5.3a

Explanation: Here, we generated three sets of random samples (without setting random seeds) with sizes ranging from 10 to 1000. The larger the sample size, the closer the sample distribution reflects the population distribution, and consequently, the closer the sample correlation to the population correlation. In practical scenarios, we often deal with limited samples. As expected, when the sample size is small, the sample correlation coefficient deviates from the population correlation, and the test fails to reject the null when it is false (lack of power). However, as the sample size increases, this error diminishes. This suggests that while the sample correlation coefficient may be biased, it is a consistent estimator of the population correlation. The p-values approach zero as more samples become available, consistent with the properties of estimators where stronger evidence emerges with larger sample sizes.

7.5.4 Power Plot

The objects from statsmodels' TTestPower class are equipped with the plot_power method for generating power plots (see Figure 7.3 below) across various effect sizes and sample sizes. This visualization is valuable for illustrating how test power varies with changes in these parameters.

The following code demonstrates how test power is affected by different values of these inputs. →C7NB 7.5.4a

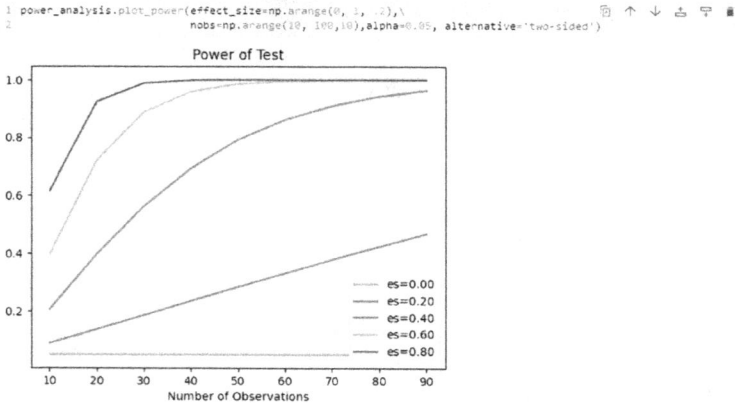

```
1 power_analysis.plot_power(effect_size=np.arange(0, 1, .2),\
2                 nobs=np.arange(10, 100,10),alpha=0.05, alternative='two-sided')
```

Figure 7.3 Jupyter Notebook screenshot for implementation of power plot on python

Explanation: The plot illustrates the relationship between test power (vertical axis) and sample size (horizontal axis) for five different tests, each with effect sizes ranging from 0 to 0.8. The effect size in these tests, using the sample Pearson correlation coefficient, approximates the test statistic. When there is no effect in the population, the test power is close to 0 because there is little evidence against the H_0 in the sample. As the effect size increases, the test power rapidly improves with larger sample sizes. The plot demonstrates that a sample size of 50 is generally sufficient to detect effects when the population correlation is above 0.5.

7.6 Nonparametric Statistics

Nonparametric statistics offer valuable alternatives in financial analysis, particularly when assumptions about data distribution or the nature of relationships between variables cannot be guaranteed. Unlike parametric methods, which assume specific distributions and parameter characteristics, nonparametric statistics derive their power from fewer assumptions, making them robust in scenarios where data may deviate significantly from normality or when exact distributional forms are uncertain.

Applications and Benefits

Nonparametric methods are particularly useful in finance for several reasons:

a) Distributional flexibility: Financial data often exhibit non-normal distributions due to factors like market volatility or skewed returns. Nonparametric tests, such as the Wilcoxon signed-rank test or the Spearman rank correlation, do not rely on distributional assumptions, making them suitable for analyzing variables that may not follow a normal distribution.

b) Robustness: Nonparametric tests are robust to outliers and do not require assumptions about the underlying distribution of data. This robustness is crucial in financial analysis, where extreme events (e.g., market crashes) can significantly impact data distributions.

c) Suitability for small samples: Parametric tests often require large sample sizes to ensure validity. Nonparametric tests can be effective with smaller samples, making them applicable in situations where data collection may be limited.

7.6.1 Nonparametric Versions of Analysis

The median serves as a nonparametric measure of central tendency in a distribution, as demonstrated in our previous code examples. To assess the dispersion of a distribution nonparametrically, we can use the interquartile range (IQR), derived from the difference between the third and the first quartile of the data set. The code cell below compares the performance of sample std and IQR in estimating population dispersion. →C7NB 7.6.1a

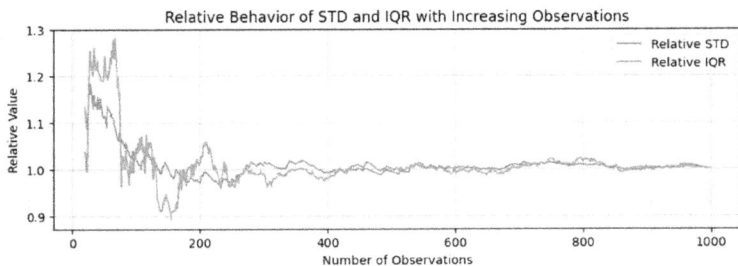

Figure 7.4 Jupyter Notebook screenshot for the result of compares the performance of sample standard deviation and IQR in estimating population dispersion

Explanation: The code generates a plot of sample std and IQR values with gradually increasing sample sizes (see Figure 7.4). These values are standardized using the last values in their respective arrays. A relative value of 1 indicates that the sample estimate is close to the "population" value. The IQR is calculated using the quantile method, which is available for both Pandas and NumPy array objects.

The plot illustrates that the sample std tends to be more stable and consistently approaches the population value compared to the IQR. This difference arises because the IQR relies on less information from the data than the sample std. However, in the presence of extreme outliers, this trend may reverse (see post-chapter exercises).

Wilcoxon Signed-Rank Test

The Wilcoxon signed-rank test (w-test) is a nonparametric test used as an alternative to the one-sample t-test when the data does not meet the assumptions of normality required for the t-test. The following code cell demonstrates the implementation of the nonparametric test on our ROE data: →C7NB 7.6.1b

Explanation: One-sample W-test is expected to outperform its parametric counterpart (one-sample t-test) only with small sample sizes. As sample sizes increase, the CLT levels the playing field for parametric tests. However, the W-test should be avoided when there are many tied observations due to its computation method.

Two-Sample Wilcoxon Signed-Rank Test

The two-sample Wilcoxon signed-rank test (ww-test) is a nonparametric statistical test used to determine if two related groups differ significantly from each other in terms of their median values. It is particularly useful when the data do not meet the assumptions required for a parametric test (like normality of distribution or equal variances), or when the data are ordinal rather than interval/ratio scale. Be aware that compared to its parametric counterpart, ww-test generally has less power given the same sample size. →C7NB 7.6.1c

Explanation: When two equal-size arrays are provided to the function, Wilcoxon performs a two-sample nonparametric test on the data. Focusing on the p-value, we observe that the two-sample t-test yields a slightly more significant result compared to the Wilcoxon test.

Spearman Rank-Order Test

To perform a nonparametric version of a correlation test, we can use the Spearman rank-order correlation coefficient, which assesses the strength and direction of association between two ranked variables. Here's is the implement using Python: →C7NB 7.6.1d

Explanation: As sample sizes increase, both the Spearman and Person's correlation tests converge consistently toward the population value. It's important to note that due to the lack of specified random seeds in the gen_obv functions, running the code cell multiple times will produce different outputs each time. However, the overall conclusions drawn from the analyses should remain consistent.

Conclusion

In this chapter, we delved into the essential principles of statistics as they apply to financial data science. We started by exploring the foundational concepts of financial statistics, emphasizing their critical role in decision-making processes within finance. We then moved on to probability distributions, reviewing common distributions, such as normal, lognormal, uniform, and binomial, and demonstrated how to simulate these distributions using Python.

Descriptive statistics were thoroughly covered, including measures like mean, median, variance, and std, which are fundamental for summarizing and interpreting financial data. We also examined statistical estimators, evaluating their accuracy and efficiency, and discussed graphical methods for visual data analysis.

Hypothesis testing was a significant focus, where we explored one-sample and two-sample t-tests, power analysis, and correlation testing. Additionally, nonparametric statistics were introduced as alternatives to parametric tests when data assumptions were not met, including tests like the Wilcoxon signed-rank test.

Further Exploration

For further reading, we encourage exploring additional statistical tests and techniques that were not covered in this chapter. Topics such as advanced nonparametric tests (Conover 1999), time series analysis (Tsay 2005), multivariate statistics (Hair et al. 2009), and machine learning methods in finance offer deeper insights into analyzing complex financial data sets (ZChen 2025). Engaging with these topics will enhance your ability to extract meaningful insights and make informed decisions in financial data science.

Exercise

In this exercise project, we will modify the simulation data generation process to include outliers and non-normal distributions (check the end of workbook FDSP_Chapter7_Notebook.ipynb). This modification aims to help you understand the impact of outliers and non-normal data on statistical analysis in finance. You will redo various statistical analyses covered in the chapter and describe the results in light of these modifications.

1. Generate 100 samples using gen_obv2 and analyze the ROE data for both companies. Describe the shape of the distributions and identify any possible outliers. Then, generate 1,000 samples to represent the population more accurately. Compare the descriptive statistics from the smaller sample to those from the larger sample. Discuss whether the descriptive statistics from the smaller sample accurately reflect the population parameters.

2. Using gen_obv2, create two sets of samples with sizes of 100 and 1,000. Evaluate the performance of statistical estimators (mean, median, std) as discussed in the Section **Statistical Estimators** of this chapter. Analyze the asymptotic behavior of these estimators in the two sample sizes.

3. Utilize gen_obv2 to generate a sample of 100 observations for company A's ROE data. Conduct a one-sample t-test to examine if the mean ROE differs significantly from zero. Next, perform a two-sample t-test to compare the mean ROE between company A and company B. Repeat the hypothesis testing using nonparametric methods. Compare the p-values and draw conclusions from each test. Based on your findings, discuss which testing approach (parametric or nonparametric) demonstrates better performance for these analyses.

CHAPTER 8

Financial Time Series Analysis

8.1 Financial Time Series Data

Financial time series data consists of sequential observations collected at regular intervals over time. This type of data is fundamental in finance for understanding market behaviors, asset prices, and economic indicators. Analyzing financial time series involves techniques that capture patterns, trends, and dependencies within the data to make informed decisions (Chatfield 2004).

To illustrate the practical aspects of financial time series analysis, we have prepared a real-life financial data set consisting of daily closing prices of gold futures and the US Dollar (USD) Index from January 1, 2013, to December 31, 2023. This data set captures the daily fluctuations in gold futures prices and the strength of the US dollar relative to a basket of currencies. The following code cell demonstrates how to obtain the data using the Yahoo Finance API package.* →C8NB 8.1a

Explanation: The API provides multiple columns of daily price and volume data. For this chapter, we focus solely on the closing prices from both data sets. Using pd.concat, we combine two Pandas Series into a DataFrame. As covered in a previous chapter, Pandas objects automatically align during concatenation operations. An alternative data source from a local csv file is also available, see

---

* Package yfinance must be installed in your Python environment. See Appendix for installation instructions. An alternative data source from a csv file is also available on the chapter notebook file.

8.2 Manipulating Time Serie Data With Pandas

The Timestamp (hereafter, TS) object in Pandas represents a point in time and serves as the fundamental building block for constructing DatetimeIndex (DI) objects. It encapsulates a specific date and time down to nanosecond precision. Key features of the class include:

- **Creation**: Instantiating a TS object from various formats like strings, datetime objects, or numeric TSs.
- **Attributes**: Accessing attributes such as year, month, day, hour, minute, second, and microsecond.
- **Operations**: Performing arithmetic operations to shift dates forward or backward.

→C8NB 8.2a

Explanation: The TS object is designed to model time and related operations. Similar to other objects, it possesses its own attributes and methods. One of its most crucial features is its compatibility with arithmetic operations. It's important to note that subtracting two TS objects yields a pd.Timedelta object, which represents the difference in time between them. However, attempting to add two TS objects together will raise an exception, as this operation is not defined.

pd.DatetimeIndex

The DI in Pandas is designed for indexing data by TSs other time references. It provides a rich set of functionalities for working with time series data, including:

- Date range generation: Easily generate sequences of dates or TSs.
- Indexing and slicing: Perform efficient selection and subsetting of data based on time intervals.
- Resampling and frequency conversion: Aggregate data over different time frequencies (e.g., from daily to monthly).
- Time zone handling: Convert time series data between different time zones.

The following code cell demonstrates the important features of DI objects. Notice that a DI object is itertable and thus it can perform certain list-like operations such as indexing and slicing. A list of TS objects can be converted into a **DI** object by using the class initializer: For example, pd.DatetimeIndex([dt_1,dt_2,dt_3,.......dt_n]). →C8NB 8.3a

Time Series DataFrame

When a DI object is attached to a DataFrame as its index, the DataFrame is referred to as a *time series DataFrame* and gains additional functionality tailored for time series analysis. It's important to note that the index in a DataFrame is both an attribute and an object itself. Therefore, when a DataFrame is created from a local file, the index is typically not a DI, even if the index data represents time. This occurs because when a DataFrame is *saved*,only the data is written to the hard disk, not the object itself. One exception to this is when saving a DataFrame object using pickle, as demonstrated in Chapter 6. →C8NB 8.2b

The DataFrame returned from the Yahoo Finance API call earlier is structured with a **DI** index attached. Consequently, we can utilize this object to perform various data operations that are specifically available in time series DataFrame.

8.3 Handling and Manipulating Time Series Data

Resampling and Frequency Conversion

Resampling and frequency conversion are essential operations in time series analysis, allowing us to aggregate or transform time series data based on different time frequencies. →C8NB 8.3a

Explanation: In this example, ts_data is resampled to a weekly frequency ('W') using the .resample('W') call. This method returns a resampler object instead of a DataFrame. It's important to note that this group-like object is designed to reduce CPU time overhead. The resampler object keeps the grouping information without performing any computation until an aggregation method, such as mean, is applied. In this code example, we call the object's mean method, which performs an averaging operation on each group (i.e., each weekly interval) created by the resampling. This operation is useful for converting daily data into weekly aggregates, providing a broader view of trends over longer periods.

Time Series Indexing and Slicing

Time series indexing and slicing enable us to select specific subsets of data based on time intervals or TSs. →C8NB 8.3b

Explanation: Here, ts_data['2023-01-01':'2023-06-30'] selects data between January 1, 2023, and June 30, 2023, inclusive. This method of indexing allows for precise extraction of data for analysis or visualization within specified time ranges. It's important to note that the data will be automatically truncated if the specified date range extends beyond the index range of the data.

Reindexing Time Series Data

Reindexing is a fundamental operation in Pandas that allows for realigning the data to match a new set of labels. This operation is particularly useful in time series analysis when you need to ensure data consistency or prepare data for further analysis. →C8NB 8.3c

Explanation: In this example, pd.date_range(start='2023-01-01', end='2023-12-31', freq='D') generates a new DI object covering daily frequencies ('D') from January 1, 2023, to December 31, 2023. ts_data. reindex(new_dates) re-indexes the ts_data object to match the new DI object specified by new_dates. It's important to note that only rows aligned with the new index are retained in the new DataFrame. Since the original ts_data index is based on trading dates in the market, when it is reindexed to a calendar day index, the rows corresponding to non-trading dates are filled with "NaN" entries.

Time-Shifting in Time Series Data

Time-shifting is a technique used in time series analysis to shift data points backward or forward in time. This operation is useful for comparing current data with historical data, aligning data for analysis, and creating lagged or lead variables for forecasting models. →C8NB 8.3d

Explanation: In this example, ts_data.shift(periods=1) shifts ts_data one period backward. This means that the time indexes aligning with the rows go backward by one period. For instance, the value originally at index t will now appear at index t-1. This kind of time-shifting is valuable for calculating changes over time or comparing current data points with their immediate past.

Time-Rolling and Expanding in Time Series Data

Time-rolling and expanding are techniques in time series analysis used to compute statistics over a rolling window of data points or expanding window that grows with time. These operations are crucial for smoothing data, calculating moving averages, and analyzing trends over time. →C8NB 8.3e

Explanation: In this example, ts_data.rolling(window=5).mean() computes the rolling mean over a window of five periods. This means that for each point in the time series, the average of the current and the previous four data points is calculated. This technique is useful for smoothing out fluctuations and identifying trends in the data.

Time-Expanding (Expanding Window Statistics)

On the other hand, ts_data.expanding().mean() computes the expanding mean, which calculates the mean from the start of the time series up to each point. As the time series progresses, the window of calculation expands, including all previous data points. This method is valuable for understanding cumulative trends and overall behavior over time. → C8NB 8.3f

Managing Missing Values in Time Series Data

Missing data can arise due to various reasons such as data collection issues, holidays, or weekends when markets are closed. Pandas provides several methods to handle missing values effectively in time series data sets. → C8NB 8.3g

Explanation: The isnull method returns a DataFrame of Boolean values indicating the null values among the cells. The sum method then adds up all the True values in each column. To find the indices of rows with null entries, we can use the DataFrame's filtering operation, as covered in Chapter 6.

Filling the NA Values

Missing values can arise due to various reasons such as data collection issues, market closures, or data adjustments. They can disrupt calculations, statistical analysis, and modeling efforts. Filling these gaps ensures that the data set remains complete and suitable for analysis.

- Forward fill (ffill): Propagates the last observed value forward to fill missing values. This method assumes that the most recent observed value is still valid for subsequent periods.
- Backward fill (bfill): Propagates the next observed value backward to fill missing values. This method assumes that the next observed value is a suitable substitute for the missing value.
- Mean or median imputation: Fills missing values with the mean or median of the observed values in the column. This method is useful when the missing values are assumed to be similar to the non-missing values.
- Interpolation: Uses linear or polynomial interpolation to estimate missing values based on neighboring data points. This method is effective for time series data where values are expected to change gradually over time.

Determining which filling method has less impact on modeling depends on the specific characteristics of your data and the requirements of your modeling approach. As a general guideline, if missing values occur sporadically and the immediate past or future values are reasonable approximations, methods like ffill or bfill can be suitable. Alternatively, interpolation methods are preferred when the missing data follows a discernible pattern that the interpolation method can accurately capture.

Filling missing values with mean or other central tendencies should be used cautiously, as this approach can alter the distribution and

variability of the data, potentially leading to biased modeling outcomes.
→C8NB 8.3h

Explanation: In older versions of Pandas (before 2.1.0), the ffill, bfill, and interpolate options were embedded within the fillna method (e.g., fillna(method= "ffill"). All filling methods included the inplace option, which allows altering the calling object directly. By default, inplace is set to False, so the method returns a new DataFrame object.

The interpolate method also offers additional algorithms, selectable via the method parameter, for inferring missing data. For instance, spline regression of a chosen order (order parameter) can be employed to interpolate missing values.

For this project, we fill the missing values with the ffill option. With the raw data prepared, we will move on to the modeling tasks.

8.4 Time Series Analysis

Time series analysis involves examining sequential data points collected over time to uncover patterns and trends that can aid in forecasting and decision making. Financial analysts and decision makers use this approach to dissect time series data into its fundamental components, each providing valuable insights.

8.4.1 Components of Time Series Data

- Trend: The long-term movement or directionality of the data over time. Example: Separating the trend from a stock price time series can reveal whether the stock is generally increasing, decreasing, or stable.
- Seasonality: Regular, periodic fluctuations in the data occurring at fixed intervals. Example: seasonal patterns in retail sales data can highlight peaks during holiday seasons or dips during off-peak periods.
- Cyclicality: Fluctuations in the data that are not fixed to specific intervals but occur over longer periods. Example: Business cycle phases (expansion, peak, contraction, trough) from economic indicators help assess broader economic conditions.

- Irregularity (noise): Random variations in the data that cannot be attributed to trends, seasonality, or cycles. Example: Random spikes or dips in daily stock prices that do not follow any discernible pattern.

How These Components Aid Financial Decision Making

- Investment strategies: By identifying trends, investors can decide whether to enter or exit positions in assets based on their long-term performance outlook.
- Business planning: Understanding seasonal patterns helps businesses adjust production, marketing, and inventory management strategies to optimize revenue and cost efficiency.
- Economic analysis: Monitoring cyclicality in economic indicators informs policymakers and businesses about the current phase of the economic cycle, guiding decisions on fiscal policies and investment plans.
- Risk management: Filtering out irregularities reduces the impact of random fluctuations in financial data, enabling more precise risk assessments and mitigation strategies.

8.4.2 Stationarity Analysis

Stationarity is a critical property of time series data where the statistical properties remain constant over time. A stationary time series is easier to model, predict, and interpret because its behavior is consistent and predictable (Tsay 2005).

Mathematical Definition of Stationarity

Stationarity in a time series context refers to a set of statistical properties that do not change over time. Formally, a time series $\{X_t\}$ is stationary if it satisfies the following conditions for all t:

- Constant mean (μ): $E[X_t]=\mu$
- Constant variance (σ^2): $Var[X_t]=\sigma^2$

- Constant autocovariance: $\text{Cov}[X_t, X_{t+k}] = \gamma(k)$. The covariance between observations at different time points depends only on the time lag between them, not on time itself.

Test for Stationarity

- The Augmented Dickey–Fuller (ADF) test helps determine if a series is stationary by evaluating the null hypothesis that the series is nonstationary.
- Kwiatkowski–Phillips–Schmidt–Shin (KPSS) test is another commonly used test for nonstationary. The null hypothesis for the test is that the series is stationary.

In practice, the ADF test often exhibits low power in rejecting a false null hypothesis (MacKinnon 1991), while the KPSS test assumes that the time series is stationary. Therefore, both tests are often used together to double-check for the stationarity of a time series (Kwiatkowski et al. 1992). →C8NB 8.4.2a

Explanation: The weekly gold futures and USD index series are both in level units perhaps with changing short-term trend; therefore, it is very unlikely that these series are stationary. The test results are as expected: the ADF test fails to reject the null hypothesis that the series are nonstationary, and the KPSS test rejects the null hypothesis that both series are stationary. Therefore, the evidence strongly indicates that the series are nonstationary.

Converting Nonstationary Series

Nonstationary time series often exhibit trends, seasonalities, or other patterns that complicate statistical modeling. Converting these series into stationary ones can simplify modeling and enhance forecast reliability. Several common techniques can be employed to achieve stationarity:

- **Differencing:** Differencing involves calculating the difference between consecutive observations. This method can eliminate trends or seasonal patterns from the series.

- **Transformation:** Transformation methods such as logarithmic or square root transformations can stabilize the variance of the series, thereby making it more stationary.
- **Seasonal adjustment:** For series with seasonal components, seasonal adjustment techniques such as seasonal differencing or seasonal decomposition (e.g., using seasonal_decompose from statsmodels) can effectively remove seasonal effects.
- **Combining techniques:** A frequently used combined method applicable to price-related time series is to compute the log difference, which approximates percentage changes in prices.

The following code cell demonstrates the implementation of these methods on our weekly gold futures and USD index prices data. The differencing and log operations are applied to the weekly prices first, followed by the combined operation—log difference. Note that the log difference operation will result in values close to the weekly percentage changes in prices.

We test each resulting series for stationarity using the ADF test and for non-stationarity using the KPSS test. The results are displayed in Figure 8.1 below. It is shown that the log difference operation is preferable over the other alternatives for transforming the data. →C8NB 8.4.2a

```
gold_futures_diff_adf_test p-value: 9.661684070757687e-25
USD_index_diff_adf_test p-value: 1.5081957645116514e-15
gold_futures_diff_KPSS_test p-value: 0.06877534606003782
USD_index_diff_KPSS_test p-value: 0.1

gold_futures_log_adf_test p-value: 0.8889712724175552
USD_index_log_adf_test p-value: 0.2389085516044085
gold_futures_log_KPSS_test p-value: 0.01
USD_index_log_KPSS_test p-value: 0.01

gold_futures_log_diff_adf_test p-value: 1.3572165576026582e-19
USD_futures_log_diff_adf_test p-value: 8.021816075177221e-16
gold_futures_log_diff_KPSS_test p-value: 0.08806339572996662
USD_futures_log_diff_KPSS_test p-value: 0.1
```

Figure 8.1 Jupyter Notebook screenshot for the result of transforming nonstationary series

8.4.3 Seasonal Decomposition

When seasonality is present in the series, simple transformation methods demonstrated above may not be sufficient to transform the series. The following code cell shows an example by simulating a time series with both trend and seasonality components. This simulation aims to show that for more complex time series with a seasonality component, seasonal decomposition operations are required to separate the stationary and nonstationary components. →C8NB 8.4.3a

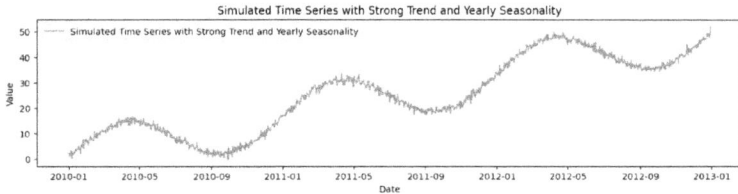

Figure 8.2 Jupyter Notebook screenshot for implementation of seasonal decomposition in Python

Explanation: pd.date_range generates the specified DI. A simulated series is constructed by adding the trend, seasonality, and noise components together. The data is displayed in a time series plot. Notice that the data frequency is daily, and the seasonal period can be inferred from the time interval between each peak or trough. In this case, based on the plot (see Figure 8.2), the period is approximately 365 days..

We now run some tests for stationarity on the raw series and transformed series. Notice that both ADF and KPSS tests are applied to each series. →C8NB 8.4.3b

Explanation: The differenced series is obtained by using the diff() method as before. Here, we use the seasonal_decompose function from statsmodels.tsa.seasonal. This function decomposes a time series into trend, seasonal, and residual components using an algorithm based on moving averages. We can configure the algorithm by adjusting the period and model inputs. Without any prior knowledge, the period is estimated using visual inspection of the time series plot. The available model inputs are "additive" and "multiplicative." The latter is used when the magnitude of the seasonality is in proportion to the data levels.

Notice that the raw series and the differenced series do not pass the stationarity test, but the residual series, which is the result of removing the estimated trend and seasonal components, passes both stationarity tests.

The following code cell displays the trend and seasonal components produced by the seasonal_decompose function in a time series plot (see

Figure 8,3 below). Notice that although the directions are correct, there are margins of error between the estimates and the true values used in our simulation. →C8NB 8.4.3c

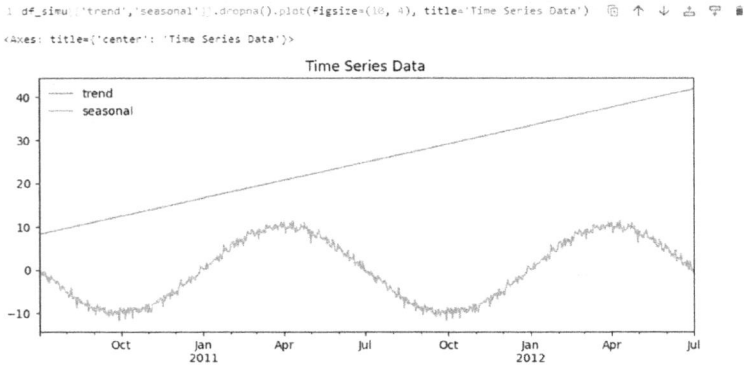

Figure 8.3 Jupyter Notebook screenshot of showing the trend and seasonal components of the simulated data

8.4.4 Autoregressive Analysis

Autocorrelation, also known as serial correlation, refers to the correlation of a time series with its own past values. In other words, it measures the relationship between an observation at a certain time and observations at previous times. This relationship is crucial in time series analysis because it can indicate patterns, trends, and cyclic behaviors that can be modeled for forecasting. There are several important terms we need to understand before moving to the implementation:

- **Order of autocorrelation:** The specific lag (or multiple lags) in a time series at which the autocorrelation is measured. In other words, it indicates how many periods back in time the data shows a meaningful relationship with the current value.
- **Autocorrelation function (ACF):** A function measures the correlation between a time series and its own past values at different lags. It helps in identifying the significant lags (orders) where autocorrelation is present.

- **Partial autocorrelation function (PACF)** measures the correlation between a time series and its own past values, removing the effects of shorter lag correlations. It helps in identifying the direct relationships between observations at different lags.

ACF Versus PACF

Without going into the mathematical details, the ACF measures the total correlation between an observation and its lagged values, including both direct and indirect effects. The PACF measures the direct correlation between an observation and its lagged values, controlling for the values of the intermediate lags.

Identifying Significant Lags

The statsmodels provide functionality that compute the map of ACF and PACF for a specific lag length. We need a guideline regarding the size of ACF/PACF values that are considered significant. For large sample size, the standard error of the autocorrelation coefficient is given by $1/\sqrt{n}$, where n is the sample size. Therefore, any autocorrelation coefficients beyond the $1.96/\sqrt{n}$ should be considered significant under 5 percent type I error.

In the following code cell, we use the ACF, PACF functions from statsmodels.tsa.stattools to compute the ACF and PACF values for our gold futures and USD index weekly return data for up to 40 lags and then compare them with the significant thresholds. →C8NB 8.4.4a

Figure 8.4 presents the computation results:

```
gold_futures_log_diff significant ACF lags & values:
  {1: 0.16, 4: -0.1, 6: 0.09, 30: 0.08}
gold_futures_log_diff significant PACF lags & values:
  {1: 0.16, 4: -0.09}
USD_index_log_diff significant ACF lags & values:
  {1: 0.22, 5: 0.09, 25: 0.09, 28: -0.09, 34: 0.09}
gold_futures_log_diff significant PACF lags & values:
  {1: 0.16, 4: -0.09}
```

Figure 8.4 Jupyter Notebook screenshot of result of computing the ACF and PACF values for gold futures and USD index weekly return (log deference) data for up to 40 lags, and then comparing them with the significant thresholds

ACF/PACF Plot

A visualization of the previous results can be obtained by using the plot_
acf and plot_pacf plot methods from statsmodels.graphics.tsaplots. →
C8NB 8.4.4b

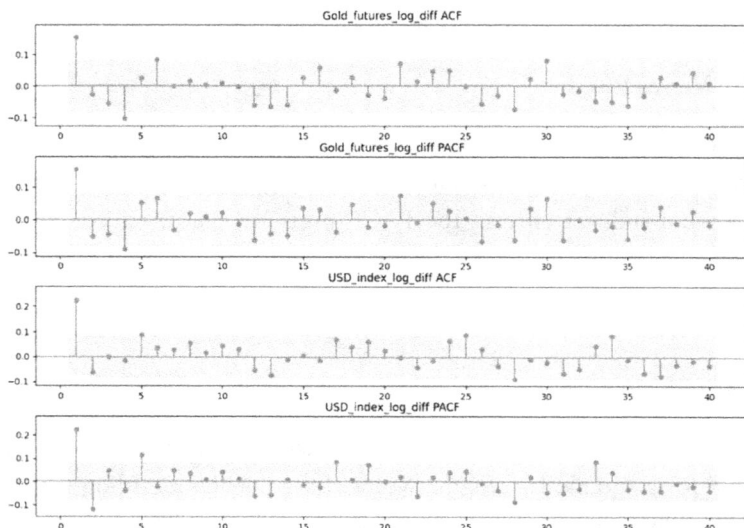

*Figure 8.5 Jupyter Notebook screenshot of visualizing of the
significant lag in ACF and PACF plots based on the log_diff weekly
returns of USD_index and Gold_futures data*

Explanation: The code for generating the ACF and PACF plots is available in the chapter workbook. In these plots (Figure 8.5), the vertical axis
shows the correlation coefficient values, and the horizontal axis shows the
lag orders. The shaded area indicates the $1-\alpha$ confidence interval for the
correlation coefficients. Any sample estimates beyond these areas are considered significant evidence against the hypothesis that the corresponding
true correlation coefficient is 0. It is shown that autocorrelation at lag one
is distinctly higher than the others in both ACF and PACF plots.

8.4.5 ARIMA Model

The ARIMA model, which stands for AutoRegressive Integrated Moving
Average, is a powerful and widely used statistical method for time series

forecasting (Box et al. 2015). The model is widely used for forecasting future values in time series data, such as predicting stock prices, sales, or economic indicators. It helps in identifying underlying patterns and making informed decisions by accounting for autocorrelations, trends, and seasonality in the data. A typical ARIMA model combines three components:

- **Autoregression (AR):**
  This component captures the relationship between an observation and a number of lagged observations (previous time steps). The AR part of the model is denoted by AR(p), where p is the number of lag observations included in the model.
  Example: AR(2) model uses the past two observations to predict the current value. $Y_t = \phi_1 Y_{t-1} + \phi_2 Y_{t-2} + \epsilon_t Y_t$, where ϕ_1 and ϕ_2 are parameters to be estimated, and ϵ_t is white noise.

- **Integration (I):**
  This component is used to make the time series stationary by differencing the observations (subtracting the previous observation from the current observation). The I part of the model is denoted by I(d), where d is the number of differences required to make the series stationary.
  Example: If $d = 1$, the model uses the first difference of the time series. $Y_t' = Y_t - Y_{t-1}$

- **Moving average (MA):**
  This component captures the relationship between an observation and a residual error from an MA model applied to lagged observations. The MA part of the model is denoted by MA(q), where q is the size of the MA window.
  Example: MA(2) model uses the past two forecast errors to predict the current value. $Y_t = \mu + \epsilon_t + \theta_1 \epsilon_{t-1} + \theta_2 \epsilon_{t-2}$, where θ_1 and θ_2 are parameters to be estimated, μ is the mean, and ϵ_t is white noise.

  The ARIMA model combining these three components is denoted as ARIMA(p, d, q)

Steps to Implement ARIMA in Python

a) Identify the parameters: Use techniques such as the ACF and PACF plots to determine the appropriate values for p, d, and q.
b) Fit the model: Fit the ARIMA model to the time series data.
c) Forecast future values: Use the fitted model to make predictions.

The following code cells fit ARIMA(1,0,1) models to our weekly gold futures and USD index returns data. The model parameters are determined based on our previous investigation into the significance of the ACF and PACF lags. No further differencing is applied to the data because we have shown that the weekly return series are stationary.

First, we separate the data into training and test sets and then translate the values into percentage units by multiplying each DataFrame by 100. We will discuss data preparation in more detail in the machine learning chapter. For now, it is important to note that we will fit the model using the training set data, make predictions about the return series over the test period, and then compare our predictions with the actual values. →C8NB 8.4.5a

The ARIMA fitting and prediction algorithms are more reliable when the time series object's index has a consistent frequency setting. In our data, a weekly frequency setting has been made in previous operation. → C8NB 8.4.5b

Explanation: The ARIMA class from statsmodels embeds many commonly used functionalities for statistical modeling with ARIMA models. First, we need to set up the model parameters. For example, order_gold = (1,0,1) are the parameters for the ARIMA's (p, d, q) configuration. We set p and q to 1 because, in our ACF and PACF plots, the lag 1 autocorrelation appears to show the most significant relationship among all the lags. The order of differencing, d, is set to 0 because we are already working with log-difference data.

The model_gold and model_usd are ARIMA objects embedded with the training data. We use the fit() method to estimate the model parameters, which returns fitted objects containing the results. For financial data scientists, being able to interpret these results is essential.

```
==============================================================================
Dep. Variable:              gold_futures   No. Observations:                  568
Model:                     ARIMA(1, 0, 1)   Log Likelihood             -1120.779
Date:                    Thu, 18 Jul 2024   AIC                         2249.558
Time:                            19:30:38   BIC                         2266.927
Sample:                        01-11-2013   HQIC                        2256.336
                             - 11-24-2023
Covariance Type:                      opg
==============================================================================
                 coef    std err          z      P>|z|      [0.025      0.975]
------------------------------------------------------------------------------
const          0.0311      0.089      0.352      0.725      -0.142       0.205
ar.L1         -0.0841      0.200     -0.421      0.674      -0.476       0.308
ma.L1          0.2460      0.198      1.240      0.215      -0.143       0.635
sigma2         3.0297      0.094     32.090      0.000       2.845       3.215
==============================================================================
Ljung-Box (L1) (Q):                 0.00   Jarque-Bera (JB):             929.88
Prob(Q):                            1.00   Prob(JB):                       0.00
Heteroskedasticity (H):             0.70   Skew:                          -0.42
Prob(H) (two-sided):                0.02   Kurtosis:                       9.21
==============================================================================
```

Figure 8.6a Jupyter Notebook screenshot of outputs after implementing ARIMA models for fitting the Gold Futures weekly return data

```
==============================================================================
Dep. Variable:                 USD_index   No. Observations:                  568
Model:                     ARIMA(1, 0, 1)   Log Likelihood              -625.571
Date:                    Thu, 18 Jul 2024   AIC                         1259.141
Time:                            19:30:38   BIC                         1276.509
Sample:                        01-11-2013   HQIC                        1265.919
                             - 11-24-2023
Covariance Type:                      opg
==============================================================================
                 coef    std err          z      P>|z|      [0.025      0.975]
------------------------------------------------------------------------------
const          0.0449      0.037      1.230      0.219      -0.027       0.116
ar.L1         -0.3995      0.105     -3.787      0.000      -0.606      -0.193
ma.L1          0.6559      0.090      7.282      0.000       0.479       0.832
sigma2         0.5297      0.023     22.678      0.000       0.484       0.576
==============================================================================
Ljung-Box (L1) (Q):                 0.05   Jarque-Bera (JB):              75.41
Prob(Q):                            0.83   Prob(JB):                       0.00
Heteroskedasticity (H):             0.96   Skew:                           0.24
Prob(H) (two-sided):                0.77   Kurtosis:                       4.72
==============================================================================
```

Figure 8.6b Jupyter Notebook screenshot of outputs after implementing ARIMA models for fitting USD index weekly return data

Explanation: The side-by-side tables in Figures 8.6a & Figures 8.6b above display the estimation results of fitting ARIMA(1,0,1) models to the gold futures and USD index weekly returns data. The first part of each table provides basic information about the estimations, including the name of the dependent variable, the model setup, the date and time of the analysis, the time range of the data, and the number of valid observations. The likelihood, AIC (Akaike Information Criterion), BIC (Bayesian Information Criterion), and HQIC (Hannan-Quinn Information Criterion) are all model comparison and selection indicators. They are used to compare different models for the same data. Generally, a higher log likelihood or lower AIC/BIC/HQIC values indicate a more preferred model compared to alternatives.

The middle part of the tables discloses the estimation results for the model parameters. Since we opted for the ARIMA (1,0,1) model, we have estimates for the coefficients of θ_1 and ϕ_1 and the model constant. The coef column displays the estimates, and the p-value for testing the significance of the coefficient is shown in the $P>|z|$ column. Based on the outputs, we can see that the ARIMA model coefficients are found insignificant for the futures gold data but significant for the USD index data.

Sigma2 represents the variance of the residuals (or the white noise) in the model. It measures the variability of the model's error terms, indicating how much the actual values deviate from the predicted values. A lower sigma2 value generally indicates a better fit of the model to the data, as it suggests that the model's predictions are closer to the actual observations. The test for sigma2 is based on the null hypothesis that the distribution of the model error is centered at zero. The table also provides the 95 percent confidence intervals for all the estimates of the model parameters.

The lower part of the table provides results for the diagnostic tests, which check whether the model assumptions are valid based on the model residuals. It is important to go over each of them.

The Ljung–Box (L1) (Q) test checks for significant lag-one autocorrelation among the residuals. A significant result indicates that the model is mis-specified, casting doubt on the estimation results.

The Jarque–Bera (JB) test examines whether the residuals follow a normal distribution. A significant result (see the p-value Prob(JB)), indicates that the residuals are not normally distributed. This undermines the validity of the model. Data scientists should consider this result as a warning that the estimation results and predictions may be unreliable, rather than a definitive rejection. Further investigations, such as visualizing the residuals for patterns and checking the original data, are required. The table also provides the skewness and kurtosis (peakedness) statistics of the model residuals. Comparing these values to those of a normal distribution (skewness = 0, kurtosis = 3) offers a quick assessment of the degree of deviation from normality. For example, the results suggest that the model residuals for gold futures are slightly skewed to the left and leptokurtic.

The heteroskedasticity (H) Test indicates whether the residuals exhibit constant variance across the observations. A significant test result (check Prob(H) for the *p*-value) indicates that the variance of the residuals is not constant. Similar to the issue of deviation from normality, nonconstant variance can lead to biased standard errors, unreliable prediction intervals, and inefficient parameter estimates. This issue must be further investigated to understand its undermining effects.

Prediction With ARIMA

We are now ready to make some predictions using our estimated models. The following code cell demonstrates how to make predictions using the fitted models. →C8NB 8.4.5c
Explanation: The model_gold_fitted and model_usd_fitted are ARIMA-fitted model objects returned from the fit() method. These objects offer two interfaces for making predictions:

1. Predict method: If the frequency of the data is well specified, such as weekly or daily frequencies, you can use the predict method with the start and end dates of the prediction period.
2. Forecast method: Alternatively, you can use the forecast method and specify the number of steps to forecast as input to the method.

Here, we generate a five-week forecast beyond the training data set. Long-term forecasts are generally not reliable when unpredictable noise is present. Comparing the actual values with the predicted values, we can see that the forecasts beyond the first week of the forecasting window tend to turn flatten as the influence of past terms diminishes. This further highlights the limitations of the model's long-term predictive power.

8.4.6 GRACH Model

Some model estimators derive their statistical properties based on the homoskedasticity assumption (Greene 2018), which means that the variance of model errors is constant. When this assumption is violated (heteroskedasticity), statistical inference based on the assumption, such as hypothesis testing and confidence intervals, becomes invalid (White 1980).

Heteroskedasticity is common among financial time series observed from the financial markets (Engle 1982). It has been well-documented that market volatility exhibits clustering, meaning that periods of high volatility are followed by high volatility and periods of low volatility follow low volatility. The generalized autoregressive conditional heteroskedasticity (GARCH) model is particularly useful in financial time series where volatility clustering is common (Bollerslev 1986). In this chapter, we will look at the GARCH(1,1) model as it has been widely used to model asset returns (Engle 2001).

Mathematical representation of GARCH(1,1) Model:

Conditional mean equation: $y_t = \mu + \epsilon_t$, where y_t is a stationary series for asset return, μ is the mean of the series, and ϵ_t is the error term.

Conditional variance equation: $\sigma_t^2 = \omega + \alpha\epsilon_{t-1}^2 + \beta\sigma_{t-1}^2$

where σ_t^2 is the conditional variance, ω is a constant term, α is the coefficient of the lagged squared residual from the mean equation (i.e., the ARCH term), and β is the coefficient of the lagged conditional variance (i.e., the GARCH term).

For more complex models, μ can be expanded to include other predictors. The GARCH model allows for autocorrelation in error variance, making it effective in modeling variance clustering.

Implementation of GARCH Model

Below is the code to fit a GARCH model using the arch package in Python on the gold futures and USD index weekly return data: →C8NB 8.4.6a

Explanation: Similar to the interfaces covered in the previous section, the arch model object provides the fit method, which returns fitted objects. The summary method delivers the results in a similar fashion (R language output).

We should focus on looking at estimates for the conditional variance equations which are displayed under "Volatility Model" as shown in Figure 8.7a, b.

```
                        Volatility Model
==============================================================================
            coef     std err           t     P>|t|         95.0% Conf. Int.
------------------------------------------------------------------------------
omega     0.0832   5.749e-02       1.446     0.148     [-2.953e-02,  0.196]
alpha[1]  0.0196   2.421e-02       0.810     0.418    [-2.784e-02,6.706e-02]
beta[1]   0.9495   3.645e-02      26.048 1.409e-149     [ 0.878,   1.021]
==============================================================================
```

Figure 8.7a Jupyter Notebook screenshot of outputs from fitting a GARCH model for gold futures weekly return data

```
                        Volatility Model
==============================================================================
            coef     std err           t     P>|t|         95.0% Conf. Int.
------------------------------------------------------------------------------
omega     0.0295   1.803e-02       1.638     0.102   [-5.813e-03,6.487e-02]
alpha[1]  0.1254   5.878e-02       2.133 3.289e-02     [1.020e-02,  0.241]
beta[1]   0.8298   6.973e-02      11.901 1.172e-32     [ 0.693,   0.966]
==============================================================================
```

Figure 8.7b Jupyter Notebook screenshot of outputs from fitting a GARCH model for USD index weekly return data

The side-by-side tables above display the estimation results of conditional variance equations of GARCH(1,1) models for gold futures (left table) and USD index (right table) weekly returns data. The GARCH terms (β) are significant in both time series, indicating the presence of volatility clustering. The ARCH term (α) is significant in the conditional variance equation of USD index returns, indicating that past squared returns significantly impact current volatility.

Although not shown in the table screenshot, the reported R-squared values are close to 0 for both time series. This is expected because the mean equation is oversimplified, as the primary goal of our investigation in using the GARCH model is to analyze the conditional variance equation.

Predicting Variance With GARCH

Forecasting future variance using a GARCH-fitted model object is straightforward. Simply use the forecast method and specify the number of steps as input to the horizon parameter. Be aware that long-term forecasts generated by GARCH models are generally unreliable. →C8NB 8.4.6b

8.4.7 Cointegration Model for Lead-lag Relationship

To study the lead-lag relationship between two time series, you can use cointegration analysis. Cointegration indicates a long-term equilibrium relationship between two or more time series. If two series are cointegrated, they move together over time despite short-term deviations (Johansen 1991).

In finance, cointegration is particularly useful for modeling relationships between different financial assets or economic indicators that move together over time. Common applications include:

Pairs Trading, Hedging Strategies, Arbitrage, Modeling Interest Rates and Economic Indicators.

Steps to Perform Cointegration Analysis

1. Check for stationarity: Ensure that both time series are nonstationary in levels but become stationary after differencing (i.e., they are integrated of order 1, or I(1)).
2. Perform cointegration test: Use tests like the Engle–Granger two-step method or the Johansen test to check for cointegration.
3. Estimate the cointegration relationship: If the series are cointegrated, estimate the long-term relationship using a vector error correction model (VECM).

To illustrate a practical implementation of cointegration, we conduct an analysis of basis trade using the futures and spot prices of the USD index. A basis trade involves taking a long position in one market and a short position in another, anticipating that the price gap will close. A necessary condition for this trading strategy to work is that the price series are cointegrated. Since we have been working with the spot index price (symbol: DX-Y.NY) since the beginning of this chapter, we will download the futures price of the same instrument. →C8NB 8.4.7a

Explanation: Both the futures and spot daily prices of the USD index are downloaded from the Yahoo Finance API. The NA entries are forward-filled, and two DataFrame objects are prepared: one for the original data and the other for the differenced data.

Next, we need to perform stationarity tests on the original and differenced series to ensure that the original series are nonstationary but become stationary after first-order differencing. →C8NB 8.4.7b

As the results suggest that the data qualifies for further cointegration analysis, we test for cointegration using the coint function from statsmodels.tsa.stattools. The function performs an augmented Engle–Granger two-step cointegration test on the series. The null hypothesis of the test is no cointegration, and thus rejecting the null hypothesis favors the alternative of existing cointegration between the two series. →C8NB 8.4.7c

Explanation: The test results strongly suggest that the spot and futures price series are cointegrated. This further enables us to model the relationship with VECM. → C8NB 8.4.7d

```
Det. terms outside the coint. relation & lagged endog. parameters for equation USD_index
==========================================================================================
                  coef    std err         z      P>|z|      [0.025      0.975]
------------------------------------------------------------------------------------------
L1.USD_index    0.6030      0.146     4.116      0.000       0.316       0.890
L1.USD_Futures  -1.0530      0.142    -7.427      0.000      -1.331      -0.775
Det. terms outside the coint. relation & lagged endog. parameters for equation USD_Futures
==========================================================================================
                  coef    std err         z      P>|z|      [0.025      0.975]
------------------------------------------------------------------------------------------
L1.USD_index    0.4611      0.150     3.068      0.002       0.166       0.756
L1.USD_Futures  -0.9362      0.145    -6.436      0.000      -1.221      -0.651
              Loading coefficients (alpha) for equation USD_index
==========================================================================================
                  coef    std err         z      P>|z|      [0.025      0.975]
------------------------------------------------------------------------------------------
ec1            -1.8977      0.240    -7.899      0.000      -2.369      -1.427
              Loading coefficients (alpha) for equation USD_Futures
==========================================================================================
                  coef    std err         z      P>|z|      [0.025      0.975]
------------------------------------------------------------------------------------------
ec1            -0.3521      0.247    -1.428      0.153      -0.835       0.131
              Cointegration relations for loading-coefficients-column 1
==========================================================================================
                  coef    std err         z      P>|z|      [0.025      0.975]
------------------------------------------------------------------------------------------
beta.1          1.0000          0         0      0.000       1.000       1.000
beta.2         -0.9653      0.003  -368.192      0.000      -0.970      -0.960
==========================================================================================
```

Figure 8.8 Jupyter Notebook screenshot of result after fitting the VECM model for the spot and futures USD price series

Explanation: The summary output provides several important test results indicating the lead-lag relationship between the two series. The first table displays the estimates for the spot price (USD index) equation. L1.USD_index refers to the lagged value of the spot price, and L1.USD_Futures refers to the lagged value of the futures price. A positive (negative) coefficient indicates a positive (negative) relationship, and the *p*-value indicates the statistical significance of the relationship. Translating all the results into plain language, the tables show:

- The lagged spot price has a positive and statistically significant effect on the current spot price. A one-unit increase in the lagged spot price increases the current spot price by approximately 0.6343 units.
- The lagged value of the futures price has a negative and statistically significant effect on the current value of the USD spot price. A one-unit increase in the lagged futures price decreases the current spot price by approximately 1.0817 units.

The next table delivers the same kind of messages for modeling USD futures prices (details left for exercise).

The third table provides estimates for the adjustment coefficient (*α*). The coefficient quantifies the speed at which the dependent variable returns to its long-run equilibrium following a deviation. The estimated coefficient is significant and negative, indicating that the spot price adjusts towards the long-run equilibrium with a speed of approximately 1.9554 units (describe the results for USD futures in the exercise).

The last table shows the estimates for the cointegration relationship coefficients (*β*), which represent the long-term equilibrium relationship between the spot and futures prices. The estimate indicates that the spot and futures prices are cointegrated with a long-run equilibrium relationship. The normalized cointegration coefficient for the spot price is 1, and for the futures price, it is –0.9645. This means that in the long run, the spot price is approximately 0.9645 times the futures price. The difference is consistent with the arbitrage pricing relationship between the prices.

Conclusion

In this chapter, we explored various aspects of financial time series data. We delved into managing time series data using Pandas, including resampling, indexing, and handling missing values. We then moved on to time series analysis, covering key concepts such as stationarity, transformation methods, and seasonal decomposition.

We introduced autoregressive models and the significance of ACF and PACF in identifying patterns in time series data. The ARIMA model was discussed in detail for forecasting, and we demonstrated fitting and interpreting GARCH models for volatility analysis. Lastly, we covered cointegration analysis to understand the long-term equilibrium relationships between financial time series, such as the USD index spot and futures prices.

Exercise

1. Create a DataFrame of the USD index's spot and futures prices at a monthly frequency. Use the resample method to take the average closing price for each month. Refer to this DataFrame as "mdata" in your code.

2. Check whether mdata is a time series DataFrame by examining the type of its index object.

3. Reverse the direction of mdata's index from ascending to descending (hint: use the sort_index method of the DataFrame object).

4. Extract the data for the year 2018 from mdata.

5. Create two new columns in mdata by applying the log-difference operation on the spot and futures prices.

6. Perform hypothesis tests to check whether the price and log-return series (four of them) are stationary. Describe the null hypotheses of your test and indicate the evidence supporting your conclusion.

7. Analyze the ACF and PACF of the spot and futures log monthly returns by showing the ACF/PACF plots. Which lags in these plots appear to be the most significant (or none)?

8. Fit an appropriate GARCH model to the log monthly returns and compare the results with those for weekly returns. Does the volatility clustering get stronger or weaker as the frequency increases? Venture an explanation using common sense.

9. Complete the interpretation of the cointegration report in the chapter for the USD futures prices equation. In particular, describe the roles of lagged spot and futures prices on current futures prices. Are these roles statistically and economically significant? Highlight the empirical evidence that supports your judgment.

CHAPTER 9

Data Visualization

In this chapter, we will explore various data visualization techniques using Jupyter Notebook. Visualizing financial data can help us uncover trends, patterns, and insights that are not immediately apparent from raw data. We will use popular Python libraries such as Matplotlib, Seaborn, and Plotly to create both static and interactive visualizations.

9.1 Plotting With Matplotlib

Matplotlib is a powerful library for creating static visualizations in Python. It consists of various classes and objects that allow for a high degree of customization (Matplotlib Documentation 2023). The core components include Figure, Axes, and various plotting functions. It is important to understand the following conceptual terms before moving on:

- **Figure:** The entire window or page that holds all the plot elements.
- **Axes:** The area where the data is actually plotted. A single figure can contain multiple Axes objects.
- **Axis:** An object that represents one of the reference lines in a plot, typically the horizontal (x-axis) or vertical (y-axis) line, which defines the coordinate system of the Axes.

It is important to note that Axes and Axis are entirely different objects. The Axis object handles the tick marks, tick labels, grid lines, and the scaling of the plot. It helps in setting the range and scale of the plot. Axis objects are created automatically when an Axes object is created. You interact with the Axis through the Axes object's methods

9.1.1 Basic Plotting

Here is an example of using Matplotlib to create a simple line plot:
→C9NB 9.1.1

Figure 9.1 Jupyter Notebook screenshot of using Matplotlib to create a simple line plot

Explanation: In this code example:

- plt.subplots(figsize=(10, 3)) returns (in a tuple) a Figure and the associated Axes object. The number of inputs here represents the figure's width and height in inches.
- ax.plot(apple_data ['Close'], label='AAPL Closing Price') plots the data on the Axes.
- ax.set_title, ax.set_xlabel, and ax.set_ylabel set the title and labels for the plot of the Axes.
- ax.legend() and ax.grid(True) add a legend and a grid to the plot of the Axes.

It is important to note that, Jupyter Notebook automatically display the Figure when it is caught in the output. This can be turned off by executing plt.ioff().

9.1.2 Building Subplot

The plt.subplots function generates the Figure and Axes objects for display. To place multiple plots in one figure, use the nrows and ncols parameters. For example, nrows=2, ncols=1 will create a 2 × 1 arrangement of plots(Axes), and nrows=2, ncols=2 will create a 2 × 2 grid of plots. The function returns the Figure and Axes objects for further implementation.

The following example generates a candlestick chart, commonly seen on many market price quote platforms. Notice that an external module called mplfinance is imported and the module's plot function is called to elaborate on the two passing Axes objects. This demonstrates the flexibility of working with the Figure and Axes objects. There are many packages, each specializing in certain domains, that interact with these objects, allowing users to generate advanced plots without knowing the details of the implementation. →C9NB 9.1.2

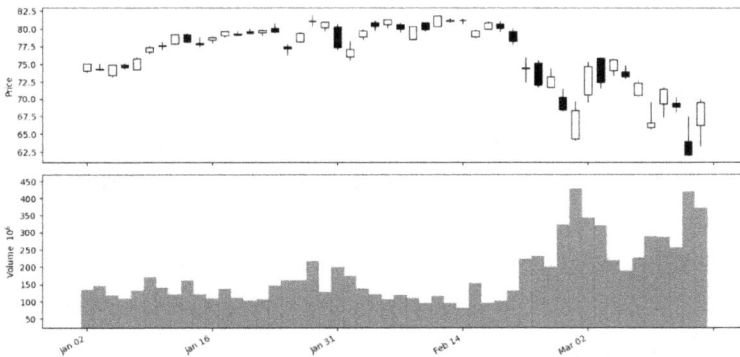

Figure 9.2 Jupyter Notebook screenshot of generating a 2 × 1 candlestick chat subplots using Matplotlib and mplfinance

Explanation: The candlestick chart uses the Open, High, Low, Close prices provided in the DataFrame (apple_data). The function automatically looks for the related price columns and constructs the plot internally. It also optionally provides the volume plot, which is also handled by the function. Users simply need to set up the figure and then plug in the Axes objects for the function.

9.1.3 Customizing Plots

Matplotlib allows extensive customization of plots. You can customize the appearance of the plot elements, add annotations, and create subplots. The following code cell redecorates the line chart using the Axes object's interface for customizing plot. →C9NB 9.1.3

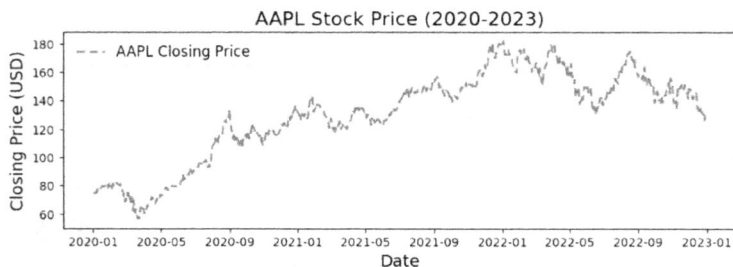

Figure 9.3 Jupyter Notebook screenshot of customizing the appearance of the plot elements, adding annotations, and creating subplots

Explanation: The output of the code is displayed in Figure 9.3. Within the source code, the Axes objects retain their attributes (the plot) unless an interaction clears the content. To clear the plot content manually, the object's cla method is called. In this example, the line chart is customized by using the Axes object's methods for plot customization.

9.1.4 Other Commonly Used Plots

In the previous examples, we demonstrated the line plot (price), bar plot (volume), and candlestick chart, which are frequently used for time series data. There are other plots commonly used by financial data scientists for data visualization. The setup and configuration of these plots are similar to each other.

Histogram

Histograms are used to represent the distribution of a data set. In financial data science, they can be used to analyze the distribution of returns, volumes, or other metrics. The following code cell displays the distribution of returns for Apple Inc. (AAPL) in Figure 9.4. The vertical axis represents the frequency of each return range (bin) over the horizontal axis. We can see that the returns exhibit an approximately normal distribution centered at 0 with several extreme outliers (fat-tails). →C9NB 9.1.4a

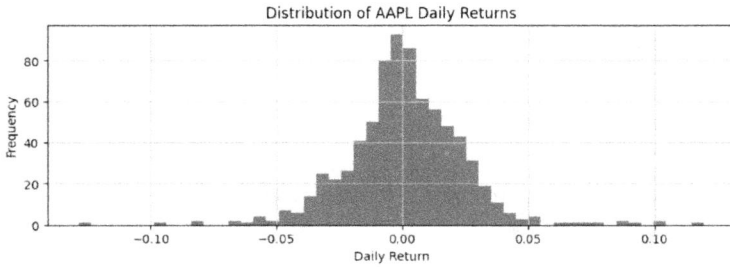

Figure 9.4 Jupyter Notebook screenshot of using histogram to display the distribution of returns for AAPL

Scatter Plot

Scatter plots are used to display the relationship between two variables. They can be used to visualize correlations, such as between returns and volumes. The following code cell creates a scatter plot using daily returns and volume from the AAPL data set. This plot does not reveal any linear relationship between the two variables. The outliers pose a potential issue for using relationship statistics, as their positions are influential. Without visualizing the data, users may jump to conclusions based on distorted statistics. →C9NB 9.1.4b

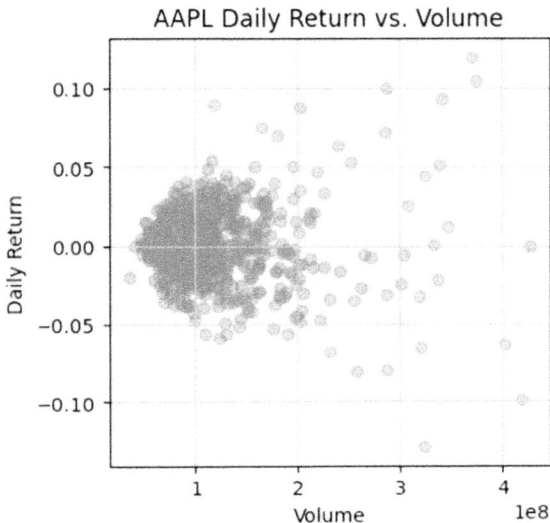

Figure 9.5 Jupyter Notebook screenshot of creating a scatter plot using daily returns and volume from the AAPL data set

Box Plot

Box plots are used to represent the distribution of data through their quartiles. They are useful for identifying outliers and understanding the spread of the data. As shown in Figure 9.6 below, the middle line of the box plot represents the median, while the top and bottom edges of the box represent the third (upper) and first (lower) quartiles, respectively. The whiskers extend to the smallest and largest values within 1.5 times the interquartile range from the quartiles, and data points outside this range are considered outliers. →C9NB 9.1.4c

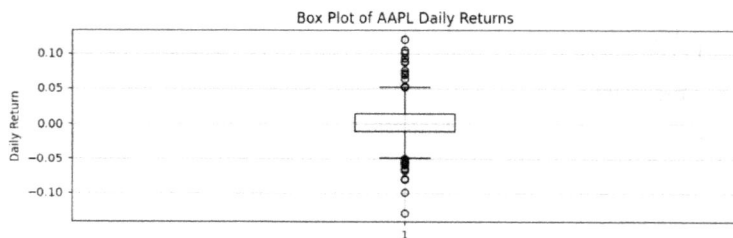

Figure 9.6 Jupyter Notebook screenshot of creating a box plot using daily returns of the AAPL data set

9.2 Advanced Visualization With Seaborn

Seaborn is a powerful Python data visualization library based on Matplotlib. It provides a high-level interface for drawing attractive and informative statistical graphics.

Distribution Plot

A distribution plot is used to show the distribution of a single variable. It combines a histogram and a kernel density estimate (KDE).

Kernel Density Estimate

A KDE is a way to estimate the probability density function of a random variable. In simpler terms, it's a way to smooth out the data to show where the data points are concentrated, giving you a continuous curve that represents the distribution of data.

Imagine you have a bunch of data points, and you want to understand how they are spread out. A histogram can give you a rough idea by grouping data into bins. However, a histogram is somewhat crude because it depends on the choice of bin width and bin edges. KDE, on the other hand, provides a smoother and more flexible way to visualize the data distribution.

Here is an example of generating a histogram with KDE: →C9NB 9.2a

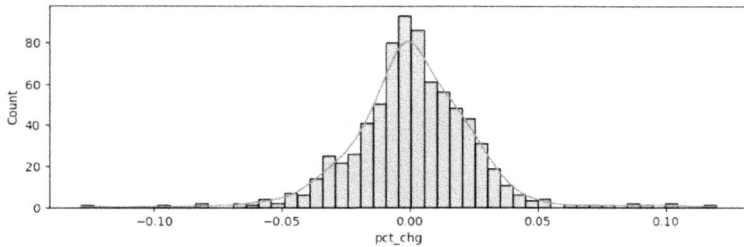

Figure 9.7 Jupyter Notebook screenshot of generating a histogram with KDE using Seaborn

Explanation: It is important to note that in this example the histplot method returns a new sub-plot object which is automatically displayed by Jupiter Notebook (other IDE may not perform this action). Alternatively, the plot can be attached to an existing sub-plot object by passing it as an input to the function (*ax = sub-plot)*

Pair Plot

A pair plot is used to visualize the pairwise relationships between multiple variables in a data set. It is especially useful for exploring correlations. The following code cell generates a pair plot between the Close prices, Volume, and Returns (percentage change) from the AAPL data. Notice that the diagonal plots are distribution histograms, and the remaining plots are scatter plots for each pair of the selected features. We can observe a negative relationship between Close price and Volume, indicating that higher stock prices are associated with fewer shares being traded. →C9NB 9.2b

```
1 selected_features = apple_data [['Close', 'Volume', 'pct_chg']].dropna()
2 sns.pairplot(selected_features)
1 plt.suptitle('Pair Plot of AAPL Stock Features',y=1.01) #y=1.02 move the suptitle up by 2%
```

Text(0.5, 1.01, 'Pair Plot of AAPL Stock Features')

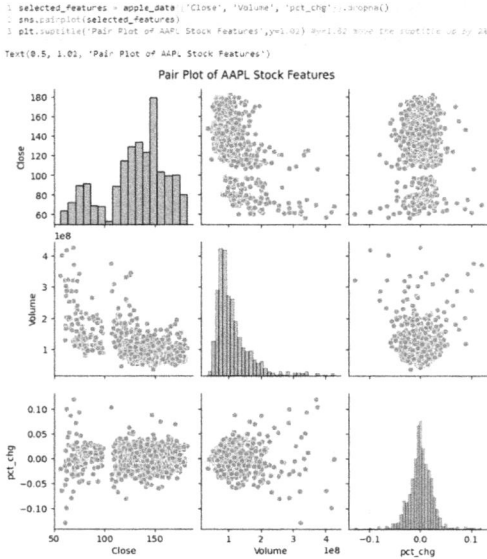

Figure 9.8 Jupyter Notebook screenshot of generating pair plot of AAPL stock features using Seaborn

Heatmap

A heatmap is used to show the correlation between different variables. It uses color to represent the values. A heatmap is often preferred over a pair plot when many features are presented. →C9NB 9.2c

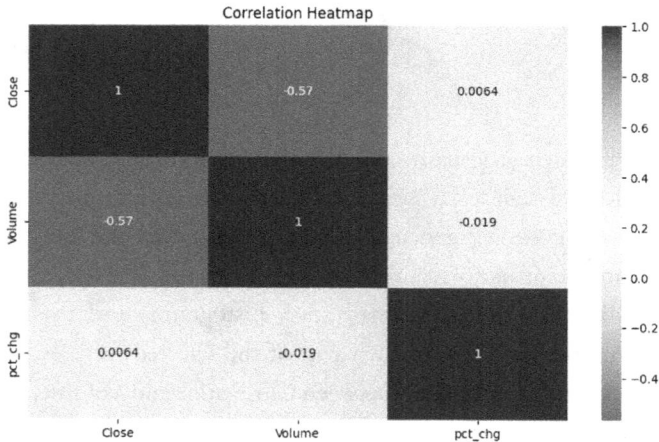

Figure 9.9 Jupyter Notebook screenshot of generating correlation Heatmap of AAPL stock features using Seaborn

9.3 Interactive Visualizations

Interactive visualizations provide a more engaging and dynamic way to explore data. Unlike static plots, interactive visualizations allow users to zoom, pan, and hover over data points to gain deeper insights. plotly is a popular library for creating interactive visualizations in Python.

9.3.1 Building Interactable Plots With plotly

plotly is a graphing library that enables the creation of interactive, publication-quality graphs online (Plotly 2023). The library supports a wide range of chart types and is particularly useful for financial data analysis. There are some important terms in plotly that we need to be familiar with before getting into the code.

- **Figure** is the top-level container for all plot elements. It can be thought of as the entire canvas on which plots are drawn. A figure encompasses the following components:
- **Trace** represents a single plot element within a figure. Each trace corresponds to a specific type of chart (e.g., scatter plot, bar chart, line chart, etc.) and contains the data and styling options for that element. Multiple traces can be combined in a single figure to create complex visualizations.
- **Frames**: Used for creating animations by defining different states of the figure.

Basic Line Plot With plotly

Let's start with a basic interactive line plot using plotly. We'll plot the closing prices of AAPL. It is important to note that plotly and jupyter-dash must be installed in your Python environment; otherwise, plotly interactive figures may not display. →C9NB 9.3.1a

Figure 9.10 Jupyter Notebook screenshot of generating interactive price plot using plotly

Explanation: The go.Scatter is the initializer for creating a scatter interactive plot object (trace) from the plotly package. For other plot types, simply find the right initializer and attach it to the figure using the add_trace method. The update_layout method is the interface for customizing the figure.

Subplots.   Building subplots with plotly is similar to creating subplots in Matplotlib. The process involves using the make_subplots function from the plotly.subplots module to create a grid layout for multiple plots within a single figure. You can specify the number of rows and columns, as well as whether the subplots should share axes (shared_xaxes=True). After creating the subplot structure, you can add individual plots (traces) to each subplot using the add_trace method. →C9NB 9.3.1b

Figure 9.11 Jupyter Notebook screenshot of a 2 × 1 plotly subplots after executing the source code from C9NB 9.3.1b

9.3.2 Animated Plot

Another interesting feature of plotly is its capacity to enable animation in plot. The basic idea is to build a playable animation using a sequence of frame, with each frame pointing to a figure to be displayed when the frame is active.

In the following code cell, the animation is enabled by passing a list of frame objects to the Figure initializer (highlighted in the red rectangle box). Each frame object contains a trace (a candlestick plot in this example) to be displayed when the frame is active. Notice that in the initial state, before the play button (arrow) is pressed, the figure displays the candlestick plot passed to the figure initializer. Once the animation is active, the sequence of candlestick objects passed to the frame initializers is displayed in turn. →C9NB 9.3.2a

Figure 9.12b Jupyter Notebook screenshot of result showing an animation of candlestick plot of AAPL's stock prices using plotly after running source code C9NB 9.3.2a

Conclusion

In this chapter, you have explored the foundational and advanced techniques of data visualization using three powerful Python libraries: Matplotlib, Seaborn, and Plotly. Starting with Matplotlib, you learned the basics of plotting, building subplots, and customizing plots to fit specific needs. You then advanced to using Seaborn for more sophisticated statistical visualizations, which simplifies complex data representations. Finally, you delved into Plotly, mastering the creation of interactive and animated plots that enhance the interactivity and engagement of your data presentations. By combining these tools, you can create compelling visual narratives that effectively communicate your data insights.

Exercise

Finish the following tasks with your own code:

1. Intraday returns calculation:
    a) Define intraday return as the percentage change from the opening price to the closing price of the same trading day.

    b) Write a Python function to calculate the intraday returns for a given stock data DataFrame.

2. Regular returns calculation:

    a) Define regular return as the percentage change from the closing price of the previous trading day to the closing price of the current trading day.

    b) Write a Python function to calculate the regular returns for a given stock data DataFrame.

3. Comparative histogram plotting:

    a) Create a subplot of histograms comparing the regular returns and intraday returns using Matplotlib.

    b) Plot the histograms one above the other (2 × 1 layout) to visually compare the distributions.

    c) Analyze which type of return appears to have higher volatility based on the histogram spreads.

4. Interactive box plot with Plotly:

    a) Build an interactive box plot using Plotly to visualize the distribution of intraday returns and regular returns. Hint: Use the go.Box.

    b) Ensure the plot allows the user to hover over the outliers to see detailed information (the date) about the data points.

CHAPTER 10

Financial Modeling With OOP

Introduction

In this chapter, we will demonstrate how to build object-oriented models to tackle practical problems in finance. We will illustrate the basic principles behind the development of many financial Python packages. In the first section, we will construct a family of classes for modeling fixed-income securities and use instances of these classes to perform financial analytics. Through these exercises, we will gain insights into how to build models for real-life financial problems using Python and its extensive financial libraries.

10.1 Object-Oriented Modeling for Fixed-Income Securities

10.1.1 *Introduction to Fixed-Income Securities*

Fixed-income securities are financial instruments that provide a return in the form of fixed periodic payments and the eventual return of principal at maturity. These instruments include bonds, treasury bills (T-Bills), and other debt instruments. They are called *fixed-income* because the payments are typically set at a fixed amount or rate (Choudhry 2010).

Interest Rate, Yield Rate and Discount Rate

- **Interest rate** is the percentage charged by a lender to a borrower for the use of assets, typically expressed annually. It is the cost of borrowing money or the return on investment for lending money.

- **Yield rate** refers to the rate of return earned on a bond or other investment over a specific period, considering all interest payments and capital gains or losses if held to maturity. It reflects the bond's internal rate of return.
- **Discount rate** is the rate used to convert future cash flows into their present value, reflecting the time value of money. It represents the investor's required rate of return and includes the risk-free rate plus a risk premium.
- In fixed-income securities valuation, these rates are closely related and sometimes used interchangeably, especially when only monetary returns from the asset are considered and credit risk is not in the context.

Yield Curve

The yield curve graphically represents the relationship between interest rates and bond maturities, typically for government bonds. It can be upward sloping (normal), downward sloping (inverted), or flat, reflecting market expectations about economic conditions. To discount short-term bonds, use the yield corresponding to their short maturities; for long-term bonds, use the yield for their longer maturities. For example, a one-year bond would use the one-year yield, while a 10-year bond uses the 10-year yield. This allows investors to accurately calculate the present value of bonds based on the appropriate discount rates provided by the yield curve.

10.1.2 Model Construction Under OOP Framework

To model fixed-income securities, we can use object-oriented programming (OOP). OOP allows us to create classes that encapsulate data and methods for different types of bonds. This approach makes the code modular, reusable, and easy to maintain. The following steps highlight the idea:

Step 1: Creating the Parent Class

The FixedIncome class will serve as the base class for all fixed-income securities. It will include common attributes and methods that can be inherited by more specific children classes.

Basic Attributes

- **issue_date**: The date on which the bond was issued.
- **maturity_date**: The date on which the securities will mature, and the principal will be repaid.
- **evaluation_date**: The date on which the bond's value is assessed.
- **yield_gen**: A function for generating the annualized discount rate for different terms of bonds.
- **period_offset**: A private Python object for offsetting pd.Timestamp objects so that they can move in time for the fixed period.

Methods

- **yield_gen**: Returns the discount rate reading at a point in time.
- **set_evaluation_date**: Sets the instance's evaluation date for pricing and analytics functions.
- **get_period_offset**: Returns the Pandas DateOffset object for a given period.

These are the basic attributes and methods that will be commonly applied to all subclasses. For example, the DateOffset object will serve as a handy tool for the subclasses to move in fixed periods along the calendar to determine the schedule of payments.

When setting up the base class, we also need to consider the features of subclass objects, which are usually the end-products for the user. In this project, our models incorporate nonconstant yield curve. This requirement can affect many functionalities of the subclasses where pricing and analytical functions are delivered. At the parent level, we need to decide on the framework solution for addressing this challenge.

The following code cell screenshot exhibits the setup of the basic attributes and methods. →C10NB 10.1.2a

Before diving into the code, we need to briefly introduce the use of decorators for building Python classes. A **decorator** in Python is a design pattern that allows you to modify or extend the behavior of functions or methods without changing their actual code. Decorators are commonly used for tasks like logging, access control, memoization, and more. They are applied using the @decorator_name syntax placed above a function definition.

In Python, **getters** are methods used to access the value of an attribute. They provide a way to add logic to the process of retrieving an attribute, enabling actions such as validation or logging. Python uses the @property decorator to define getters, allowing attribute access to behave like standard variable access while incorporating additional logic when needed.

Now, going back to the code, notice that the issue_date, maturity_date, and evaluation_date have been made private, but getter decorators (@property) have also been implemented so the value of these private attributes is available to subclass users. A setter interface for the evaluation date is provided for input validation. The yield_gen function serves as a framework for users to set up the term structure of discount rates (as a function).

Step 2: Creating the Bond Subclass

A bond is a fixed-income instrument that represents a loan made by an investor to a borrower (typically corporate or governmental). Bonds can have different attributes, such as coupon rates and maturity dates, which influence their pricing and yield.

- **Zero-coupon bond**: This type of bond does not make periodic interest payments. Instead, they are issued at a discount to their face value and mature at par value, with the difference representing the interest earned.
- **Fixed-rate bond**: This type of bond pays a fixed interest rate (coupon) over its life. The interest payments are made periodically until maturity, when the face value of the bond is repaid.
- **Floating-rate bond**: This type of bond has variable interest payments that are tied to a reference interest rate, such as

SHIBOR (Shanghai Interbank Offered Rate). The coupon payments fluctuate based on changes in the reference rate.

The following code cell implements the Bond class. →C10NB 10.1.2b

Notice that inheritance is declared in the class definition statement. The underscore at the front of the variable name indicates that the attribute is intended to be internal (but is still accessible to the user). When an instance of the Bond class is initialized, the super() function refers to the parent instance and calls the parent's initializer. In addition to the parent's implementation of its initializer, the Bond class now has its own implementation of extra attributes and methods, which reflect the characteristics of the subclass. For example, a bond should have a face value, a bond type, and a schedule of coupon payments. These additional attributes are assigned after the parent's initializer is called. The coupon_schedule method is defined to generate a list of ex-coupon dates, which means that buyers of the bonds on such dates are not entitled to any accrued interest. This method is likely (but not necessarily) reusable in every subclass, so it is better to define such a method at the parent level.

ZeroCoupon Bond. We now start building the model that represents a particular type of bond. Let's begin with the simplest type of bond, the zero-coupon bond.

A zero-coupon bond is a type of bond that does not pay periodic coupon payments and is sold at a discount to its face value. The bondholder receives a single payment, which is the face value, at maturity. The formula for the present value (price) of a zero-coupon bond is:

$$P_{zero} = \frac{F}{(1+r)^n}$$

Common practical examples of zero-coupon bonds include:

- **T-Bills**: Issued by the government with maturities ranging from a few days to one year. They are sold at a discount to their face value and do not pay periodic interest.

- **Separate Trading of Registered Interest and Principal Securities**: These are U.S. Treasury securities that have been separated into their individual interest and principal components, each of which is sold as a zero-coupon bond.
- **Municipal zero-coupon bonds**: Issued by state and local governments, these bonds are sold at a discount and mature at face value. They can be used to finance public projects like schools and highways.
- **Corporate zero-coupon bonds**: Issued by corporations to raise capital, these bonds do not pay periodic interest and are sold at a discount. The investor receives the face value at maturity.

Here is the example of code for ZeroBond class: →C10NB 10.1.2c

Notice that the only subclass implementation is to calculate the net present value (NPV), based on the yield rates available on the evaluation date, and the yield of the bond at a given market price. Newton's method is utilized for solving the yield rate. The number 365.25 (considering leap years) is used for calculating the length of time to maturity (in years).

Fixed-Rate Bond

A coupon-paying fixed-rate bond is a type of debt security that pays the bondholder periodic interest payments, known as coupons, until maturity, at which point the face value (principal) is repaid. The coupon payments are typically made semi-annually, annually, or at other regular intervals, providing a steady income stream to the investor. The coupon rate, which is the annual interest rate paid on the bond's face value, is determined at the time of issuance. Coupon-paying bonds are widely used by governments, municipalities, and corporations to raise capital for various purposes. The value of a coupon-paying bond is influenced by interest rates, the creditworthiness of the issuer, and the time to maturity. In order to fully understand the calculation of bond prices, we need to get into some terminology about fixed-rate bonds.

Year Conventions in Finance

In finance, year conventions standardize how interest and other time-based calculations are performed. Common conventions include:

Actual/actual: Uses the exact number of days in each period and accounts for leap years (365 or 366 days).

30/360: Assumes each month has 30 days and each year has 360 days, simplifying calculations for bonds and loans.

Actual/360: Uses the actual number of days in the period divided by 360, commonly used in money market instruments.

Actual/365: Uses the actual number of days divided by 365, often applied in UK markets.

These conventions ensure consistency and accuracy in financial calculations, particularly for interest accrual and bond pricing.

Accrued Interest Calculation

While many financial calculators can perform simple analytics for fixed-rate bonds when the transaction occurs on the issue date or the coupon dates and the discounting rates are fixed, in practice, secondary market transactions can occur between coupon dates, and the transaction prices should reflect the accrued interest the seller has forgone and the buyer will be entitled to for trading the bond. In practice, accrued interest is estimated using simple or compound methods. Here, we will utilize simple linear interpolation to calculate the accrued interest as follows:

$$\text{Accrued Interest} = C \times \frac{Days\ since\ last\ coupon\ payment}{Total\ Days\ in\ coupon\ period}$$

Clean and Dirty Prices

The full transaction price includes the accrued interest and the "clean" price of the bond, as if the bond has not accrued any interest. This transaction price is often referred to as the "dirty price." To be consistent with financial practice, our fixed-rate bond class should provide the functionality for calculating the clean and dirty prices. In other instances, bond prices are not quoted by their monetary units but by the annualized yields implied by the listing prices. This adds another requirement for our project.

Net Present Value

The NPV for a bond represents the present value of all expected future cash flows (coupon payments and the principal repayment). It reflects the fair value of the bond in today's terms, accounting for the time value of money. The discount rates should be chosen in such a way that they reflect the tradeoff between the time value of money and the risk associated with future cash flows. Thus, the discount rates may vary by different terms of maturity.

The formula for NPV of a bond is as follows:

$$P_{fixed\_rate} = \sum_{t=1}^{n} \frac{C}{(1+r)^t} + \frac{F}{(1+r)^n}$$

where C = coupon payment, r = discount rate,
F = face value of the bond, t = time period in years, and n = total number of periods.

Duration

Duration measures the sensitivity of a bond's price to changes in interest rates, representing the weighted average time until the bond's cash flows are received. It is used to assess the interest rate risk of a bond. The formula for Macaulay duration is:

$$D = \frac{\sum_{t=1}^{n} \frac{tC}{(1+r)^t} + \frac{nF}{(1+r)^n}}{P}$$

Macaulay duration can be interpreted as the weighted average time for receiving the principal and interest payments of the bond.

Where C = coupon payment, r = discount rate, P = bond price based on NPV,
F = face value of the bond, t = time period in years, and n = total number of periods.

An alternative measure of duration based on the Macaulay duration is called the Modified duration, calculated as follows:

$$\text{Modified duration} = \frac{D}{1 + y/n}, \text{ where } y \text{ is the YTM for the bond}$$

Modified duration is an estimate of how much the bond's price will change for a 1 percent change in yield. Notice that the NPV of the bond since the issue date or last coupon date is utilized as a reference to the clean price of the bond.

The part of the code that demonstrates the calculation of the yield quote and the Macaulay duration is displayed in the following code cell. →C10NB 10.1.2d

Notice that when a yield curve function is specified in the model, the function must take the term of years as an input and return the corresponding annualized discount rate. The shape of the yield curve is assumed to be unchanged when changing the evaluation date. The parent-class method self.year_count is utilized to calculate the remaining term of the bond in years when the evaluation date is set between the bond's issue and maturity dates. →C10NB 10.1.2d

Floating-Rate Bond.   Floating-rate bond is a type of debt security whose coupon payments vary based on a reference interest rate or index. Unlike fixed-rate bonds, where the coupon rate remains constant, the coupon rate for variable-rate bonds is periodically adjusted, typically every three or six months, to reflect changes in market interest rates. This adjustment mechanism helps protect investors from interest rate risk, as the bond's yield adjusts with fluctuations in the broader market. Variable-rate bonds are commonly issued by governments, municipalities, and corporations to attract investors seeking interest rate protection.

In practice, floating-rate bonds are issued with a spread to the reference rate. For example, a Chinese corporation may issue a floating-rate bond with a 2 percent spread to the SHIBOR rate. This means that if SHIBOR is at 3 percent at a coupon reset date, then the coupon rate for the upcoming payment date will be 5 percent. The following code cell presents the first half of the implementation of the floating-rate bond class. Notice that the key difference of the floating-rate bond class compared to its sibling classes is how the variable coupon amount is determined in each period. The formula for the amount of the coupon at time t is:

$C_t = F(r_t + s)$, where C_t and r_t are the coupon payment discount rate at time t and s is the spread.

The formula for calculating the NPV of the floating-rate bond is given by:

$$P_{float\_rate} = \sum_{t=1}^{n} \frac{C_t}{(1+r_t)^t} + \frac{F}{(1+r_n)^n}$$

Notice that in our model r_t and r_n are the annualized discount rates (also the reference rate) observable through the yield curve available at the evaluation date. The NPV, full_price, and yield_gen methods require redefinition because we need to set up a handle (delta) to allow shocks to the reference rate. The yield_rate method, which calculates the implied discount rate given a market price, is not implemented for the VariableRateBond class because the result would be misleading when the future coupon rates are variable and related to the reference discount rates. Here is an example of the code implementation for the VariableRateBond class: →C10NB 10.1.2e

The second half of the implementation focuses on the analytics functions for the floating-rate bond class. Before going into the code, we need to introduce three different measures of duration:

- **Macaulay duration**: Measures the average time to receive cash flows.
- **Modified duration**: Measures price sensitivity to yield changes, based on Macaulay duration.
- **Effective duration**: Measures price sensitivity to yield changes, accounting for changes in cash flows due to options or floating rates.

The calculation of Macaulay duration has been implemented in the FixedRateBond class, but this measure is not suitable (same for Modified duration) for analyzing floating-rate bonds because the bond, by design, has low sensitivity to interest rate changes. In this case, effective duration should be utilized as a replacement for the parent's duration method. The formula for calculating effective duration is:

$$D_{eff} = \frac{P_- - P_+}{2P_0 \Delta r},$$ where P_- / P_+ = bond price if yields decrease/increase by Δr, P_0 Initial bond price.

10.2 Model Testing and Analysis

The following code cells implement a series of tests for the three end-user classes for bonds. In each test, we change the evaluation date from the issue date to some dates between coupon dates and a date near the maturity date. By comparing the results, we aim to study the behavior of the bond prices and their sensitivity to shocks to the yield curve. This information is often crucial for bond investors.

Testing Zero-Bond Model

→C10NB 10.2a

Explanation: For a zero-coupon bond, the coupon is always 0, and the duration equals the remaining time to maturity. This means that the sensitivity of the bond price to interest rate shocks is at its maximum at the issue date. Our test for the zero-coupon bond model mainly focuses on the calculation of NPV and yield. The results show that the NPV of the bond approaches the face value, and the bond yield increases (for a fixed market price) as time moves toward the maturity date.

Testing Fixed-Rate Bond Model I: Constant Yield

The test of our fixed-rate bond model focuses on the calculation of bond prices and duration. The behavior of the bond prices as the term to maturity decreases can be analyzed through our model by setting different evaluation dates along the bond's maturity horizon. Notice that changing the evaluation date is equivalent to buying a floating bond in the secondary market, where only the remaining coupons and principal payments should affect the bond's prices and risk metrics. The term structure of the yield curve is assumed to be unchanged when switching the evaluation date.

In the following test section, we calculate the clean and dirty prices and the duration of a 10-year annual fixed-rate bond with a 5 percent coupon rate. Two constant yield scenarios (5 and 2 percent) are utilized in the test code. The results are organized and generated as a reporting DataFrame. →C10NB 10.2b

Explanation: When the yield rate is the same as the coupon rate, the clean price (NPV at coupon dates) is expected to be the same as the bond's face value. On the other hand, the clean price is expected to be higher than the bond's face value when the coupon rate is higher than the yield rate (assuming no credit risk). This difference reflects the premium for higher-than-expected interest returns. As the bond approaches the maturity date, this difference should be reduced because there are fewer future coupons. Moreover, since accrued interest increases as the evaluation date approaches a coupon date (on which accrued interest resets to 0), we should expect to see the dirty price become higher as it approaches the coupon date. Lastly, the duration of the bond should approach 0 as the evaluation time approaches the maturity date.

Our results are consistent with the aforementioned principles of fixed-rate bonds. Furthermore, it is shown that the duration is higher when the market yield is low. This inverse relationship can be inferred from the formula for Macaulay duration, where a high discount rate results in smaller terms in the summation.

Testing Fixed-Rate Bond Model II: Nonconstant Yield

In the real-world scenario, the yield curve is hardly flat. An upward-sloping yield curve reflects expectations of future economic growth and potential inflation, while a downward-sloping curve indicates expectations of economic slowdown or recession. Our models have been built with the capacity to allow for a nonconstant yield curve. The following code cell reproduces the test for our fixed-rate bond model by customizing a function that generates a linearly increasing yield curve. →C10NB 10.2c

Explanation: The linear_yield function represents an upward-sloping yield curve, with the discount rate starting from 2 percent at the issue date and reaching a maximum of 7 percent at the maturity date. This means that longer-term cash flows are discounted at higher rates than shorter-term cash flows. The results show that the initial clean price is at a discount to the par value. As we move the evaluation date forward, the high discount rates for longer terms no longer apply to the bond's future cash flows. Thus, the price discount reverses to a premium, eventually converging back to the face value as maturity approaches.

The upward-sloping yield curve specified in this example should result in a duration lower than the two yield curve scenarios demonstrated in previous code cells because the longer-term yield rates are high. As fewer coupon payments remain and the corresponding yield rates flatten, the behavior of the bond's duration becomes unclear. Our model provides a clear answer: it shows that at the midpoint of the investment horizon, the duration of the bond is close to the case where a 5 percent constant yield rate is assumed. As the bond approaches maturity, all duration measures converge to 1.

Testing Float-Rate Bond Model

The next code cell uses the same setting of a nonconstant yield curve, but this time the coupon rates are linked to rates generated by the yield curve plus a 2 percent spread. This setting resembles a floating-rate bond for hedging interest rate risk, and thus the price of the bond is expected to be less sensitive to shocks to the yield curve. →C10NB 10.2d

Explanation: The most interesting aspect of the result is that the bond has a negative duration when it is issued. This means that the bond price will rise in response to a positive shock to the yield curve. This conclusion is counterintuitive but can be explained by the larger increase in all coupon amounts compared to the offsetting effect of higher discount rates.

The role of the floating-rate bond as an instrument for hedging interest rate risk is shown in this example, as the readings of the bond's effective duration have been low in all evaluation windows.

In principle, the floating-rate bond should be priced higher than its par value because of the higher coupon rate due to the positive spread. The behavior of bond prices as the bond reaches maturity is similar to the fixed-rate bond example. The clean price initially increases and then converges back to its par value as the bond reaches maturity.

Conclusion

In this chapter, we demonstrated how to build object-oriented models to tackle practical problems in finance using Python. We illustrated the basic principles behind developing financial Python packages. Initially, we constructed a family of classes for modeling fixed-income securities, creating a FixedIncome parent class with common attributes and methods, and extending it to specific bond subclasses like zero-coupon, fixed-rate, and floating-rate bonds.

We used these models to calculate key financial metrics, including NPV, yield, clean price, dirty price, and duration. Testing under various scenarios, including constant and nonconstant yield curves, showed consistent results with financial theory, demonstrating expected behaviors of bond prices and sensitivity to interest rate changes. Floating-rate bonds highlighted their role in hedging interest rate risk, showing lower sensitivity to yield curve shocks.

By building and testing these models, we applied theoretical concepts to practical problems and showcased the power of Python's OOP capabilities. This approach ensures that our code is modular, reusable, and easy to maintain, providing a robust framework for future financial modeling tasks.

Exercise

1. Class design for semi-annual bond:
   a) Write a Python class SemiAnnualBond that inherits from the FixedIncome class. This bond should pay interest semi-annually, with the total amount consistent with the annual coupon rate.
   b) Implement methods to calculate the clean price, dirty price, and duration for the semi-annual bond.
   c) Compare the behavior of the prices and durations of the semi-annual bond with an annual-paying bond (paying once a year) with the same coupon rate and yield assumptions as they approach maturity.
   d) Discuss the differences in the behavior of the two bonds as they approach maturity.

2. Yield curve analysis:
   a) Design a downward-sloping yield curve and modify your yield curve function to simulate this market condition.
   b) Re-run the tests for the fixed-income bond models using the downward-sloping yield curve.
   c) Compare the results with those obtained from the upward-sloping yield curve example.
   d) Analyze how the prices and durations differ between the two scenarios and explain the underlying reasons for these differences.

3. Interest rate sensitivity:
   a) Add a method called modified_duration to the bond classes. The calculation should be consistent with the formula of modified duration introduced in the text.
   b) Compare the interest rate sensitivity of the semi-annual and annual-paying bonds using the modified duration method.
   c) Evaluate the differences in interest rate sensitivity between the two bonds under various yield scenarios.

CHAPTER 11

Introduction to Machine Learning

Introduction

In previous chapters, we have learned various data processing techniques. We have explored how to handle missing data, filter and aggregate data sets, and manipulate data frames to prepare our data for analysis. These skills are crucial for transforming raw data into a usable format.

Now, think about a situation in finance where the multitude of market data provides a wealth of information but also poses a significant challenge: how do we extract useful insights and actionable signals from this data?

In the following chapters, we will explore machine learning (ML) techniques that can help us address these challenges. We will learn how to apply these methods to financial data, allowing us to make predictions, identify patterns, and ultimately make better-informed decisions.

What Is Machine Learning?

ML is a subset of artificial intelligence that focuses on developing algorithms that allow computers to learn from and make predictions or decisions based on data (Murphy 2012; Alpaydin 2020). Unlike traditional programming, where explicit instructions are given to the computer, ML models learn patterns from data through a process called training. Training involves feeding the model a data set with input features (variables) and corresponding output labels (answers) (Bishop 2006). The model makes predictions and calculates errors using a loss function, which measures the difference between the predicted values and the actual values. The model then adjusts its parameters iteratively to minimize these errors using optimization techniques. This iterative process continues until the model's performance stabilizes.

11.1 Comparing Machine Learning With Traditional Quantitative Methods

To understand the advantages of ML, let's compare it with traditional quantitative methods, specifically traditional regression analysis. Consider a situation where we have various types of market data, such as historical stock returns, trading volumes, and economic indicators (e.g., interest rates, GDP growth). Using traditional regression analysis, we would attempt to create a linear model to predict future stock returns based on these variables. However, several challenges arise:

- Multicollinearity: If the independent variables are highly correlated (e.g., trading volumes and stock returns often move together), traditional regression can produce unreliable estimates. Multicollinearity can inflate the variance of the coefficient estimates and make the model sensitive to small changes in the data. This issue leads to difficulties in determining the individual effect of each variable on the target variable.

- Nonlinearity: Assumption of linearity: Financial data often exhibit nonlinear relationships. Traditional regression assumes a linear relationship between the independent and dependent variables, which may lead to poor model performance if the true relationship is nonlinear. Nonlinear patterns in the data can be missed, resulting in a model that fails to capture the complexity of the financial markets.

- Misspecification: If the chosen model does not accurately reflect the underlying data structure (e.g., omitting important variables or using an incorrect functional form), the predictions will be biased and inaccurate. Traditional regression methods are less flexible in addressing model misspecification problems. They rely heavily on the correct specification of the model, and any deviation from this can significantly impact the accuracy of the predictions (Hastie et al. 2009).

ML techniques offer several advantages over traditional regression methods, particularly in handling the challenges mentioned above:

- Handling multicollinearity: ML methods, such as Ridge and Lasso regression, can handle multicollinearity by adding a penalty term to the loss function. This penalty term shrinks the coefficient estimates towards zero, reducing the impact of multicollinearity and helping to identify the most important features (Tibshirani 1996).
- Capturing nonlinear relationships: ML algorithms, such as Decision Trees, Random Forests, and Neural Networks, can capture complex, nonlinear relationships in the data. These models do not assume a linear relationship and can adapt to the true underlying patterns in the data, providing more accurate predictions in the presence of nonlinearities (Breiman 2001).
- Flexibility and robustness: ML methods are highly flexible and can model complex interactions between variables. Techniques like support vector machines and ensemble methods can handle a wide range of data structures and relationships, reducing the risk of model misspecification (Vapnik 1999).
- Hyperparameter tuning: ML models often come with hyperparameters that can be tuned using validation data. This tuning process helps to find the best model configuration, improving the overall performance and robustness of the predictions (Bergstra and Bengio 2012).

ML also differs from traditional modeling methods in terms of how parameters are turned. Traditional models often rely heavily on evaluating the model using the same data that was used to train it, using metrics like the R^2 score and hypothesis tests for statistical significance. In contrast, ML models focus on evaluating performance using new data that was not part of the training process.

11.2 Overview of Model Training

Model training involves teaching an ML algorithm to make predictions or decisions based on data, and a loss function plays a crucial role in the functioning of the algorithm.

Loss Function

A loss function (also known as a cost function or objective function) is a mathematical function that measures the difference between the "the predicted value ($\hat{y}_i$) and the actual values (y_i) in an ML model. The purpose of a loss function is to quantify how well the model's predictions match the actual data. In the training algorithm, models with smaller loss function scores are prioritized as they indicate better performance.

Common Types of Loss Functions:

Mean squared error (MSE) penalizes larger errors more severely due to the squaring term, making it sensitive to outliers.

$$\text{Formula: MSE} = \frac{\sum_1^n \left(y_i - \hat{y}_i \right)^2}{n}$$

Mean absolute error (MAE): MAE treats all errors equally, making it more robust to outliers compared to MSE.

$$\text{Formula: MAE} = \frac{\sum_1^n \left| y_i - \hat{y}_i \right|}{n}$$

Cross-entropy loss (log loss): Used primarily in classification tasks, cross-entropy loss measures the performance of a classification model whose output is a probability value between 0 and 1.

$$\text{Formula: Cross-entropy loss} = \frac{\sum_1^n [y_i Log(\hat{y}_i) + (1 + y_i) \log \left(1 - \hat{y}_i \right)]}{n}$$

11.3 Data Preparation

Data preparation involves transforming raw data into a clean and structured format that can be used to train and evaluate ML models. Here's an overview of the data preparation process:

- Data collection: Gather the relevant data required for the task.
- Data cleaning: Handle missing values, remove duplicates, and correct inconsistencies.
- Feature engineering: Create new features from the existing ones and select the most relevant features for the model.
- Feature standardization(optional): When applying ML algorithms, it is crucial to transform the feature data so that it has a mean of zero and a standard deviation of one because many ML algorithms are sensitive to the scale of the input features
- Data splitting: Divide the data into training, validation, and test sets. The training set is used to train the model, the validation set is used for hyperparameter tuning, and the test set is used for final evaluation. This involves splitting the data into training sets, validation sets, and test sets.

Training, Validation, and Test Sets

- The **training set** is used to train the model, where it learns patterns by adjusting parameters to minimize prediction errors.
- The **validation set** is used for tuning hyperparameters—parameters set before training that control the learning process—by evaluating the model's performance and making adjustments to improve generalization to unseen data.
- The **test set** is used to evaluate the model's performance after training and validation, ensuring it can handle new, unseen data effectively.

11.4 Model Selection

Model selection involves choosing an appropriate ML algorithm based on the problem type (e.g., regression, classification) and data characteristics (e.g., structure, time-series, text. Audio). There are two general categories of ML models:

- Supervised learning is typically used for prediction tasks,
  such as regression and classification. This approach allows the
  model to learn the relationship between input features and
  the target variable.
  Example: Develop an ML model for the credit spread of corporation bonds using features extracted from the company's financial
  statements, managers' profiles, and bond market data.
- Unsupervised learning is typically used for clustering and
  dimensionality reduction tasks. The model is trained on
  unlabeled data, where the outcome is not known. The
  goal is to identify patterns or structures within the data.
  Unsupervised learning is typically used for clustering and
  dimensionality reduction tasks.
  Example: Grouping similar stocks (winners versus losers) based on
  their price movements without any predefined labels. The model
  analyzes the features of the stocks to identify clusters of similar
  stocks

11.5 Hyperparameter Tuning

Hyperparameters are parameters that are not learned from the data but
are set prior to the training process. These parameters control the learning process and affect the behavior and performance of the ML model.
Hyperparameter tuning involves finding the optimal combination of
hyperparameters to maximize the performance of the model. The tuning
process aims to improve model accuracy and generalizability by selecting
the best hyperparameters.

Grid Search is a hyperparameter tuning technique that systematically
works through multiple combinations of parameter values, cross-validat-
ing as it goes to determine which combination provides the best performance. Grid Search evaluates all possible combinations of the specified
hyperparameters. This exhaustive search ensures that the optimal hyperparameter set is found within the provided grid. Grid Search can be computationally expensive, especially if the grid of hyperparameters is large.
Evaluating every combination can be time-consuming.

11.6 Performance Evaluation

Once the model is trained, it is important to evaluate its performance in predicting new and unseen data. This is accomplished using the test set, which was not used during the training or validation process. The model should not be deployed in practical usage if its performance on the test set is weak. The results and patterns of the prediction errors can provide guidelines for correction and improvement of the model.

Cross-validation is a technique used to assess the generalizability of an ML model. It involves splitting the data into multiple subsets, training the model on some subsets (training set), and validating it on the remaining subsets (validation set). This process is repeated several times, and the performance is averaged to get a more robust estimate of the model's performance (Hastie et al. 2009).

11.6.1 Evaluation Metrics

Evaluation metrics are used to quantify an ML model's performance. The choice of a particular metric should be based on the data characteristics (e.g., presence of outliers) and the project's objective. Commonly used metrics include:

For Regression ML Models

- MAE
- MSE
- Root Mean Squared Error: The square root of the MSE. It is in the same units as the target variable, making it easier to interpret.
- R^2 score (coefficient of determination) represents the proportion of the variance for a dependent variable that's explained by an independent variable or variables in a regression model.

$$\text{Formula: } R^2 = 1 - \frac{\sum_i^n \left(y_i - \hat{y}_i \right)^2}{\sum_i^n \left(y_i - \overline{y}_i \right)^2}$$

For Classification ML Models

- Accuracy: The proportion of true results (both true positives and true negatives) among the total number of cases examined.
  Formula:

$$\text{Accuracy} = \frac{TP + TN}{TP + TN + FP + FN}$$

  where TP = true positives, TN = true negatives, FP = false positives, FN = false negatives.
- Precision: The ratio of correctly predicted positive observations to the total predicted positives. It answers the question: How many of the positively predicted cases were correct?
  Formula:

$$\text{Precision} = \frac{TP}{TP + FP}$$

- Recall (sensitivity): The ratio of correctly predicted positive observations to all observations in the actual class. It answers the question: How many of the actual positive cases were predicted correctly?
  Formula:

$$\text{Recall} = \frac{TP}{TP + FN}$$

- F1 score: The weighted average of Precision and Recall. It takes both false positives and false negatives into account. It is particularly useful when the class distribution is imbalanced.
  Formula :

$$\text{F1 score} = 2 \times \frac{\textbf{Precision} \times \textbf{Recall}}{\textbf{Precision} + \textbf{Recall}}$$

- Area under the receiver operating characteristic curve (AUC - ROC): This represents the ability of the model to discriminate

between positive and negative classes. An excellent model has
an AUC close to 1, while a poor model has an AUC close to
0. ROC is a probability curve and AUC represents the degree
or measure of separability.

- Confusion matrix: a table used to describe the performance of
a classification model on a set of test data for which the true
values are known. It shows the distribution of predicted and
actual classifications.

11.6.2 Other Evaluation Criteria

Overfitting and Underfitting

Overfitting: The model performs well on the training data but poorly
on the test data. This indicates that the model has learned the noise
in the training data rather than the underlying pattern.

Underfitting: The model performs poorly on both the training and
test data, indicating that it has not learned the underlying pattern
in the data.

Model Interpretability

Assess the interpretability of the model. Simple models like linear regression and decision trees are easier to interpret, while complex models like
deep neural networks may require techniques like SHAP (SHapley Additive exPlanations) values or LIME (Local Interpretable Model-agnostic
Explanations) to understand feature importance and model decisions.

Conclusion

In this chapter, we transition from traditional data processing techniques to the realm of ML, a powerful subset of artificial intelligence.
ML involves developing algorithms that learn from data to make predictions or decisions, a stark contrast to traditional programming which
relies on explicit instructions. We start by comparing ML with traditional
regression methods, highlighting the challenges of multicollinearity, nonlinearity, and model misspecification in financial data. ML techniques,

with their ability to handle these challenges, offer advantages such as capturing complex relationships and providing flexibility in model tuning. Key concepts such as model training, loss functions, data preparation, model selection, hyperparameter tuning, and performance evaluation are introduced.

CHAPTER 12

Regression Machine Learning Models in Finance

Introduction

Regression ML models are commonly used for predicting continuous target variables. In this chapter, we will demonstrate the practical implementation of regression ML models using Python with the Shanghai Stock Exchange (SSE) Daily Index data (see reference for details). Our goal is to predict stock index returns using the previous trading day's index returns, abnormal trading volume, and a measure of recent market volatility. Additionally, we will incorporate weekday effects in our feature collection. These features are selected based on the documented behavior of the stock market. However, the traditional Efficient Market Hypothesis suggests that none of these features should be useful in predicting the target variable. We will examine the evidence generated by our ML models.

We'll begin with data cleaning and restructuring, followed by setting up the data for machine learning. Finally, we'll implement and compare several regression models. We will need the following external packages for this project: yfinance, sklearn (scikit-learn). The instruction for installing these packages is supplied in the appendixes.

12.1 Importing and Preparing Data

12.1.1 Data Description

The data set consists of daily data from the SSE Index, including the following columns:

- Date: The date of the observation.
- Open: The opening price of the index.

- High: The highest price of the index during the day.
- Low: The lowest price of the index during the day.
- Close/adj close: The closing price of the index.
- Volume: The trading volume of the index.

12.1.2 Defining the Target Variable and Features

Target Variable

- Daily index returns.

Features

- Past daily returns: The returns from the previous day.
- Abnormal trading volume: Previous day's volume divided by the simple moving average of over the past 30 days.
- Recent market volatility: The average absolute percentage change over the past five days.
- Weekday flag: Dummy variables for each weekday.

12.1.3 Data Preparation

Step 1: Import data* →C12NB 12.1.3a
Step 2: Data cleaning
Invalid or incomplete entries, if any, should be removed from the data. →C12NB 12.1.3b
Step 3: Data restructuring →C12NB 12.1.3c
Explanation: The "get_dummies" method from Pandas generates dummy variables to represent the categorical variable 'Weekday,' The drop_first setting generates c–1 dummy variables for a categorical variable with c levels of outcomes. In the case of the weekday effect, the Monday effect becomes the base case (all dummies equal to 0). The shift method in pandas is used to shift the values in a DataFrame or Series by a specified number of periods along the

---

*An alternative approach for downloading data from the Yahoo Finance API is provided in the Jupyter Notebook file accompanying this chapter.

index. This method is commonly used in time series data analysis to create lagged versions of data for various purposes, such as calculating differences or creating lagged features for modeling.

Step 4: Setting up training, validation, and test sets →C12NB 12.1.3d

Explanation: The train_test_split method from sklearn.model_selection is a handy tool for dividing the data into training and validation sets. In the above code block, the method is called twice—once on the full data set and then on the validation set generated in the first call. As a result, 70 percent of the data is allocated to the training set, while the remaining 30 percent is split equally into the validation and test sets. The "shuffle=False" setting orders the method to split the data without shuffling the order of the data. This setting is required for the current project because the data is time series indexed.

Step 5: Feature standardization

To perform feature standardization in Python, we use the Standard-Scaler class from sklearn.preprocessing. Only the continuous features are standardized. →C12NB 12.1.3e

Explanation: In the code block above, the fit_transform method is applied to the continuous feature values of the training set. The transform method is then applied to the validation and test sets, using the mean and standard deviation calculated from the training set.

Now, let's take a quick look at the final data set for training. Notice that four dummy variables have been generated for modeling the effect of each weekday on stock returns. All the continuous features are standardized with a mean zero and a standard deviation equal to 1. →C12NB 12.1.3f

We now have the training, validation, and test data sets with features and the target variable clearly defined. We will implement various ML models on these data sets and evaluate their performance.

12.2 Linear Models

12.2.1 Linear Regression

Linear regression is a fundamental and widely used method for predictive modeling. The basic principle is to model the relationship between a dependent variable (target) and one or more independent variables (features) by fitting a linear equation to the observed data. Traditionally, the model is expressed as follows:

$$y = \beta_0 + \beta_1 X_1 + \beta_2 X_2 + \ldots + \beta_p X_p + \varepsilon$$

where y is the dependent variable (daily returns); β_0 is the intercept; $\beta_0, \beta_1, \ldots, \beta_p$ are the regression coefficients; $X_1, X_2, \ldots, X_p$ are the independent variables (features); ε is the error term.

Parameters Trained

- Regression coefficients (weights): These represent the relationship strength between each feature and the target variable.
- Intercept: This represents the value of the target variable when all feature values are zero.

Hyperparameter

The basic linear regression does not explicitly include hyperparameters for tuning. Traditionally, the model parameters are tested for significance, and a better model may result after removing some of the features. Therefore, we can expand the traditional model by adding an indicator for each model parameter as the hyperparameters as follows:

$$y = \beta_0 + I_1 \beta_1 X_1 + I_2 \beta_2 X_2 + \ldots + I_p \beta_2 X_p + \varepsilon$$

where $I_1, I_2, \ldots, I_p$ are indicator variables.

The process of removing some features to improve the model is called feature selection. Models with fewer features are referred to as sub-models.

Without any prior preference for features, we will generate all possible sub-models: →C12NB 12.2.1a

Note that in the above code cell, each element in feature subsets is a list of features included in a sub-model. For example, sub-model 20 includes only the features of Abnormal Volume and the Thursday Effect.

In the following code block, we will train each of these sub-models using the data of the training set and then evaluate their performance using the data of the validation set. →C12NB 12.2.1b

Explanation: After comparing the performance of the full model and the sub-models, the algorithm finds that the sub-model with features ['Lag_Daily_Return,' 'Abnormal_Volume,' 'Recent_Volatility,' 'Weekday_3,' 'Weekday_4'] is the best-performing trained model based on the validation set data. This model achieves an R^2 score of 4.3 percent, which means that it explains 4.3 percent of the variation in the target variable in the validation set.

It is important to note that although we use R^2, a more interpretable metric, as the reporting metric for model evaluation, the training algorithm by default minimizes the mean squared error (MSE) of the predictions. The same training and reporting metrics will be used consistently in the rest of this chapter.

Finally, we will see how the best one performs on the test set. →C12NB 12.2.1c

Explanation: The R^2 score can be negative, in contrast to the traditional coefficient of determination, because it is calculated based on out-of-sample predictions. A negative value indicates that the optimized model after validation does not perform as well as a simple prediction model based on the average of the target variable. When the performance metric drops significantly from the validation set to the test set, it generally indicates the model's limited ability to generalize to new data, and thus its practical value should be questioned. One common cause for such a result is that the model is overfitted during the training stage, making it too sensitive to random patterns that only exist in the training set.

12.2.2 Ridge Lasso, Elastic Net Regressions

ML models are trained by minimizing the loss function. For traditional linear regression, the loss function is the sum of square errors:

$$\sum_i (y_i - \beta_0 - \sum_j \beta_j X_{ij})^2$$

The coefficients that minimize this loss function are called the ordinary least squares estimators. Note that with this loss function, a more parsimonious model will always have a higher loss score(in-sample) and thus will not be selected by the algorithm over a more complex model, which tends to result in overfitting. Ridge and Lasso regression add a regularization term to the loss function to penalize extra features that add little to reducing the loss score (Hoerl and Kennard 1970; Tibshirani 1996).

The loss function for Lasso regression (L1 regularization) can be expressed as follows:

$$L_1(\beta) = \sum_i (y_i - \beta_0 - \sum_j \beta_j X_{ij})^2 + (\lambda \sum_j |\beta_j|)$$

The loss function for Ridge regression (L2 regularization) can be expressed as follows:

$$L_2(\beta) = \sum_i (y_i - \beta_0 - \sum_j \beta_j X_{ij})^2 + (\lambda \sum_j \beta_j^2)$$

In both expressions, λ serves as the regularization parameter that controls the amount of shrinkage applied to the coefficients. As λ increases, the penalty for larger (but less important) coefficients becomes stronger, leading to more shrinkage of the coefficients.

Both Ridge and Lasso regression are particularly useful for automatic feature selection, where the algorithm reduces or completely removes the contributions of less useful features.

The difference between Ridge and Lasso regression mainly rests on whether feature coefficients can be shrunk to zero, thereby completely removing the feature. In Ridge regression, all the features will remain, while in Lasso regression, coefficients of less significant features can shrink to zero, making it useful when a more parsimonious model is preferred.

Elastic Net Regularization

Elastic Net is a regularization technique that combines both L1 (Lasso) and L2 (Ridge) penalties. It is particularly useful when dealing with highly correlated features, as it combines the strengths of both Lasso and Ridge regularization.

The loss function L3 for Elastic Net can be expressed as:

$$L_3(\beta) = \sum_i (y_i - \beta_0 - \sum_j \beta_j X_{ij})^2 + (\lambda_1 \sum_j |\beta_j|) + (\lambda_2 \sum_j \beta_j^2)$$

Notice that Elastic Net has two hyperparameters: λ_1 and λ_2, which control the strength of the L1 and L2 regularization, respectively.

Hyperparameter Turning.   Before writing the code, it is important to consider how the trained models are tuned. In the case of the three ML models, the hyperparameters are λ (Ridge and Lasso) and λ_1 and λ_1 (Elastic Net). In this context, tuning the parameters means finding a setting for the hyperparameters such that the trained model achieves a better loss function score (MSE in our case) on the validation set. If there is no prior information regarding the preferred setting of the parameters, we can perform a grid search over a range of the parameter space. A larger set of potential values for the parameters can result in better tuning but will require more computing resources. For this project, we will set the following grids for the λ values:

Ridge regression: [0.01, 0.1, 1, 10, 25, 50, 75, 100]
Lasso regression: [0.001, 0.01, 0.1, 0.5, 1, 5, 7.5, 10]

Ridge regression typically requires exploring a wider range of λ values because the L2 penalty impacts all coefficients more uniformly and does not lead to zero coefficients. →C12NB 12.2.2a

The following function calculates the MSE for each trained model covered by the grids, finds the best model based on the validation result, and then calculates the best model's R^2 score on the test set. The key step is to pass the ML class initializer to the function so that it can produce an instance of an ML model with parameters specified by the grid internally. →C12NB 12.2.2b

The following code block applies the tune_and_evaluate function to each of the ML models, and the results are incorporated into f-strings before printing. Key messages are highlighted by red rectangles. →C12NB 12.2.2c; C12NB 12.2.2d; C12NB 12.2.2e

Explanation: Ridge regression shrinks all coefficients to very small numbers when the highest alpha is chosen after parameter tuning. The tuned model does not perform well on both the validation and test sets, as indicated by the negative R^2 scores. The likely reason is that some features are insignificant, but Ridge regression still retains them in the model. On the other hand, Lasso and Elastic Net regressions can shrink insignificant parameters to zero, effectively performing feature selection. The results suggest that only Recent Volatility is useful for predicting next-day index returns. Both Lasso and Elastic Net regressions exhibit positive R^2 scores on the test set, with Elastic Net regression achieving the highest R^2 score of 1.75 percent. Since Elastic Net regression is the most flexible model among the linear ML models we have covered, it is likely that the underlying feature-target relationship is more complex than a simple linear relationship.

While features such as lagged daily returns, recent volatility, and week-day effects are categorized as insignificant predictors, they may still have a significant relationship with the target variable. This is because Ridge, Lasso, and Elastic Net regressions assume a linear relationship between the features and the target variable.

Bias-Variance Tradeoff.   There are two sources of error that affect a model's performance:

- Bias error: Caused by overly simplistic assumptions in the learning algorithm, leading to underfitting.
- Variance error: Caused by excessive complexity in the learning algorithm, leading to overfitting.

In our regression models, we have utilized feature selection and parameter shrinking to control variance error. However, in doing so, we also introduce bias error to our model. The goal of parameter tuning is, therefore, to optimize the bias-variance tradeoff so that the model can achieve the best performance on unseen data.

12.3 Nonlinear Models

When the relationship between features and the target variable is complex, such as the presence of structural breaks and nonlinearity, linear models will perform poorly in making out-of-sample predictions (Hastie et al. 2009). In the remainder of this chapter, we will look into two popular nonlinear ML regression models that are ideal for capturing nonlinear relationships.

12.3.1 K-Nearest Neighbors Regression

K-nearest neighbors regression (KNNR) is a powerful, flexible algorithm that can model complex, nonlinear relationships without making strong assumptions about the data (Cover and Hart 1967). Unlike linear models, which assume a specific relationship between features and target variables, KNNR is a nonparametric model and does not require such assumptions (Bezdek et al. 1986). Additionally, KNNR does not involve an explicit training phase. Instead, it memorizes the training data and makes predictions based on the distances to the training points, characteristic of instance-based learning models (Aha et al., 1991).

To make a prediction for a new data point, KNN computes the distance between the new point and all the points in the training data set. Common distance metrics include Euclidean distance, Manhattan distance, and Minkowski distance. The algorithm selects the k-nearest neighbors (the k points in the training set that are closest to the query point) and then predicts the target value by averaging the target values of the k-nearest neighbors. Since KNNR needs to compute the distance between the new point and all the points in the training data set every time it makes a prediction, the algorithm does not scale well for large training data sets.

The parameter k in KNNR plays a crucial role in controlling the bias-variance tradeoff. When k is small (e.g., $k = 1$), the model uses only the closest neighbor to make predictions. A small k makes the model sensitive to noise in the training data. It can capture very specific patterns and outliers, leading to high variance. The model may perform well on the training data but poorly on unseen data. When k is large, the model averages the target values of many neighbors to make predictions. When *k* equals the size of the training set, the algorithm simply uses the mean of the target variable in the training set for all predictions. A large *k* thus smooths out the predictions, potentially ignoring small but important patterns in the data. This can lead to high bias and a model that fails to capture the underlying trends in the data, resulting in poor performance on both the training and test data (underfitting). Therefore, the optimal *k* strikes a balance between bias and variance. It captures the essential patterns in the data without being too sensitive to noise.

Implementation

The code cell below first sets up the grid search for finding the optimal *k*. In practice, *k* is often chosen between 1 and 20. The KNNR class from scikit-learn package also provides additional configuration windows for model optimization. For example, when 'weight' = 'distance,' closer neighbors will have a greater influence on the algorithm.

The code reuses the tune_and_evaluate function we have created for testing the linear models. → C12NB 12.3.1a

Explanation: Despite being simple and robust, KNNR does not perform well in predicting daily index returns. The R^2 score for the test set is significantly lower than the score from validation, even though a high value of *k* was chosen by the grid search. One possible explanation for this result is that the KNNR algorithm does not preserve the intertemporal order of the time-series data, which is related to the regime-switching patterns within the data. This means that if the relationship between feature and target variables changes over time, KNNR's algorithm cannot detect when the change occurs. For example, some features, such as Recent_Volatility, may exhibit different predictive roles during bull and bear markets. In conclusion, the KNNR algorithm is not suitable for modeling time-series data where multiple structural breaks in the feature-target relationship are present.

12.3.2 Random Forest Regression

Random Forest Regression (RFR) is a versatile and powerful algorithm capable of handling both linear and nonlinear data effectively (Breiman

2001). Before diving into the details, it is important to introduce some key concepts and techniques in machine learning first:

Decision Trees: Think of a decision tree as a series of yes/no questions leading to a prediction. For example, if you were predicting stock prices, a tree might first ask if the stock has a regular dividend policy, then ask the amount of the regular dividends, and finally come up with a fair value of the stock. In a decision tree, each path down the tree leads to a predicted value.

Random Forest: Random Forest builds many decision trees (often hundreds or thousands). Each tree is created using a different random subset of the data and a random subset of the features (input variables). This randomness helps ensure that the trees are diverse.

Bagging (Bootstrap Aggregating): To create each tree, the algorithm takes a random sample of the data (with replacement). This means some data points may be used multiple times in a single tree, while others might be left out. This process is called "bagging." Because each tree sees a different set of data, they each learn slightly different patterns.

Ensemble Learning: Ensemble learning means combining multiple models to make a better prediction. Instead of relying on just one tree, Random Forest uses many trees and combines their results. The idea is that multiple trees working together can make more accurate predictions than any single tree. Once all the trees are built, they each make a prediction for a new data point. The Random Forest algorithm then averages all these predictions to come up with a final prediction. This averaging process helps smooth out any odd predictions from individual trees, leading to a more accurate and robust result.

Model Configuration

To apply RFR to the SSE daily index data, we need to set up a grid search for tuning the hyperparameters. Compared to the previously introduced ML methods, configuring an RFR model is more complex as both the tree and the forest require tuning. The sklearn library provides a comprehensive interface for adjusting the model. In Table 12.1 below, we cover the most important parameters mostly related to controlling overfitting. Notice that the default settings and the meanings of the parameter values may change in different versions of the package.[†]

Table 12.1 Summary of RFR model parameters for overfitting control under sklearn library

Hyperparameter	Default setting	Description
n_estimators	100	The number of trees in the forest; increasing the number of trees enforces the quality of the ensemble learning but also increases computational cost.
max_features	None	The number of features to consider when looking for the best split. Lower values reduce model complexity but may increase bias.
max_depth	None	The maximum depth of the tree, if None nodes are expanded until all leaves are pure or until all leaves contain less than min_samples_split samples.
min_samples_split	2	Controls overfitting. Higher values prevent the model from learning overly specific patterns.
min_samples_leaf	1	The minimum number of samples required to be at a leaf node. Higher values prevent the model from learning overly specific patterns but may increase bias.

The following code cell sets up the parameter tuning range for four hyperparameters related to overfitting. The tune_and_evaluate function is reused to perform the grid search. Notice that the option bootstrap is set to false. → C12NB 12.3.2a

Explanation: The results show significant improvement in out-of-sample prediction over the linear ML models, as the optimized RFR models explain 2.3 percent of the variation of the test set. For a simple demonstration, our parameter tuning program only performs grid search over

---

† For complete documentation, check https://scikit-learn.org/ for the latest updates.

a limited range. In a practical project, when time and computational resources are allowed, it is advised to expand the operation of grid search for a better-optimized model.

12.3.3 Interpretation of Feature Effects

Although the RFR model is better shaped in hashing the computing power, its major drawback lies in model interpretation (Molnar 2020). It is impossible to read the marginal effect of individual features on the target variable in a clean mathematical format as we have in linear models. RFR, being an ensemble of decision trees, doesn't provide coefficients like a linear model does. This is because it does not assume a linear relationship between the features and the target variable. However, there are methods to interpret the model and understand the relationship between features and the target variable in more detail. Here are a few approaches.

Feature Importance

Feature importance scores indicate the relative importance of each feature in making predictions. The more a feature is used to make key decisions within the forest of trees, the higher its importance score. However, they do not provide a direct interpretation of how changes in a feature affect the target variable.

We can extract the feature importance score from our trained RFR mode by accessing the feature_importances attribute. In sklearn, this score is normalized to sum to 1. →C12NB 12.3.3a

The output suggests that in the optimized RFR model, Recent Volatility is the most important feature, followed by Lag Daily Return for predicting the index returns. The weekday effects and Recent_Volatility are treated as insignificant features by the RFR algorithm.

Partial Dependence Plots (PDP).   PDPs provide insights into the relationship between a particular feature and the predicted outcome of a machine learning model, while marginalizing over the effects of all other features. The following code cell generates the PDPs for optimized RFR model. →C12NB 12.3.3b

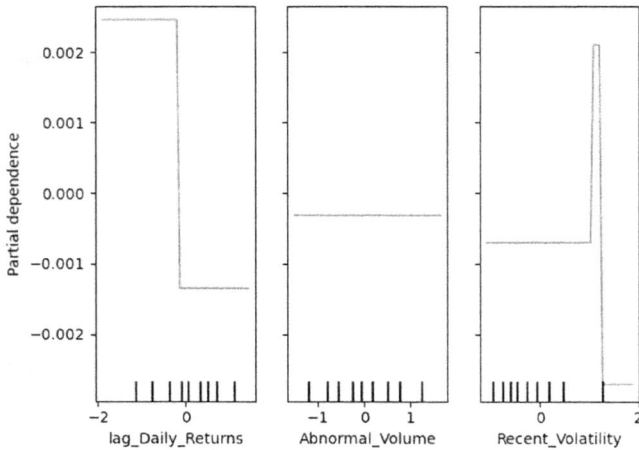

Figure 12.1 Jupyter Notebook screenshot for code for obtaining the Partial Dependence Plots (PDP) for the trained RFR mode

Explanation: The program generates three plots in one graph as shown in Figure 12.1 above. For each plot, the *x*-axis represents the standardized feature value, and the *y*-axis represents the predicted outcome (partial dependence) averaged over all other features.

- Abnormal Volume: The plot for Abnormal Volume suggests that the predicted outcome does not depend on the value of this feature, as indicated by the flat line. This implies that abnormal trading volume has little to no impact on the daily index returns in the model.
- Lag Daily Returns: The plot for Lag Daily Returns shows a nonlinear relationship. The effect of lagged returns is mostly dependent on the direction of the lagged returns, suggesting that the index returns exhibit positive lag-one autocorrelation. This insight can be useful for further developing the prediction model, as it indicates that past returns can be predictive of future returns.
- Recent Volatility: The plot for Recent Volatility also indicates a nonlinear relationship. It suggests that both extremely high and low levels of recent volatility predict negative daily index returns, with a stronger effect on the high side. This

means that periods of high volatility are associated with lower future returns, which can be critical for risk management and strategy development.

Overall, the plots explain why RFR outperforms the linear models, as the evidence indicates that the relationship between the features and the target variable is nonlinear.

Conclusion

In this chapter, we explore the complete workflow of applying regression models to financial data. The chapter begins with importing and preparing data, including defining the target variable and features, and necessary data preparation. It then delves into linear models, covering linear regression and advanced techniques like Ridge, Lasso, and Elastic Net regressions, emphasizing the bias-variance tradeoff. Nonlinear models such as K-nearest neighbors and RFR are also examined. The chapter concludes with methods for interpreting feature effects, determining feature importance, and utilizing PDP to visualize feature-target relationships, ensuring robust model insights and predictions.

Exercise

In this exercise, you will apply the concepts and techniques learned in this chapter to a new feature derived from the SSE Daily Index data. Follow the steps below, implement the solution for each question, and provide your analysis.

1. Create a new column in the data set named Day_range, calculated as follows:
   Day_range = (High-Low)/Low
2. Preparing the data:
   a) Prepare the data by defining the target variable and features (use "lag_Daily_return," "lag_Day_range," and the Weekday effects).
   b) Describe the steps you took to clean and restructure the data.

   c) Write the code to split the data into training, validation, and test sets.

   d) Standardize the continuous features.

3. Implementing models:

   a) Implement the sample ML models demonstrated in the chapter (Linear Regression, Ridge, Lasso, Elastic Net, k-nearest neighbors, and Random Forest) using the new data set with the Day_Range feature.

   b) Write the code to implement and evaluate these models.

4. Does the target variable (daily index returns) appear to be predictable with the inclusion of the Day_Range feature?

5. Which model performs the best in predicting the target variable?

6. Which features appear to be the most useful in predicting the target variable?

7. Does the relationship between the features and the target variable appear to be linear or nonlinear?

8. Does the relationship between the features and the target variable appear to be stable or changing over time?

9. Does the target variable (daily index returns) appear to be autocorrelated? If it does, how might you improve the performance of the machine learning models?

CHAPTER 13

Classification Machine Learning Models for Finance

Introduction

Classification is a type of supervised machine learning where the objective is to categorize data points into predefined classes or labels based on input features (Murphy 2012). Unlike regression, which predicts continuous values, classification predicts discrete outcomes. The core idea is to learn a mapping from input features to output labels using historical data, training the model to classify new, unseen data accurately.

13.1 Introduction of ML Classification and Applications

How Classification Differs From Other Machine Learning Problems

a) Output type:
  - Classification: The output is a categorical label, such as *spam* or *not spam* in email filtering.
  - Regression: The output is a continuous value, like predicting stock prices or house prices.
b) Evaluation metrics:
  - Classification: Metrics include accuracy, precision, recall, F1 score, and ROC-AUC (Receiver Operating Characteristic - Area Under the Curve).
  - Regression: Metrics include mean squared error, root mean squared error, mean absolute error, and R-squared.

c) Decision boundaries:
- Classification: The model learns decision boundaries that separate different classes in the feature space.
- Regression: The model fits a continuous curve or line that best represents the relationship between input features and the output.

d) Applications:
- Classification: Used in applications like fraud detection, medical diagnosis, and image recognition.
- Regression: Applied in fields like finance for predicting stock prices, in real estate for estimating property values, and in economics for forecasting economic indicators.

Examples of Classification Applications in Finance

a) Credit risk assessment:
- Problem: Predict whether a loan applicant will default on a loan (Thomas 2000).
- Input features: Credit score, income, employment status, loan amount, and payment history.
- Output: A binary label indicating "default" or "no default."
- Impact: Helps financial institutions evaluate the risk associated with lending money and make informed decisions.

b) Fraud detection:
- Problem: Identify fraudulent transactions among millions of credit card transactions (Bhattacharyya et al. 2011).
- Input features: Transaction amount, transaction location, merchant category, time of transaction, and historical transaction patterns.
- Output: A binary label indicating "fraudulent" or "non-fraudulent."
- Impact: Protects financial institutions and customers from financial losses and reduces fraudulent activities.

c) Customer segmentation:

- Problem: Classify customers into different segments based on their purchasing behavior (Maddumala et al. 2022).
- Input features: Purchase history, demographic information, income, and engagement level.
- Output: Multiple labels representing different customer segments, such as "high-value customers," "bargain hunters," and "loyal customers."
- Impact: Enables targeted marketing campaigns and personalized offers, improving customer retention and increasing sales.

d) Market movement prediction:
- Problem: Predict whether a stock price will go up or down the next day.
- Input features: Historical stock prices, trading volume, market indicators, and economic news.
- Output: A binary label indicating "up" or "down."
- Impact: Assists traders and investors in making buy or sell decisions, potentially increasing their returns.

13.2 Data Preparation for Classification ML

In this chapter, we will explore a data set that contains various features about individuals applying for bank loans,* including demographic information, financial status, and loan details. Our primary goal is to use this data to predict the risk rating of loan applicants. We will delve into the nuances of handling different types of data, including continuous and categorical variables, and explain why different treatments are necessary for each. Finally, we will standardize the data and prepare it for machine learning models.

---

* This data set is a modified version of the original dataset from Kaggle. Some of the data in the current version have been generated through computer simulations for educational purposes. The original dataset is available at www.kaggle.com/datasets/preethamgouda/financial-risk. Full credit for the original dataset goes to the respective owner(s).

Loading Data

The following code cell loads the original data set into the Jupyter Note-book session. A preliminary examination of the data set is conducted to provide an overview of the data. From the summary information of the DataFrame, we observe that the data set contains nine numerical fea-tures and possibly seven categorical features. Some features appear to have missing values, which will require further handling. →C13NB 13.2a

Data Set Features

The data set comprises the following features:

a) Age: The age of the individual (continuous variable).

b) Gender: The gender of the individual (categorical variable with cate-gories Male, Female, and Nonbinary).

c) Education level: The highest level of education achieved (categorical variable with levels ranging from High School to PhD).

d) Marital status: The current marital status (categorical variable with categories Single, Married, Divorced, and Widowed).

e) Income: The annual income in USD (continuous variable).

f) Credit score: A numeric value indicating creditworthiness.

g) Loan amount: The amount of loan requested by the individual (con-tinuous variable).

h) Loan purpose: The purpose of the loan (categorical variable with categories Home, Auto, Personal, and Business).

i) Employment status: The employment situation of the individual (categorical variable with categories Employed, Unemployed, and Self-employed).

j) Years at current job: The duration of employment at the current job (continuous variable).

k) Payment history: Historical payment performance (categorical vari-able with categories Excellent, Good, Fair, and Poor).

l) Debt-to-income ratio: The ratio of debt to income (continuous vari-able).

m) Assets value: The total value of assets owned by the individual (con-tinuous variable).

n) Number of dependents: The number of dependents supported by the individual (continuous variable).

o) Previous defaults: The number of previous loan defaults (continuous variable).

p) Marital status change: The number of changes in marital status (continuous variable).

The primary objectives of applying machine learning models to this data set are:

a) Risk prediction: To predict the risk rating of loan applicants based on their demographic, financial, and loan-related features. This helps financial institutions assess the risk associated with loan applicants and make informed decisions.

b) Improving loan approval processes: By accurately predicting the risk rating, financial institutions can streamline their loan approval processes, reduce the likelihood of defaults, and enhance their decision-making capabilities.

c) Identifying key factors: Machine learning models can help identify the key factors that influence the risk rating of loan applicants. This can provide valuable insights into which features are most important in predicting risk and allow institutions to focus on those areas when assessing applications.

Target Variables

The primary objective is to classify loan applicants' risk ratings, which will serve as the target variable for our classification model. Since machine learning models for handling binary and multi-class targets differ, we will create two target variables from the original column to demonstrate techniques for handling both types of target variables.

As displayed in the code cell below, two target variables, namely Risk_Rating_2Cat and Risk_Rating_3Cat, are derived from the same original column but serve different purposes in demonstrating how to handle classification problems with binary and multiple categories. →C13NB 13.2b

a) Risk_Rating_3Cat: This target variable indicates the risk rating of the individual in three coded categories:

0: Low risk

1: Medium risk

2: High risk

b) Risk_Rating_2Cat: This target variable indicates the risk rating of the individual in two coded categories:

0: Low risk

1: Medium risk

13.2.1 Handling Categorical and Continuous Variables

Categorical variables, such as Gender and Loan Purpose, represent distinct groups or categories. These variables need to be encoded into numerical values to be used in machine learning models. This is typically done using one-hot encoding, which creates binary (0 or 1) columns for each category. One-hot encoding avoids imposing any ordinal relationship between categories, which is not present in categorical data.

Continuous variables, such as Age and Income, can take any numerical value within a range. When preparing continuous variables for machine learning models, it is important to **standardize** them to ensure they have a mean of 0 and a standard deviation of 1. This is done by subtracting each observation from the estimated mean and dividing the result by the estimated standard deviation. The data set used to calculate these estimates must be selected carefully to reflect the actual conditions under which the models will be tested. We will demonstrate this important step in conjunction with the discussion on training and test sets. It's important to note that standardization is crucial for models sensitive to the scale of input data, such as logistic regression and neural networks. Standardization improves the convergence of gradient-based optimization algorithms and ensures that features contribute equally to the model.

The following code cell splits the original data set into two based on the number of categories in the target variables. All categorical variables are encoded into numerical values, and rows with missing values are dropped. The final result is two clean data sets (fr_data_2cat and fr_data_3cat)—one with a binary target variable and the other with a three-category target variable. →C13NB 13.2.1a

The drop_first=True setting in pd.get_dummies is an essential part of our data preprocessing. Without this specification, each class in a categorical feature would be represented by a separate binary column. For example, if a categorical feature has three classes ('A,' 'B,' 'C'), one-hot encoding would create three binary columns, each indicating whether the observation belongs to 'A,' 'B,' or 'C.' However, this introduces redundancy. If an observation is not in 'A' and not in 'B,' it must be in 'C.' This redundancy creates a multicollinearity issue for machine learning models, where the feature columns become highly correlated, potentially leading to problems in linear models like logistic regression.

13.2.2 Data Partitioning

The next step in the data preparation process is to partition the data into training, validation, and test sets. In the previous chapter, we discussed handling time series data by retaining the temporal order and avoiding randomization. However, for the current project, the data is cross-sectional, with each row representing a single loan application. Therefore, randomization should be applied when forming the training, validation, and test sets to ensure that the samples are representative of the entire data set.

The following code cell uses the train_test_split function from sklearn. model_selection to partition the data: →C13NB 13.2.2a

Before getting into the code for partitioning data, we first need to understand the part of the code for standardizing the numerical features. Standardization is essential because many machine learning algorithms perform better when numerical features are on a similar scale. This is particularly important for models that rely on distance measurements, such as **k-nearest neighbors**, **support vector machines (SVM)**, and **logistic regression**, where the magnitude of the feature values can influence the model's performance.

The numerical features are standardized using instances of sklearn's StandardScaler class. A similar procedure was used in the previous chapter for regression models. It is crucial to apply the fit_transform method to the training set. Once fitted, the scaler "remembers" the standardization parameters (mean and standard deviation), which can then be applied to the test set or any out-of-sample data for prediction.

The train_test_split function divides the data set into training and test sets randomly, using an 80:20 split. The random_state parameter is arbitrarily assigned to allow readers to replicate the results. Note that there are two parallel sets of training and test data for the two target variables: Risk_Rating_2cat and Risk_Rating_3cat.

13.2.3 Descriptive Statistics and Preliminary Analysis

At this stage, before deploying machine learning models, it is important to examine the data through exploratory analysis. The goal is to identify any abnormal patterns in the original data that may indicate issues with the sampling or data collection process and to gather insights that can inform the choice of machine learning models and configurations. For categorical variables, any extreme imbalance among categories may indicate problems with the initial classification or issues in the data source. For numerical features, we can quickly check for the presence of outliers by looking for observations outside the range of [–3, 3] after standardization. One easy way of performing a quick check on data is to use a DataFrame object's describe () method, which calculates the basic descriptive statistics for each data column. Based on the max and min statistics for numerical features and the mean statistics for categorical features (available in the chapter notebook file), we can conclude that the original feature data appears to be free of extreme outliers. →C13NB 13.2.3a

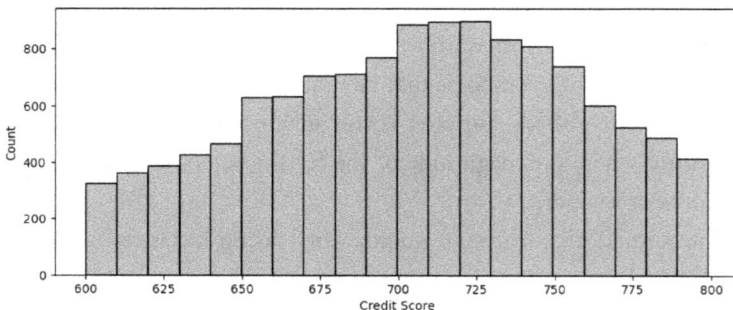

Figure 13.1 Jupyter Notebook screenshot for code and result that generate the histogram for the original credit score feature data

Visual inspection of the original data distribution can also reveal potential issues that might undermine the predictive power of our machine learning models. For continuous data, extreme skewness or heavy tails warrant further investigation. For example, the histogram of **Credit Score** (before standardization) shows that values are bounded between 600 and 800, with a center around 715. This range is inconsistent with the typical FICO score system (300 to 850). This discrepancy may suggest a restriction in the bank's application process that is not reflected in the data set, potentially limiting the accuracy of any machine learning model trained on this data.

It is also important to check the distribution of classes in the target variable. Specifically, we need to identify whether there is a class imbalance, as this can significantly affect the performance of machine learning models, as we will demonstrate later. A frequency plot, created using the sns.countplot method, reveals a highly noticeable class imbalance in the target variable outcomes. Most loan applications are considered low risk, while only a small portion (7.94%) are categorized as high-risk applicants. We will later discuss how this imbalance can influence the performance of our ML models and explore techniques for addressing this issue.
→ C13NB 13.2.3b

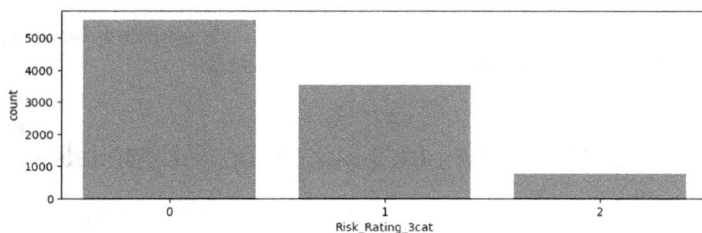

Figure 13.2 Jupyter Notebook screenshot for code that generates the frequency plot for three-categorical target variable

13.2.4 Correlation Analysis

Performing a correlation analysis among the feature variables can provide insights into the relationships between different features. This can help identify multicollinearity issues, where some features are highly correlated with each other, potentially impacting the performance of certain machine learning models (James et al. 2013).

For an efficient report of correlation between the numerical variables, we can use the heatmap correlation matrix (see Chapter 9.2). The plot is presented in Figure 13.3. It is shown that multicollinearity is not presented among these variables. →C13NB 13.2.4a

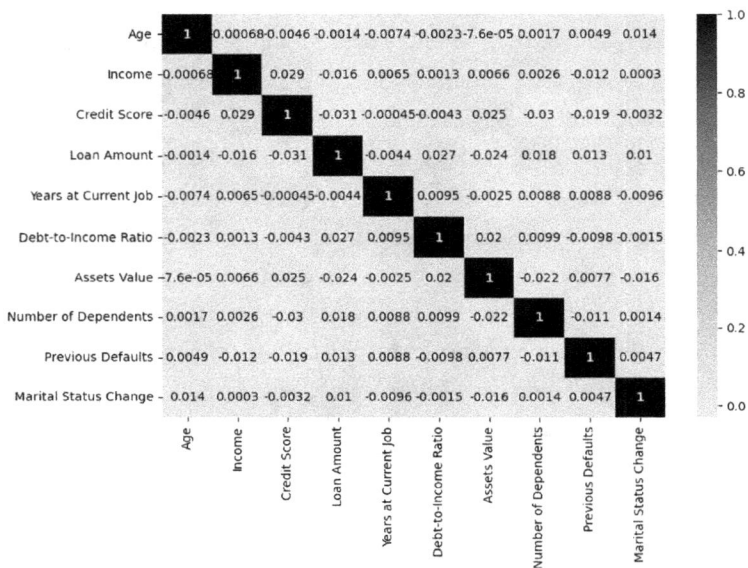

Figure 13.3 Jupyter Notebook screenshot for code output of heatmap correlation matrix among the numerical variables

13.3 Overview of Classification ML Models

Once the data is prepared with features and the target variables defined, we can move on to the ML training stage. The sklearn package provides a comprehensive toolbox for ML classification models, we will cover the most popular ones in this chapter.

13.3.1 Logistic Regression

Logistic Regression is a statistical method used for binary classification problems, where the goal is to predict one of two possible outcomes based on one or more predictor variables. It is an extension of linear regression that applies a logistic function to model the probability of a binary dependent variable (Hosmer and Lemeshow 2000). The logistic function, also known as the sigmoid function, transforms the linear combination of input features into a value between 0 and 1, which can be interpreted as a probability.

Principle Behind Logistic Regression

Logistic Regression models the relationship between the dependent binary variable and one or more independent variables by estimating probabilities using the logistic (sigmoid) function:

$$P(y=1|X) = \frac{1}{1 + e^{-(B_0 + B_1 X_1 + B_2 X_2 + \ldots + B_n X_n)}}$$

where:

$P(y=1|X)$ is the probability that the target variable y equals 1 given the feature variable X.

$\beta, \beta, \ldots,$ and β_n are the coefficients estimated from the data.

$X, X, \ldots,$ and X_n are the feature variables.

The model predicts the probability of the positive class (e.g., success, event occurrence) and uses a threshold (commonly 0.5) to classify observations into binary outcomes.

Advantages of Logistic Regression

- Simplicity and interpretability: Logistic Regression coefficients βs represent the relationship between the predictor variables and the log-odds of the dependent variable.
- Probabilistic output: It provides probabilistic estimates that can be useful for decision making.
- Efficiency: It is computationally efficient and performs well when the relationship between the dependent variable and independent variables is approximately linear.

Limitations of Logistic Regression

- Linear decision boundary: Logistic Regression assumes a linear relationship between the predictors and the log-odds of the response. It may not perform well if the true decision boundary is nonlinear.
- Multicollinearity: The presence of high correlation among predictors can lead to unstable estimates and affect the model's performance.
- Outliers: Logistic Regression can be sensitive to outliers, which can disproportionately influence the model parameters.

Interpretation of the Coefficients in Logistic Regression

In Logistic Regression, the coefficients (also known as weights) represent the relationship between the predictor variables and the log-odds of the dependent variable. Here's a detailed interpretation of these coefficients:

Log-Odds Interpretation

Each coefficient in a logistic regression model represents the change in the log-odds of the outcome for a one-unit increase in the predictor variable, holding all other variables constant.

The log-odds are the natural logarithm of the odds, where the odds are the probability of the event occurring divided by the probability of the event not occurring.

Mathematically:

$$\log\left(\frac{P(y=1)}{P(y=0)}\right) = B_0 + B_1 X_1 + B_2 X_2 + \ldots + B_n X_n$$

β_i = a positive coeffcient indicates that as X_i increases, the odds of the outcome occurring increase.

β_i = a negative coefficent indicates that as X_i increases the odds of the outcome occurring decrease.

β_i = zero indicates no effect of X_i on the odds of the outcome.

Hyperparameter Tuning of Logistic Regression

The technical details of the hyperparameters can be overwhelming for readers who prefer to focus on the practical applications of machine learning. Fortunately, with the aid of Python and its developers' community, these details have been thoughtfully handled by the developers. As users, we simply need to understand the functional aspects of these hyperparameters.

a) **Regularization terms:**

   Description: The regularization term in logistic regression is similar to the one used in Lasso, Ridge, and Elastic Net regressions, which were covered in previous chapters. It is the penalty term added to the loss function to prevent overfitting. This penalty discourages the model from fitting too closely to the training data, thereby improving its generalization to new, unseen data. The two most common regularization techniques in logistic regression are L1 (Lasso) and L2 (Ridge) regularization. Elastic Net regularization, which combines both L1 and L2 regularization, is also used. Typical Values: 'l1,' 'l2,' 'elasticnet,' None. The default value in scikit-learn is 'l2.'

b) **C (inverse of regularization strength):**

   Description: This hyperparameter controls the strength of the regularization (controls for overfitting). It is the inverse of the regularization parameter lambda (λ). Smaller values of C correspond to stronger regularization, which helps to prevent overfitting by penalizing large coefficients. Larger values of C reduce the regularization strength, potentially leading to overfitting.
   Typical values: Common values range from 0.01 to 100. The default value in scikit-learn is C = 1.0.

c) **Solver (optimization algorithm):**

   Description: This parameter specifies the algorithm to use for optimization (minimizing the loss function). Each solver has unique compatibility with different settings and other hyperparameters.

The detailed descriptions can be found in the scikit-learn official documentation.[†] For a simple introduction, it is important to note that the default setting (lbfgs) is robust for unscaled feature data but is not suitable for different penalty terms (only good for L2 and None). On the other hand, the saga solver is robust for different penalty terms but not robust for unscaled data. For the purpose of grid search over all possible penalty terms, saga is the preferred choice of solver.

Typical values: 'lbfgs,' 'liblinear,' 'newton-cg,' 'newton-cholesky,' 'sag,' 'saga.' The default value in scikit-learn is 'lbfgs.'

13.3.2 Decision Trees

Decision Trees are nonparametric supervised learning models used for both classification and regression tasks. They work by recursively splitting the data into subsets based on the value of input features. Each internal node represents a "test" on an attribute, each branch represents the outcome of the test, and each leaf node represents a class label (in classification) or a continuous value (in regression) (Breiman et al. 1986). The path from the root to a leaf represents the decision rules applied to the input features.

Principle Behind Decision Trees

A **Decision Tree** splits the data into subsets to minimize a specific criterion, which typically reflects the impurity of the split. Below, we provide a brief and easy-to-understand introduction to two commonly used measures:

- **Gini impurity**: When a decision tree splits the data, it aims to create groups (or nodes) that are as pure as possible. The tree uses Gini impurity to evaluate how well each split separates the data. It seeks splits that minimize Gini impurity, striving

---

† See the Appendix.

for the most homogeneous groups—like trying to get bags of candy with only one color.

- **Entropy for classification**: Entropy is another measure used to evaluate impurity or disorder in a data set, commonly applied in decision trees for classification tasks. Simply put, entropy measures how mixed a group of items is. Borrowed from information theory, it quantifies the uncertainty or randomness in the data.

The tree continues to split the data until a stopping condition is met, such as reaching a maximum depth or a minimum number of samples per leaf.

Advantages of Decision Trees

- Simplicity and interpretability: Easy to visualize and interpret.
- Nonlinearity: Can model nonlinear relationships without requiring feature scaling.
- Handling of categorical data: Naturally handles both numerical and categorical data.
- Robustness to outliers: Less sensitive to outliers compared to some other models.

Limitations of Decision Trees

- Overfitting: Prone to overfitting, especially with deep trees.
- Instability: Small changes in the data can lead to different splits, making the tree unstable.
- Bias: May not perform well with some data sets compared to more sophisticated models.

Key Hyperparameters

- max_depth: The maximum depth of the tree. Limits the number of splits to prevent overfitting.

- min_samples_split: The minimum number of samples required to split an internal node.
- min_samples_leaf: The minimum number of samples required to be at a leaf node.
- criterion: The function to measure the quality of a split (e.g., 'gini' for Gini impurity, 'entropy' for information gain).

13.3.3 Support Vector Machines (SVM)

SVM are powerful and versatile supervised learning models used for both classification and regression tasks. SVMs are particularly well-suited for the classification of complex but small- or medium-sized data sets (Cortes and Vapnik 1995). They work by finding the hyperplane that best separates the data points of different classes in the feature space. The "best" hyperplane is the one that has the largest margin, which is the distance between the hyperplane and the nearest data points from any class.

Principle Behind SVM

SVM aims to find a hyperplane (e.g. a line or boundary) that maximizes the margin between two classes. The data points that are closest to the hyperplane are called support vectors. SVM can also handle nonlinear classification by using kernel functions to project the data into higher dimensions where a linear separation is possible.

Advantages of SVM

- Effective in high-dimensional spaces: SVM is effective in cases where the number of dimensions is greater than the number of samples. In other words, SVM is robust to small sample.
- Memory efficient: Uses a subset of training points (support vectors) in the decision function.
- Versatile: Different kernel functions can be specified for the decision function, providing flexibility in handling various types of data.

Limitations of SVM

- Computational complexity: Training can be time-consuming for large data sets.
- Choice of kernel: The performance of SVM depends on the choice of the kernel and its parameters.
- Not probabilistic: SVM does not directly provide probability estimates.

Key Hyperparameters

- C: Regularization parameter that controls the trade-off between achieving a low training error and a low testing error. Smaller values specify stronger regularization.
- kernel: Specifies the kernel type to be used in the algorithm (e.g., 'linear,' 'poly,' 'rbf,' 'sigmoid').
- gamma: Kernel coefficient for 'rbf,' 'poly,' and 'sigmoid.' It defines how far the influence of a single training example reaches.

Understanding Kernel Functions in SVM. The key to understanding the applications of SVM lies in the meaning of their Kernel Function. In plain and simple language, the kernel function is the tool given to the computer for drawing the boundary line. Imagine a 2D coordinate system with two groups of points, each point having its x–y coordinates similar to the feature data of each observation. If you need to draw a line on the coordinate system to separate the two groups, it would be easy if they are clearly separable, such that a straight line will do the job. However, if there is an overlap between the two groups, you will need to draw a more complex line to fulfill the task.

The kernel function is closely related to the algorithm that the computer uses to draw the line. A linear kernel function, for example, will always result in a straight line and thus will make poor classification decisions for overlapping cases. The other kernel functions available in scikit-learn (and probably other ML packages) can handle nonlinear classification tasks. When considering other aspects of our modeling project, we can focus on two main candidates: the "rbf" and "sigmoid" kernels.

RBF vs Sigmoid

RBF Kernel (Radial Basis Function).

- Also known as the Gaussian kernel.
- One of the most popular and widely used kernels in SVM.
- Maps the input data into an infinite-dimensional space, making it capable of handling very complex relationships.
- Parameter: γ (gamma) controls the model's complexity.

Sigmoid Kernel

- Similar to the activation function used in neural networks.
- Can be used to model relationships that have a logistic-like pattern.
- Parameters: γ and coef0 control the model's complexity and flexibility.
- Guidelines for choosing the Kernel Function for SVM.

RBF Kernel

- Use if the relationship between features and targets is unclear but possibly nonlinear and complex.
- Suitable when computational resources are not an issue.

Sigmoid Kernel

- Use if the features and target have a logistic-like relationship.[‡]
- Suitable when the sample size is large enough that computational burden becomes a concern.

13.4 Evaluation of ML Classifiers

As we studied in the previous chapter on Regression ML models, the training process involves configuring the hyperparameters to achieve

---

‡ This means that as the value of the predictor changes, the probability of the outcome changes in a nonlinear fashion

the highest evaluation score. For classification projects, the commonly employed model evaluation metrics include:

Precision

Precision measures the proportion of correctly predicted positive instances out of the total predicted positive instances. Precision is important when the cost of false positives is high, such as in spam detection.

Recall (Sensitivity or True Positive Rate)

Recall measures the proportion of correctly predicted positive instances out of the total actual positive. Recall is important when the cost of false negatives is high, such as in disease detection.

F1 Score

The F1 score is the harmonic mean of precision and recall, providing a balance between the two metrics.

$$\text{Formula: F1 score} = 2\,\frac{Precision \times Recall}{Precision + Recall}$$

The F1 score is useful when you need a balance between precision and recall, especially in cases of imbalanced classes.

Accuracy

Accuracy is one of the most commonly used metrics for evaluating the performance of classification models. It measures the proportion of correctly classified instances among the total instances. However, it can be misleading in cases of class imbalance, as it doesn't account for the distribution of the classes.

Formula:
Accuracy = Number of Correct Predictions/Total Number
of Prediction = (TP + TN)/(TP+TN+FP+FN)

where TP = true positives, TN = true negative, FP = false positive
FN = false negative

Confusion Matrix

A confusion matrix is a table that shows the number of true positives, true negatives, false positives, and false negatives. It provides a comprehensive view of the performance of a classification model.

Structure.

	Predicted positive	Predicted negative
Actual positive	True positive (TP)	False negative (FN)
Actual negative	False positive (FP)	True negative (TN)

Risk Management Consideration

In a bank loan application scenario with a target variable indicating the risk level of applicants, **recall** and **precision** are critical metrics for effective risk management.

1. **Recall (true positive rate, TPR)**: Recall is crucial for minimizing loan defaults, as it measures the model's ability to correctly identify high-risk applicants. A high recall reduces the chances of approving risky loans that could default. For example, a model with a high recall ensures that most high-risk applicants are correctly flagged, which is vital for managing default risk (Noriega et al. 2023; Dong et al. 2024).

2. **Precision**: Precision ensures that most predicted high-risk loans are genuinely risky. This is essential for avoiding unnecessary rejections of low-risk applicants, which could lead to lost business opportunities. High precision minimizes false positives, ensuring that the bank doesn't wrongly classify low-risk applicants as high-risk (Dong et al. 2024).

By balancing both precision and recall, or using the **F1-score** (a combination of both metrics), banks can effectively minimize defaults while maximizing loan approvals to low-risk applicants (Noriega et al. 2023).

13.5 Training Implementation for Binary Classification

Let's proceed with training three classification models: Logistic Regression, Decision Tree, and SVM with the financial risk assessment data. The ML model training and parameter tuning under binary and multiple outcomes scenarios are different and thus we will look into each scenario separately.

13.5.1 Training Logistic Regression for Binary Classification

A binary classification scenario refers to a target variable that has two possible outcomes (e.g., True or False, Pass or Fail). For the financial risk assessment data, this is represented by the target variable Risk_Rating_2Cat, which specifies whether a loan application has been evaluated as Safe (low risk rating) or Risky (medium risk rating).

It is important to note that logistic regression is a widely used traditional statistical method for classification problems. Its training process assumes certain parametric assumptions. Violating these assumptions will result in sub-optimal performance. These assumptions include:

a) Linearity of logits: The relationship between the independent variables (features) and the log-odds (logit) of the dependent variable (target) is assumed to be linear. This means that the logit of the probability of the positive class should be a linear combination of the features.

b) Independence of errors: Observations should be independent of each other. The error terms should not be correlated, meaning that there should be no autocorrelation in the residuals. This is particularly important in time series data or spatial data.

c) No multicollinearity: The model assumes that the independent variables are not highly correlated with each other. High multicollinearity can make it difficult to determine the individual effect of each predictor. Variance inflation factor can be used to detect multicol-linearity.

d) Large sample size: Logistic regression requires a sufficiently large sample size to produce reliable estimates. Small sample sizes can lead to overfitting and unreliable estimates of the coefficients.

e) Absence of outliers: Assumes no significant outliers that could distort the results. Outliers can disproportionately influence the model parameters.

The following code cell demonstrates the training and tuning of a Logistic Regression model to our project data. →C13NB **13.5.1a**

```
Beta Coefficient of Loan Amount 0.10091201290993354
Best Hyperparameters for Logistic Regression: {'C': 0.1, 'l1_ratio': 0, 'penalty': 'l1'}
Logistic Regression Confusion Matrix Report on Test:
              precision    recall  f1-score   support

           0       0.62      0.87      0.73      1106
           1       0.48      0.18      0.27       715

    accuracy                           0.60      1821
   macro avg       0.55      0.53      0.50      1821
weighted avg       0.57      0.60      0.55      1821
```

Figure 13.4 Jupyter Notebook screenshot of result of code from training and testing of a Logistic Regression model to the chapter data (binary target)

Explanation: The sklearn package provides a suite of tools for training commonly used machine learning models for classification problems. The GridSearchCV function from sklearn.model_selection encapsulates the n-fold cross-validation method within its grid search algorithm, finding and returning the model with the best set of hyperparameters. Using the best model, we apply an L2 penalty (Ridge regularization) with a regularization strength of 1 to make predictions based on the test set data. The results are then summarized in a confusion matrix as shown in Figure 13.4.

For logistic regression in classification tasks, we can examine the marginal effect of each feature on the log-odds of the positive class (risky applicants) by interpreting the estimated model coefficients (Beta). For example, the coefficient for **Loan Amount** is 0.1, which indicates that for a 1 standard deviation increase in Loan Amount the log-odds of being classified as risky increase by approximately 0.10, holding all other variables constant and assuming the linear relationship persists across observations.

Regarding the confusion matrix results, overall, the model exhibits an accuracy of 60 percent, meaning it correctly classified 60 percent of the loan risk levels in the test set, which is better than the expected result from random guessing. From a risk management perspective, particular attention should be given to the positive class (risky loan applicants). The trained logistic regression model achieves an accuracy of 0.48 in predicting risky loans, which is higher than the percentage of risky applicants in the population. However, the model's low recall rate, indicating that it correctly identifies only 18 percent of risky applicants, reveals a practical insufficiency. This drawback may result from the class imbalance in the target variable or limitations of the classification algorithm.

13.5.2 N-Fold Cross-Validation and Grid-Searching

The previous code example demonstrates an important technique in machine learning called N-fold Cross-validation. This technique is used to assess the performance and generalizability of a machine learning model. It involves partitioning the data set into N equal-sized subsets or "folds." The model is trained and evaluated N times, each time using a different fold as the validation set and the remaining folds as the training set. The benefits of N-fold Cross-validation include:

- Decrease in risk of overfitting: Each data point gets to be in the training set (N-1) times and in the validation set exactly once.
- More reliable performance estimate: Provides a more reliable estimate of model performance compared to a single train/test split.

The cost of implementing this technique is computational time, especially for large data sets and complex models.

GridSearchCV is a tool in scikit-learn that performs hyperparameter tuning using cross-validation. It automates the process of searching for the best combination of hyperparameters for a given model by evaluating different combinations using N-fold cross-validation.

In the previous (and the following) code example, an instance of GridSearchCV is initialized. At the same time, a machine learning model instance (e.g., log_reg in previous code cell), the search space for the hyperparameters (param_grid_log_reg), and the number of folds in cross-validation (provided as the input for cv) are defined. The scoring input allows users to specify the criteria for model selection. Common options for scoring include[§]:

a) Accuracy (enter as "accuracy"): Measures the proportion of correctly classified instances among the total instances.

b) Precision: Measures the proportion of true positive predictions among all positive predictions.

c) Recall (sensitivity): Measures the proportion of true positive predictions among all actual positives.

d) F1 score: The harmonic mean of precision and recall, providing a balance between the two.

e) ROC-AUC("roc_auc"): Measures the area under the receiver operating characteristic (ROC) curve, evaluating the trade-off between TPR and false positive rate (FPR).

13.5.3 Training Decision Trees for Binary Classification

Unlike Logistic Regression, Decision Trees are nonparametric models (James et al. 2013). This means they can handle nonlinear relationships, are robust to multicollinearity and outliers, and are flexible with small sample sizes. However, a common problem with Decision Trees is their tendency to overfit small samples, making them less interpretable than Logistic Regression in terms of feature effects. The following code cell demonstrates how to train and tune a Decision Trees model using our project data. →C13NB 13.5.3a

---

§ For a complete list: https://scikit-learn.org/stable/modules/model_evalua-tion.html#scoring-parameter.

```
Best Hyperparameters for Decision Tree Classifier (2cat) :
DecisionTreeClassifier(max_depth=10, min_samples_leaf=10, min_samples_split=20)
Decisoin Tree Confusion Matrix Report on Test:
              precision    recall  f1-score   support

           0       0.77      0.76      0.77      1106
           1       0.64      0.64      0.64       715

    accuracy                           0.71      1821
   macro avg       0.70      0.70      0.70      1821
weighted avg       0.72      0.71      0.72      1821
```

Figure 13.5 Jupyter Notebook screenshot of for training and tuning of a Decision Trees model to the chapter data (binary target)

Explanation: The output of source code is provided in Figure 13.5. The decision tree model, optimized with the best hyperparameters (max_depth=10, min_samples_leaf=10, min_samples_split=10), demonstrates significantly better classification performance than the logistic regression model. For low-risk loans (class 0), the decision tree achieves an F1-score of 0.77, indicating strong performance in identifying low-risk loans while maintaining a balance between precision and recall. In classifying risky loans (class 1), the model achieves both precision and recall of 0.64, compared to 0.48 and 0.18, respectively, from the logistic regression model.

The significant improvement in out-of-sample predictions from the decision tree over logistic regression suggests the presence of nonlinear relationships between the features and the target variable. Unlike logistic regression, decision trees do not assume linearity or independence of errors and are robust to multicollinearity and outliers. They can also handle small sample sizes better than logistic regression, though they are prone to overfitting if not properly regularized. The use of n-fold cross-validation to tune the model's regularization parameters has played an important role in reducing the risk of overfitting.

13.5.4 Training SVM for Binary Classification

The sklearn.svm module in scikit-learn offers a flexible and efficient implementation of SVMs for classification tasks. The SVC class within this module supports both linear and nonlinear classification using different kernel functions, such as linear, polynomial, RBF(Radial Basis Function), and sigmoid kernels. Kernels help machine learning models handle complex, non-linear data by mapping it into a higher-dimensional space

without extra computation overhead. The following code cell demonstrates training an SVM classifier for our binary classification data set.
→C13NB 13.5.4a

```
Best Hyperparameters for SVM(2cat): SVC(C=10, gamma='auto')
SVM Confusion Matrix Report on Test:
                 precision    recall  f1-score   support

            0        0.73      0.75      0.74      1106
            1        0.60      0.58      0.59       715

     accuracy                            0.68      1821
    macro avg        0.67      0.66      0.67      1821
 weighted avg        0.68      0.68      0.68      1821
```

Figure 13.6 Jupyter Notebook screenshot of code cell demonstrating the training and testing and the result of SVM for binary classification on the chapter data

Explanation: The output of the source code is provided in Figure 13.6. In this example, we use the **F1** score as the scoring criterion for model selection, configuring GridSearchCV to find the model that achieves the highest F1 score for the positive class (risky loans). Despite this setting, the F1-score for class 1 produced by the SVM classifier does not outperform the one produced by the decision tree classifier. Overall, the performance of the SVM classifier is comparable to that of the decision tree, as both classifiers are based on nonparametric principles. The minor differences in performance can be attributed to sample variation, differences in model algorithms, and model configuration.

13.6 Muti-Class Classification

Logistic regression for multi-class classification is typically performed using one of two methods: One-vs-Rest (OvR) or Multinomial (Softmax) regression (Hastie et al. 2009). For a problem with k classes, OvR involves training k binary classifiers, each one distinguishing one class from the rest. During prediction, the class with the highest probability score is selected. Contrary to OvR, the Multinomial method directly generalizes logistic regression to multiple classes. Instead of modeling the probability of a single binary outcome, it models the probability distribution over the k classes using the softmax function.

For newer versions of sklearn, the Multinomial method is the default setting. Thus, for implementation, we simply need to replace the features and target data for the multi-class scenarios (e.g., X_train_3cat). Compared to OvR, the Multinomial method can handle overlapping classes (classes with similar relationships with features and thus difficult to classify) better but is computationally intensive for a large number of classes.

The algorithms of Decision Trees and SVM naturally handle multi-class classification without needing modifications (replace the X and y with the 3cat version). Here, we provide the outputs for training and testing under the scenarios of a target variable with three classes (low-, medium-, and high-risk levels). The example code associated with the outputs can be viewed in the chapter Notebook file. →C13NB 13.6a

```
Class 2 Beta Coefficient(3cat) of Loan Amount under multinomial 0.16649044346990055
Best Hyperparameters for Logistic Regression (3cat): {'C': 0.1, 'l1_ratio': 0, 'penalty': 'l1'}
Logistic Regression (3cat) Confusion Matrix Report on Test:
              precision    recall  f1-score   support

           0       0.58      0.81      0.68      1092
           1       0.48      0.23      0.31       727
           2       0.45      0.28      0.34       159

    accuracy                           0.56      1978
   macro avg       0.50      0.44      0.44      1978
weighted avg       0.53      0.56      0.52      1978
```

Figure 13.7a Jupyter Notebook screenshot of results for training and testing of multi-class classification using logistic regression on the chapter data

```
Best Hyperparameters for Decision Tree Classifier(3cat):
{'criterion': 'entropy', 'max_depth': None, 'min_samples_leaf': 10, 'min_samples_split': 10}
Decision Tree(3cat) Confusion Matrix Report on Test:
              precision    recall  f1-score   support

           0       0.68      0.72      0.70      1092
           1       0.56      0.56      0.56       727
           2       0.57      0.33      0.42       159

    accuracy                           0.63      1978
   macro avg       0.60      0.54      0.56      1978
weighted avg       0.63      0.63      0.63      1978
```

Figure 13.7b Jupyter Notebook Screenshot of results for training and testing of multi-class classification using Decision Tree on the chapter data

```
Best Hyperparameters for SVM (3cat): {'C': 10, 'gamma': 'auto'}
SVM (3cat) Confusion Matrix Report on Test:
              precision    recall  f1-score   support

           0       0.65      0.70      0.67      1092
           1       0.55      0.53      0.54       727
           2       0.36      0.23      0.28       159

    accuracy                           0.60      1978
   macro avg       0.52      0.49      0.50      1978
weighted avg       0.59      0.60      0.59      1978
```

Figure 13.7c Jupyter Notebook screenshot of results for training and testing of multi-class classification using SVM on the chapter data

Explanation: The output for fitting a logistic regression classifer is presented in Figure 13.7a. One advantage of using a logistic regression classifier is its capacity to generate estimates of the beta coefficients, which indicate the influence of each feature on the log-odds of being in a particular class. When multi_class='multinomial' is set for the LogisticRegression instance (the default setting), the coef_ array contains one set of coefficients for each class, and these coefficients explain how the features influence the log-odds of being in that class compared to all other classes combined. For example, the estimated beta coefficient for Loan Amount (enclosed by red rectangle) for class 2 suggests that a 1 standard deviation increase in loan amount is associated with a 0.16 increase in the log-odds of being classified as a high-risk loan compared to the other loan classes.

The second output screenshot (Figure 13.7b) presents the results of the Decision Tree model. The GridSearch algorithm identified the best parameter set as {'criterion': 'entropy,' 'max_depth': 20, 'min_samples_leaf': 10, 'min_samples_split': 10}. This configuration uses entropy to measure information gain, allowing for more effective splits based on impurity reduction. A max depth of 20 allows the tree to capture sufficient complexity, while the min samples leaf and min samples split parameters (both set to 10) ensure that splits occur only when there are enough samples, helping to avoid overfitting by maintaining broader, more general splits. This balance between complexity and generalization makes the model more robust and effective for the classification task.

The third output screenshot (Figure 13.7c) shows the results of the SVM classifier. The GridSearch algorithm identified the best parameters as {'C': 10, 'gamma': 'auto'}. The C parameter controls the regularization strength, with higher values like 10 allowing the model to focus more on correctly classifying the training data by reducing the penalty for misclassified points, which can lead to a more complex model. However, this increases the risk of overfitting if the model becomes too focused on the training data. The gamma='auto' setting means that the kernel coefficient is set based on the number of features, allowing the model to adjust the influence of each data point accordingly and creating a broader decision boundary. This parameter set balances flexibility (through a high C value) while controlling the influence of individual data points (through gamma='auto').

In terms of test performance, the logistic regression classifier under-performs compared to the nonparametric classifiers in both overall classification and in classifying risky loans. The low recall rates for both class 1 (medium risk) and class 2 (high risk) loans, as seen in the confusion matrix for the logistic regression model, highlight the practical limitations of this approach. Notably, the recall rates for classifying high-risk loans are low across all models, which is likely caused by the class imbalance in the target variable. As with binary classification, the marginal outperformance of the decision tree over the SVM may be attributed to sample variation and the specifics of our GridSearch settings.

13.7 Ensemble Methods

Ensemble methods combine multiple machine learning models to improve overall performance (Hastie et al. 2009). By leveraging the strengths of individual models and mitigating their weaknesses, ensemble methods can achieve better generalization and robustness. The three main ensemble techniques are Bagging, Boosting, and Random Forest Classification (RFC).

13.7.1 Bagging

Bagging (Bootstrap Aggregating) is an ensemble technique that involves training multiple base models (e.g., decision trees) on different subsets of the training data and averaging their predictions (Breiman 1996). The subsets are created by sampling the training data with replacement. Bagging helps reduce variance and overfitting, especially for high-variance models like decision trees.

Procedure

  a) Create multiple subsets of the training data by sampling with replacement.
  b) Train a base model on each subset.
  c) Combine the predictions of the base models by averaging (for regression) or voting (for classification).

The implementation of the above steps for the Bagging technique is made easy by the BaggingClassifier from the sklearn package: →C13NB 13.7.1a

```
Bagging Confusion Matrix Report on Test:
              precision    recall  f1-score   support

           0       0.72      0.79      0.76      1092
           1       0.63      0.62      0.62       727
           2       0.75      0.25      0.38       159

    accuracy                           0.69      1978
   macro avg       0.70      0.56      0.59      1978
weighted avg       0.69      0.69      0.68      1978
```

Figure 13.8 Jupyter Notebook screenshot of results for training and testing of multi-class classification using Bagging Classifier on the chapter data

The output is presented in Figure 13.8. In this code example, a DecisionTreeClassifier instance using the best parameter settings found previously is provided as the estimator for the BaggingClassifier instance. Compared to our previous result from the standalone Decision Tree Classifier for multiclass classification, the current result shows an improvement in overall accuracy but underperforms in the accuracy and recall for the minority class. This result is consistent with the function of bagging, which is useful for reducing overfitting, but may not specifically address class imbalance issues.

13.7.2 Boosting

Boosting is an ensemble technique that builds models sequentially, each one correcting the errors of its predecessor (Freund and Schapire 1997). Boosting methods aim to reduce bias and variance, creating a strong model by combining the strengths of many weak models.

Types of Boosting

- AdaBoost: Adjusts the weights of incorrectly classified instances, focusing on harder cases in each iteration.

- Gradient Boosting: Builds models sequentially by optimizing a loss function, adding models that correct the residual errors of the previous models.

Procedure

a) Create multiple subsets of the training data by sampling with replacement.
b) Train a decision tree on each subset, but at each split, consider only a random subset of features.
c) Combine the predictions of the trees by averaging (for regression) or voting (for classification).

The implementation of the above steps for the Boosting technique is handled by GradientBoostingClassifier from sklearn.ensemble module. → C13NB 13.7.2a

```
   Random Forest Classifier(3cat) Confusion Matrix Report on Test:
              precision    recall  f1-score   support

          0       0.68      0.83      0.75      1092
          1       0.65      0.54      0.59       727
          2       0.73      0.14      0.23       159

   accuracy                           0.67      1978
  macro avg       0.69      0.50      0.52      1978
weighted avg       0.67      0.67      0.65      1978
```

Figure 13.9 Jupyter Notebook screenshot of code and results for training and testing of multi-class classification using decision trees under Gradient Boosting

Explanation: Figure 13.9 provides the confusion matrix report after running the source code. The GradientBoostingClassifier uses decision trees as its individual models. The parameter n_estimators specifies the number of boosting stages, or the number of weak learners (decision trees), to be added sequentially. The learning_rate controls the contribution of each tree to the final model. A lower learning rate makes the model more robust to overfitting, but it requires more trees (higher n_estimators) to achieve the same level of performance. While Gradient Boosting demonstrates stronger performance than Bagging across all measures, it still scores low on recall for the minority class.

13.7.3 Random Forest Classification

RFC is an ensemble learning method that constructs multiple decision trees during training and outputs the mode of the classes (for classification) or mean prediction (for regression) of the individual trees. It introduces randomness by selecting subsets of features and data samples, ensuring that the trees are decorrelated and the ensemble model is robust.

Random Forest extends Bagging by introducing additional randomness in the model training process, specifically in the selection of features for each split. This decorrelation between trees results in a more robust and generalizable model.

The following code cell demonstrates the deployment of RFC for the financial risk assessment data. RFC is computationally efficient. →C13NB 13.7.3a

```
Random Forest Classifier(3cat) Confusion Matrix Report on Test:
              precision    recall  f1-score   support

           0       0.68      0.83      0.75      1092
           1       0.65      0.54      0.59       727
           2       0.73      0.14      0.23       159

    accuracy                           0.67      1978
   macro avg       0.69      0.50      0.52      1978
weighted avg       0.67      0.67      0.65      1978
```

Figure 13.10 Jupyter Notebook screenshot of code and results for training and testing of multi-class classification using Random Forest Classification (RFC)

Explanation: The RandomForestClassifier instance shares a similar configuration interface with other scikit-learn ensemble classifier objects. The n_estimators parameter specifies the number of trees in the forest. Increasing the number of trees generally improves performance up to a certain point but also increases computational cost. Having too many estimators can lead to an overly complex model, which may reduce out-of-sample prediction performance. The confusion matrix results presented in Figure 13.10 suggest that the RFC underperforms other ensemble classifiers in both overall performance and minority class measures. This is expected, as Random Forest builds trees based on random samples, and if the minority class is underrepresented, the model may not give sufficient focus to that class. As a result, RFCs may not be ideal for accurately classifying minority classes.

13.8 Class Imbalance: Issues and Solutions

Class imbalance occurs when the number of instances in one class significantly outnumbers the instances in other classes. This is a common issue in many real-world data sets, particularly in fields like fraud detection, medical diagnosis, and risk assessment, where the minority class (e.g., correctly identifying risky loans, fraudulent transactions, and rare diseases) is often of greater interest.

13.8.1 Issues With Class Imbalance

Bias Toward Majority Class

Models trained on imbalanced data sets tend to be biased toward the majority class, resulting in poor performance on the minority class. This can lead to high accuracy but low recall and precision for the minority class, making the model unreliable for predicting minority class instances (Kotsiantis et al. 2006).

Poor Generalization

The model may not generalize well to new, unseen data, especially for the minority class, due to insufficient learning from minority class instances.

Misleading Performance Metrics

Accuracy is not a reliable metric in the presence of class imbalance. A model can achieve high accuracy by simply predicting the majority class most of the time. Metrics like precision, recall, and F1-score provide a more comprehensive evaluation of model performance in imbalanced settings (Davis and Goadrich 2006).

13.8.2 Addressing Class Imbalance

Reassigning Class Weight

Many machine learning algorithms, such as Logistic Regression, Random Forest, SVM, and others, offer the option to assign higher importance (or weight) to the minority class and lower importance to the majority class. This encourages the classifier to pay more attention to the minority class during training by penalizing misclassifications of the minority class more heavily than the majority class. The classifier then strives to optimize not just overall accuracy, but also performance on the minority class.

Automatic and Manual Class Weighting

Automatic class weighting (via 'balanced' option): Classifiers in scikit-learn, like LogisticRegression, SVC, and RandomForestClassifier, offer a class_weight='balanced' option. Under this option, the algorithm automatically adjusts the class weights inversely proportional to the class frequencies in the training data. This means the minority class will be assigned a higher weight, and the majority class will be assigned a lower weight based on their relative proportions.

Manual class weighting: We can specify class weights manually by passing a dictionary of class weights. This allows us to have more control over the importance we place on each class. For example: class_weights = {0: 1, 1:3} give class 1 (minority class) three times the weight of class 0

Limitation

While reassigning class weights can be a useful method for addressing class imbalance, it may not always work as expected in certain situations. For example, when the imbalance is severe, the data is noisy, or the classes overlap significantly, class weighting may not sufficiently improve performance to adequately handle the minority class. Research indicates that in cases of extreme imbalance, oversampling techniques like SMOTE (which will be introduced next) or undersampling may be more effective when combined with class weighting (Chawla et al. 2002; Japkowicz 2000). Additionally, noisy or highly overlapping data can lead to overfitting when class weighting is applied, as the model may overly focus on incorrectly labeled or ambiguous samples (He and Ma 2013). Similarly, for data sets with complex nonlinear relationships, using more advanced models like Gradient Boosting or Random Forests may provide better results (Chen and Guestrin 2016).

The following code cell demonstrates the implementation and results of class weight reassignment using the chapter data. The best version of the Decision Tree classifier, identified in a previous code example, is employed for this demonstration. For the binary classification model, a manual class weighting is applied, where the minority class is overweighted by three times. For the multi-class classification model, the balanced auto-weighting option is used. →C13NB 13.8.2a

```
Decision Tree Classifier Matrix (2cat, with manual weight) Report on Test:
               precision    recall  f1-score   support

           0       0.78      0.60      0.68      1106
           1       0.54      0.74      0.63       715

    accuracy                           0.65      1821
   macro avg       0.66      0.67      0.65      1821
weighted avg       0.69      0.65      0.66      1821

Decision Tree Classifier Confusion Matrix (3cat, with balanced weight) Report on Test:
               precision    recall  f1-score   support

           0       0.69      0.54      0.60      1092
           1       0.54      0.57      0.56       727
           2       0.28      0.64      0.39       159

    accuracy                           0.56      1978
   macro avg       0.50      0.58      0.52      1978
weighted avg       0.60      0.56      0.57      1978
```

Figure 13.11 Jupyter Notebook screenshot of result for addressing class imbalance by class weight reassignment

Compared to the previous results, the current set of outputs presented in Figure 13.11 show significant performance gains in terms of recall for the minority classes in both the binary and multi-class scenarios. However, these gains come at the cost of reducing scores for other metrics (He and Ma 2013). This outcome is consistent with the fact that recall is sensitive to class imbalance, and using class weight reassignment can shift the model's predictive power toward improving recall at the expense of other performance measures.

Resampling Techniques

Compared to class weight reassignment techniques, which adjust how the algorithm treats the classes (and are applicable only to certain classifiers), resampling techniques modify the data set itself by adding or removing data points to balance class distributions. This approach can be applied to a wide range of classifiers.

Resampling methods aim to balance the data set by either oversampling the minority class or undersampling the majority class:

- Oversampling: Increases the number of observations in the minority class by duplicating existing instances or generating synthetic ones.
- Undersampling: Reduces the number of observations in the majority class by randomly removing instances.

Both techniques can be implemented using the Python library imblearn (short for imbalanced-learn), which is specifically designed to address class imbalance issues. It is important to note that undersampling is generally not preferred in most applications, as it reduces the amount of information in the data set.

In the following code cell, the minority classes in both binary and multi-class scenarios are resampled (with replacement) to synthetically balance all classes. →C13NB 13.8.2b

We now use a synthetically balanced data set to train the same version of Decision Tree classifiers in the previous example (without the class_ weight setting), the complete code is provided in the chapter Jupyter Notebook file and the out-of-sample test results of the trained models are presented in Figure 13.12. →C13NB 13.8.2c

```
Decision Tree Classifier Confusion Matrix (2cat, with synthetically balanced classes ) Report on Test:
              precision    recall  f1-score   support

           0       0.73      0.71      0.72      1106
           1       0.57      0.60      0.58       715

    accuracy                           0.67      1821
   macro avg       0.65      0.65      0.65      1821
weighted avg       0.67      0.67      0.67      1821

Decision Tree Classifier Confusion Matrix (3cat, with synthetically balanced weight) Report on Test:
              precision    recall  f1-score   support

           0       0.69      0.53      0.60      1092
           1       0.54      0.53      0.53       727
           2       0.25      0.66      0.36       159

    accuracy                           0.54      1978
   macro avg       0.49      0.57      0.50      1978
weighted avg       0.60      0.54      0.56      1978
```

Figure 13.12 Jupyter Notebook screenshot of test result using data with synthetically balanced classes

Compared to those following the class weight reassignment methods, the results presented in Figure 13.12 following resampling techniques show further performance gain in recall measures of the minor classes, but no absolute further decrease in performance of other measures.

13.9 Performance Optimization for ML Classifiers

When applying grid search to ensemble models like Random Forests, Gradient Boosting, or Bagging, the process can become computationally expensive due to the complexity and the number of parameters involved. For example, the RandomForestClassifier has 17 parameters in total, though not all are commonly tuned. Even if only the commonly adjusted parameters (i.e., n_estimators, max_depth, min_samples_split, min_samples_leaf, max_features, and bootstrap) are included in the grid search, each with only 3 possible values(usually require more in practical projects), in a typical fivefold cross-validation, the total number of models that would need to be trained is around 3,645, which can result in hours of computing time—not to mention the memory cost involved for a large data set.

In this section, we will discuss some techniques for improving efficiency in the optimization of ML classifiers.

Parallelism and Resource Utilization

One way to reduce the computational time when performing hyperparameter optimization with methods like Grid Search is to take advantage of parallelism. Scikit-learn supports parallelism, allowing models to be trained simultaneously on multiple CPU cores.

In scikit-learn, parallelism is easily implemented using the n_jobs parameter, which is available in functions like GridSearchCV, RandomizedSearchCV, and other scikit-learn functions that involve iterative processes like model training and evaluation. The n_jobs parameter controls how many CPU cores to use:

- n_jobs=-1: This setting tells scikit-learn to use all available CPU cores. This is the most common and effective setting for maximizing performance.

- n_jobs=<positive integer>: You can specify the exact number of CPU cores you want scikit-learn to use (e.g., n_jobs=4 will use four cores).

It is important to note that while parallelism speeds up computation, it also increases memory usage because multiple models are trained simultaneously. For large data sets or complex models, this can lead to high memory consumption.

13.9.1 Strategies to Mitigate Computational Costs

Early Stopping and Depth Control

After a certain point, the incremental gains in model performance from hyperparameter tuning may not justify the computational cost. It's crucial to balance the thoroughness of the search with practical resource constraints. Some ensemble methods, like Gradient Boosting, support **early stopping**, where the training process halts if the model's performance on a validation set stops improving. Other ensemble methods often provide parameters for controlling the depth of decision tree structures. These settings can save time by avoiding unnecessary iterations (Hastie et al. 2009).

For example, most tree-based ensemble methods, including **Random Forests**, **Bagging**, and **Gradient Boosting**, offer parameters to control the maximum depth of individual decision trees. Controlling tree depth ensures that the training process stops early when further iterations yield minimal performance gains.

Randomized Search

Instead of exhaustively searching through all possible combinations of hyperparameters, the algorithm samples a fixed number of hyperparameter settings from the specified distributions. This approach significantly reduces computation time while still allowing for the exploration of a wide range of parameters.

The randomized search algorithm can be easily implemented using sklearn's RandomizedSearchCV class. The following code block demonstrates the implementation of randomized search for optimizing the parameters of an RFC: →C13NB 13.9a

The remainder of the code, available in the chapter's Jupyter Notebook file, sets up an exhaustive search for parameter optimization on the same classifier. The outputs for computation time and confusion matrices under both grid search techniques are provided in Figure 13.13.

```
total number of combinatoin of parameter values: 1872
performing randomized search
Fitting 5 folds for each of 50 candidates, totalling 250 fits
performing non-randomized search
Fitting 5 folds for each of 1872 candidates, totalling 9360 fits
time cost comparsion non-randomized vs. randomized Search 269 vs. 10
Random Forest Confusion Matrix Report(Non-randomized Search) on Test:
              precision    recall  f1-score   support

           0       0.73      0.46      0.56      1092
           1       0.58      0.63      0.61       727
           2       0.24      0.77      0.37       159

    accuracy                           0.55      1978
   macro avg       0.52      0.62      0.51      1978
weighted avg       0.64      0.55      0.56      1978

Random Forest Confusion Matrix Report(Randomized Search) on Test:
              precision    recall  f1-score   support

           0       0.77      0.44      0.56      1092
           1       0.59      0.67      0.62       727
           2       0.24      0.79      0.37       159

    accuracy                           0.55      1978
   macro avg       0.53      0.63      0.52      1978
weighted avg       0.66      0.55      0.57      1978
```

Figure 13.13 Jupyter Notebook screenshot of result of code for comparing results under randomized and unrandomized search for classifier parameter optimization

The results show that the optimized model using the randomized approach achieves a similar performance to the one obtained through an exhaustive grid search across all measures on the test set. However, it significantly reduces the computational time and burden by approximately 97 percent.

13.10 Evaluating Classification Models With ROC Curve and AUC

Receiver Operating Characteristic Curve (ROC Curve)

The ROC curve is a graphical representation of a classification model's performance across different threshold values. It plots the TPR

(Recall) against the FPR. The ROC curve helps visualize the trade-off between sensitivity (TPR) and specificity (FPR) at various threshold settings.

Area Under the Curve (AUC)

AUC is the area under the ROC curve. It measures the ability of the model to distinguish between classes. Higher AUC values indicate better model performance.

AUC interpretation:

- **AUC = 1**: Perfect model
- **0.5 < AUC < 1**: Better than random guessing
- **AUC = 0.5**: No discriminative power, equivalent to random guessing
- **AUC < 0.5**: Worse than random guessing

Comparing Logistic Regression With Random Forest Using ROC Curve and AUC

The ROC Curve and the AUC measure allow us to compare the performance of two or more classifiers under different threshold values. Let's implement the ROC Curve and AUC evaluation for Logistic Regression and Random Forest on the two-class target data set.

The key is to use the classifier object's predict_proba method to calculate the predicted probabilities for each class. The predicted probability for logistic regression is simply the output of the trained log-likelihood function. For RFC, the predicted probability for each class is calculated by aggregating the predictions from each individual decision tree in the forest. The details of the calculation are usually handled by the program, and it is the interpretation of the results that requires our careful consideration. →C13NB 13.10a

Once we have the predicted probabilities, we can generate the ROC curve using matplotlib's plot method.

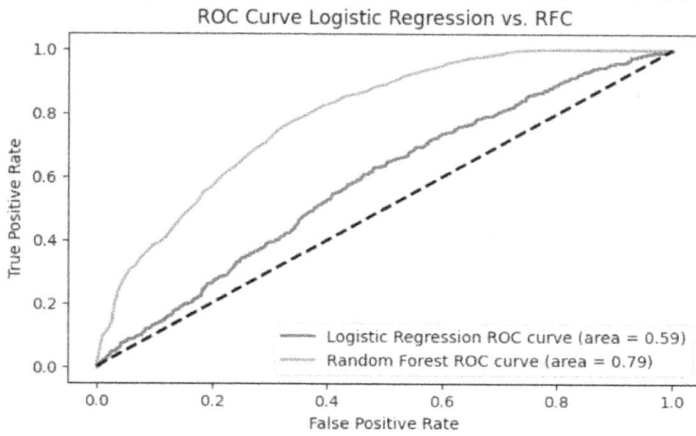

Figure 13.14 Jupyter Notebook screenshot of code output of ROC Curve for comparing logistic regression with Random Forest

Explanation: A screenshot of the plot is presented in Figure 13.14. The ROC curve plots the TPR against the FPR for various threshold settings. The black dashed line represents the line of no discrimination, where the TPR equals the FPR, indicating random guessing with an AUC of 0.5.

While both ROC corves are above the No discriminative line, the ROC curve for Random Forest (orange) hovers above the one for Logistic Regression (blue). The distance between the two curves is at its maximum around 0.3 FPR. This suggests that the **Random Forest model** consistently outperforms **Logistic Regression** in terms of distinguishing between true positives and false positives. The larger gap at a 0.3 FPR indicates that the Random Forest model achieves a significantly higher TPR (sensitivity) at this level of false positives, meaning it is better at correctly classifying positive instances (risky loans) while maintaining a low FPR. This superior performance implies that Random Forest is more capable of capturing complex patterns in the data, leading to better classification outcomes in comparison to the simpler, linear decision boundaries of Logistic Regression.

13.11 Feature Importance

Feature importance under the context of ML classifiers refers to the quantification of the impact or relevance of each feature in making predictions.

Estimating feature importance is crucial because it helps identify which features most strongly influence the outcome, allowing for a better understanding of the model's decisions and providing insights for feature selection and model refinement.

When interpreting feature importance for different types of classifiers, such as **binary classifiers** and **multiclass classifiers**, the approach and interpretation differ slightly based on the complexity of the classification task.

Feature Importance in Binary Classifiers

Feature importance under the context of machine learning classifiers refers to the quantification of the impact or relevance of each feature in making predictions. Estimating feature importance is crucial because it helps identify which features most strongly influence the outcome, allowing for a better understanding of the model's decisions and providing insights for feature selection and model refinement.

In simpler, linear models such as Logistic Regression, feature importance is straightforward to interpret. The beta coefficients (or weights) provide a direct measure of the impact of each feature. In logistic regression, the magnitude and sign of each beta coefficient indicate how much a one-unit change in a feature affects the log-odds of the outcome, while holding all other features constant. A large positive coefficient suggests that the feature increases the probability of the positive class, while a large negative coefficient indicates the opposite.

However, for nonlinear classifiers such as Decision Trees, SVM, and ensemble methods (like Random Forests and Gradient Boosting), the quantification of feature importance requires more advanced techniques because these models do not directly provide coefficients. Instead, we rely on more sophisticated approaches to extract feature importance from these models.

Permutation Feature Importance (PFI)

When interpreting feature importance for binary classifiers (where the model predicts one of two possible outcomes), a commonly used and generalizable method across nonlinear classifiers is PFI. This technique works by randomly shuffling the values of each feature and measuring how much the model's performance decreases. The more the performance drops, the more important the feature is.

PFI can be applied to nonlinear classifiers such as Decision Trees, Random Forests, and SVMs. It works as follows:

- The model is first trained on the original data, and its performance (e.g., accuracy, F1-score) is recorded.
- The values of a single feature are then randomly shuffled, breaking the association between the feature and the target variable.
- The model's performance is measured again on this shuffled data.
- If shuffling the feature leads to a significant drop in performance, it indicates that the feature is important for making accurate predictions.

This method is valuable because it is model-agnostic, meaning it can be applied to any classifiers—whether linear or nonlinear. The following code example demonstrates the calculation of permutation importance using the same RFC as in the previous example and then identifies the top three features with the highest PFI scores. →C13NB 13.11aThe results suggest that Credit Score is the most important feature for identifying risky loans, followed by the Number of Dependents and the Asset Value associated with the loan applicants.

Feature Importance in Multiclass Classifiers

In multiclass classifiers, where the model predicts one of more than two classes, estimating feature importance becomes more complex. Unlike binary classifiers, where a feature's importance can be linked to its ability to distinguish between two classes, multiclass classifiers must separate multiple classes, often requiring more nuanced interpretations.

The **PFI scores** can also be applied to multiclass classifiers. Unlike in binary classification, where a feature's importance is based on its ability to separate two classes, in multiclass classification, the importance reflects how well the feature helps classify instances into three or more categories. As a result, the importance of each feature is typically averaged or aggregated across all classes.

Tree-Based Feature Importance

In tree-based models like Random Forests and Gradient Boosting, the same method—mean decrease in impurity—is used to compute feature importance for both binary and multiclass classification tasks. However, in the multiclass case, the importance values are calculated by evaluating how well each feature helps to separate instances across all classes. The values are standardized, meaning that each reading reflects the percentage contribution to the total importance in determining the model's predictions. These values can be accessed (after fitting) by retrieving the feature_importances_ attribute of the classifier.

The following code cell uses the same classifier as in the previous example, but this time it is applied to the multiclass data set. It first computes the PFI scores for all features used by the classifier and then extracts the tree-based feature importance values from the trained classifier instance. In both steps, the code prints out the top three important features based on their importance scores. →C13NB 13.11b

Notice that the top three features highlighted by the two feature importance measures are not the same. This is expected, as they have completely different interpretations. For **Permutation Importance**, it reflects the decrease in overall model performance (in percentage) when the associated feature is shuffled. In contrast, for the **tree-based Feature Importance** measure, it reflects the proportion of total importance that each feature accounts for. The results suggest that Credit Score is likely the most important feature, followed by the applicant's Asset Value. Together, these two features account for approximately 36 percent of the total feature importance.

Conclusion

In this chapter, we explored the principles and applications of classification machine learning models in finance. Classification models, unlike regression models, predict discrete outcomes and are used in various financial applications such as credit risk assessment, fraud detection, customer segmentation, and market movement prediction.

Proper data preparation, including handling categorical and continuous variables through encoding and standardization, is crucial for effective model performance. We delved into key classification models like Logistic Regression, Decision Trees, and SVM, highlighting their advantages and limitations. Logistic Regression offers interpretability but assumes linear relationships, while Decision Trees handle nonlinear relationships and SVMs are effective for high-dimensional data. Evaluating classification models using metrics like precision, recall, F1 score, and ROC-AUC ensures robust performance assessment. Ensemble methods, such as Bagging, Boosting, and RFC, enhance model performance by reducing variance and bias, and addressing class imbalance. Techniques like resampling and careful hyperparameter tuning using Grid Search help in optimizing model performance while balancing computational cost. Lastly, feature importance analysis, particularly through permutation importance and tree-based methods, was highlighted as a valuable tool for interpreting model decisions and refining feature selection.

This chapter provides a comprehensive understanding of classification models and their practical applications in finance, laying the groundwork for effective machine learning model development and evaluation. For more advanced learning, consider exploring topics like neural networks and deep learning for classification, as well as gradient boosting machines (GBMs) and XGBoost (Brownlee, 2019).

Exercise

1. Exploratory data analysis:
   - Use sns.countplot or other plotting tools to create a plot that shows the relationship between the three classes of risk rating and Loan Amount.
   - Question: Is there a pattern between the two variables? In other words, do high-risk applicants tend to ask for more or less loan amounts?

2. Re-engineer target variables:
   - Re-engineer the two-class and three-class target variables by using high risk as the base class (0) and low-risk classes as the positive class (1 or 2). Do not change the coding for the medium-risk class.
   - Task: Modify the data set to reflect this new target variable coding.
3. Train ML models on re-engineered two-class data:
   - Using the newly created two-class target data from question 2, train the following ML models: Logistic Regression, Decision Tree, and SVM.
   - Task: Evaluate and report the performance of each model.
4. Train ML models on re-engineered three-class data:
   - Using the newly created three-class target data from question 2, train the following ML models: Logistic Regression, Decision Tree, and SVM.
   - Task: Evaluate and report the performance of each model.
5. Impact of reversed coding on class imbalance:
   - Discuss whether reversing the coding of categories for the target variable, making the minority group the negative (0) class, helps address class imbalance issues among the ML models.
   - Question: Does this approach improve model performance in terms of handling class imbalance?
6. Retrain ML models:
   - Based on your discussion in question 5, retrain the Logistic Regression, Decision Tree, and SVM models on the re-engineered two-class target data.
   - Task: Evaluate and report the performance of each model, and compare it with the previous results to see if there is any improvement.
7. Optimization of a Gradient Boosting model:
   - Hyperparameter ranges:
     n_estimators: [50, 100, 200, 500]
     learning_rate: [0.01, 0.05, 0.1, 0.2]
     max_depth: [3, 5, 7, 9]

min_samples_split: [2, 5, 7, 10]

min_samples_leaf: [1, 2, 4]

subsample: [0.6, 0.8, 1.0]

- Task: Perform the grid search and randomized search and report the best hyperparameters found using the resampled data generated in section **Class Imbalance: Issues and Solutions of this chapter**. Show the prediction results based on a test set. Discuss the importance of choosing a reasonable search space and the potential computational costs associated with each search technique.

8. Compare the best model found in question 7 with the two classifiers presented in section of ***Evaluating Classification Models With ROC Curve and AUC*** by adding the new model to the existing ROC curve plot. Discuss how the new model performs in distinguishing the positive class relative to the other classifiers.

CHAPTER 14

Unsupervised Learning in Finance

Introduction

Unsupervised learning is a type of machine learning where the algorithm is given data without explicit instructions on what to do with it. Unlike supervised learning, there are no labeled outputs to guide the learning process. Instead, the model identifies patterns and relationships within the data on its own.

14.1 Financial Applications of Unsupervised Learning

Unsupervised learning techniques have a wide range of applications in finance, helping to uncover hidden patterns and insights from complex data sets. Here, we explore some key applications.

Market Segmentation

One of the primary applications of unsupervised learning in finance is market segmentation. Financial institutions can use clustering techniques to segment their customer base into distinct groups based on various features such as transaction history, risk tolerance, or investment behavior. This segmentation helps in tailoring products and services to different market segments, improving customer satisfaction, and targeting marketing efforts more effectively. For example, high-net-worth individuals might receive personalized wealth management services, while younger, tech-savvy customers might be offered digital banking solutions (Wang et al. 2020).

Portfolio Diversification

Dimensionality reduction techniques like principal component analysis (PCA) can be employed to analyze the underlying structure of financial markets and identify factors that drive asset returns. By understanding these factors, investors can construct diversified portfolios that minimize risk and maximize returns. For instance, PCA can help identify uncorrelated factors in a large set of stocks, enabling the construction of a portfolio that is less sensitive to market fluctuations.

Anomaly Detection.   Unsupervised learning methods are particularly effective for anomaly detection in financial data. Techniques such as density-based spatial clustering of applications with noise can identify outliers that deviate significantly from normal patterns. This is crucial for detecting fraudulent transactions or unusual market movements. For example, a sudden spike in transaction volume or an unexpected price movement in a stock can be flagged for further investigation, helping to safeguard against fraud and mitigate risks.

Risk Management.   Financial institutions can use clustering techniques to identify different risk profiles within their loan portfolios. By grouping borrowers with similar risk characteristics, banks can better understand the risk distribution and take proactive measures to manage potential defaults. This can involve adjusting interest rates, setting aside capital reserves, or implementing more stringent monitoring for high-risk segments (Bessis 2015).

Customer Retention

Customer churn is a significant concern for financial institutions. By applying clustering techniques to customer transaction data, banks can identify patterns that indicate potential churn. For instance, a decrease in transaction frequency or a shift in spending patterns might signal that a customer is considering leaving. By identifying these patterns early, banks can take targeted actions to retain valuable customers, such as offering personalized incentives or reaching out with tailored communication (Fader et al. 2010).

Trend Analysis

Unsupervised learning can be used to identify trends in financial markets. By analyzing large data sets of historical price movements, trading volumes, and other market indicators, unsupervised algorithms can uncover patterns that may not be immediately apparent. These patterns can provide valuable insights for traders and investors, helping them make informed decisions based on emerging trends (Powell et al. 2008).

Sentiment Analysis

In the age of social media and online news, sentiment analysis has become an important tool for financial decision making. Unsupervised learning techniques can be used to analyze large volumes of text data, such as news articles, social media posts, and financial reports, to gauge market sentiment. This information can help investors understand how public perception might influence market movements and make more informed trading decisions.

14.2 Clustering Techniques

Clustering techniques are a cornerstone of unsupervised learning, used to group similar data points into clusters based on their features. These methods are particularly useful in finance for finding co-movement in stock returns (Aghabozorgi and Teh 2014). In this section, we will use the price and volume data of stocks from different industries. We will see if the clustering techniques can identify the natural grouping—the industry segment—and uncover any additional patterns or insights.

14.2.1 K-Means Clustering

k-Means clustering is a popular unsupervised learning algorithm used to partition a data set into k distinct, nonoverlapping clusters. The main objective of k-Means is to group similar data points together while ensuring that dissimilar data points fall into different clusters (MacQueen 1967). The algorithm works iteratively to assign each data point to one of the k clusters based on feature similarity. The central idea is to minimize the variance within each cluster while maximizing the variance between clusters.

This unsupervised ML technique is particularly useful for market segmentation and anomaly detection problems. The algorithm requires calculating the distance between each data point to the group means, and thus it is sensitive to outliers. It also does not perform well when the shape of the clusters is not spherical and the sizes of the clusters differ significantly.

Principle of K-Means

To explain the algorithm behind k-means without going into the mathematical details. We will demonstrate in a case of two-feature clustering. Imagine you have a scatterplot with points representing different stocks. Each point has two coordinates: YoY EBITDA Growth for 2021 (x-axis) and YoY EBITDA Growth for 2022 (y-axis). Your goal is to group these points into clusters so that stocks with similar growth patterns are grouped together. Here are the steps to follow:

a) Initialization:
   You start by randomly placing k points on the scatterplot. These points are called centroids and will serve as the center of the clusters. Let's say you choose $k=3$, so you place three centroids.

b) Assignment:
   For each point on the scatterplot, you look at the distance to each of the centroids. The point is then assigned to the cluster of the nearest centroid. So, if a stock is closest to centroid 1, it becomes part of cluster 1.

c) Update:
   Once all points are assigned to clusters, you update the position of each centroid. This is done by calculating the average position (mean) of all points in each cluster and moving the centroid to this new position.

d) Iteration:

Steps b and c are repeated. Points are reassigned to the nearest centroid, and centroids are moved to the average position of their assigned points. This process continues until the centroids no longer move significantly, indicating that the clusters have stabilized.

e) Convergence:

The algorithm stops when the centroids have stabilized and do not change much with further iterations. At this point, you have your final clusters, with each stock assigned to the cluster whose centroid it is closest to.

Loading Data

Now, let's apply this algorithm for grouping stocks exhibiting clustering in price and vol changes. We will use the daily stock price and volume data from the Chinese stock market. The original data set is available on the book's website. The following code cell loads the data from the file and presents its original structure. →C14NB 14.2.1a

Explanation: The original data set has nine columns, namely 'date,' 'pct_ chg,' 'vol,' 'open,' 'high,' 'low,' 'close,' 'code,' and 'sector.' There are 22,505 rows, with each row as one observation on a particular trade date for a stock code. After further examination of the unique values from the 'code' and 'sector' columns, we can see that there are 93 stock codes from three business sectors. There is also a 'nan' entry in the output, which indicates that the data may require careful cleaning.

Data Cleaning and Preprocessing for K-Means Clustering

The original format of the data is structured but not ready for our ML models. First, we need to separate the features and the objects for clustering analysis. In this data set, the objects are the stocks represented by their exchange symbols (e.g., 000166.SZ). The features are changes in volume and closing prices. Our goal is to find clusters within these stocks that exhibit co-movement over our study period. Therefore, we need to restructure the data so that each row represents one object and each column represents one feature.

Our first task is to determine how to prepare the features. The original data is in daily frequency with unstandardized scales (price and volume) and some missing values. This data is not friendly for our machine learning models, which require scaled data with no missing entries. There are many ways to address the problems in the original data; here, we opt for resetting the frequency of the data to weekly to eliminate the missing entries. This approach also allows us to convert our feature data into weekly percentage values, which are well-scaled and standardized.

The details of the operations applied to the original data are available in the chapter notebook file. Here is the end result after the operations: →C14NB 14.2.1b

Now, we have 102 rows, with each row representing one stock. For each stock, we have two sets of features. The first set is the percentage changes in closing prices over all weeks within the study period, and the second set is the weekly percentage change in volumes. We are interested in knowing whether there are clusters within those stocks based on the distribution of these feature data.

One possible clustering among these stocks is their affiliation to their business sectors. As shown at the beginning, we have this information in the original data set but is not carried to the training set. We intend to use the business sector as a reference to evaluate our training results.

The following code cell screenshot demonstrates the implementation of k-mean clustering (k=3) in Python. →C14NB 14.2.1c
Explanation: k-Means clustering is handled by sklearn's KMeans class. When creating an instance, we need to specify the number of clusters for the algorithm. The random_state parameter specifies the random seed for the initial search. The fit_predict method requires a prepared data set with feature data formatted in a way as we have demonstrated. The method returns an array of cluster labels with positions corresponding to the rows of the input DataFrame (pro_data), and thus we can just place the clusters back into pro_data(line 6 in the source code). The code cell generates a scatter plot of points (see Figure 14,1) using the feature data from the first week only. The complete code for generating the plot can be viewed in the chapter Jupyter Notebook file.

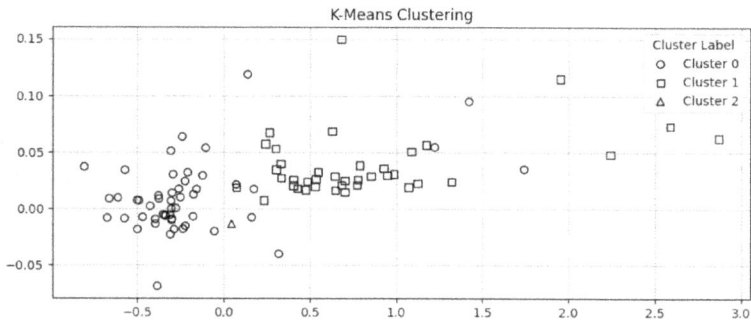

Figure 14.1 Jupyter Notebook screenshot of scatter plot of points using the feature data(pct changes in stock price and volume) from the first week.

Explanation: It is important to note that for a 2D scatter plot, it can only show the distribution of the first week's feature data points for the stocks. The points' color codes represent the clusters rendered by the algorithm, which does not know the financial context behind the clusters, and thus they are labeled as 0, 1, and 2. If we cross-reference with the information on business sectors for the stocks, we can see that cluster 0 appears to be the Semiconductor industry, 1 to be the Securities industry, and 2 to be the Airport industry. The k-Means algorithm is able to uncover 93.41 percent of the business sectors based on the features data (calculation provided in the chapter notebook).

Evaluation of Clustering Quality. In many practical projects, we don't know how many clusters are there. We need to explore the data and find the best value of k as in k-Mean clustering that best describes the similarity among the objects. Here are the commonly used metrics and methods for evaluating the clustering results:

Elbow Method

The Elbow Method helps to determine the optimal number of clusters (k) in a data set. It does this by plotting the sum of squared distances from each point to its assigned cluster center (inertia) against the number of clusters. Notice that this sum of distances from the center should decrease as the number of clusters increases. The optimal k is usually at the "elbow" point where the inertia starts to decrease at a slower rate (in a linear pattern).

The following code cell calculates the inertia in our weekly stock feature data for values of k ranging from 1 to 10 and then generates a scatter plot as shown in Figure 14.2for the result. →C14NB 14.2.1d

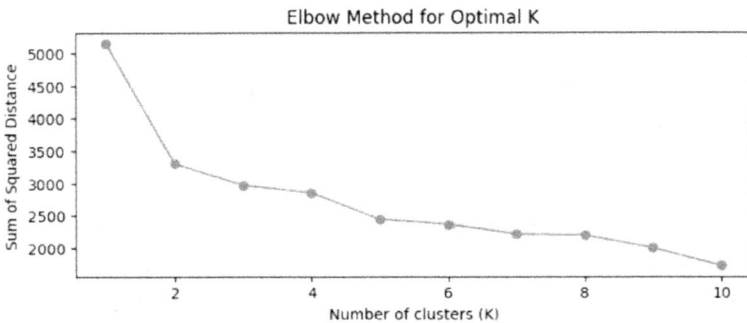

Figure 14.2 Jupyter Notebook screenshot of result of Elbow Method for Optimal k

Explanation: In this plot, the location of the "Elbow" where the sum of distance to inertias starts to drop in reducing speed is unclear. This problem is actually common when the Elbow Method is used in practice. It Elbow appears (subjectively) to be between 3 and 5 inclusively.

Silhouette Score.   The Silhouette Score measures how similar each data point is to its own cluster compared to other clusters. The score ranges from −1 to 1, where a higher value indicates better-defined clusters (Rousseeuw 1987). The mean of all data points' Silhouette Scores can be used as an indicator of the overall quality of the clusters. The metric is undefined for there is only one cluster. As a rule of thumb, an average score over 0.7 is considered high quality, 0.5 is reasonable, and 0.25 and below is considered low quality. However, this value must be interpreted together with the number of features (dimensions) employed by the clustering algorithm. The more features we provide to the algorithm, the more difficult it becomes to achieve a higher Silhouette Score, as it becomes harder for each data point to reduce dissimilarity with other clusters.

Davies–Bouldin Index (DBI).   The DBI evaluates the quality of clustering by comparing within-cluster distances to between-cluster distances (Davies and Bouldin 1979). Lower DBI values indicate better clustering performance. This metric complements the Silhouette Score, providing another perspective on clustering quality. As a rule of thumb, DBI < 1 is considered indicative of good clustering quality, 1 < DBI < 2 is acceptable, and DBI > 2 indicates poor clustering quality.

It is essential to compare the mean Silhouette Score and DBI values relative to different clustering solutions based on the same set of features of the same data set rather than relying on an absolute threshold. In other words, the evaluation of clustering quality should be used as an indicator for the appropriate number of clutters and a measure of the quality of the resulting clustering.

The following code cell shows the Silhouette Score and DBI values for different arrangements of k for our data set. →C14NB 14.2.1e

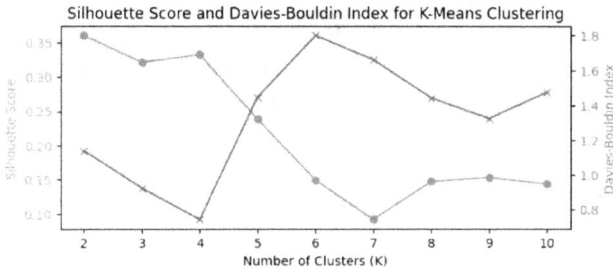

Figure 14.3 Silhouette score and Davies–Bouldin index for k-means clustering

Explanation: The output plot generated by the source code is presented in Figure 14.3. The blue line indicates the average Silhouette Score, and the red line represents the values of the DBI across different settings of k from 2 to 10. A higher Silhouette Score or a lower DBI suggests better clustering quality. Based on this plot, it appears that four clusters may be the best choice given the data, despite the fact that the stocks belong to three different business

14.2.2 Hierarchical Clustering

Hierarchical clustering is an unsupervised learning technique used to group similar data points into clusters based on their hierarchy (Murtagh and Legendre 2014). Unlike k-Means, which requires specifying the number of clusters upfront, hierarchical clustering creates a tree-like structure (dendrogram) that helps visualize the data's natural grouping. This method is particularly useful for exploratory data analysis, where the number of clusters is unknown or varies at different levels of hierarchy.

Principle of Hierarchical Clustering

Hierarchical clustering works by iteratively merging or splitting clusters based on their similarity. There are two main types of hierarchical clustering:

Agglomerative (Bottom-Up) Clustering

- Starts with each data point as a single cluster.
- Iteratively merges the closest pairs of clusters until all data points are in a single cluster.
- The process is visualized using a dendrogram, where the y-axis represents the distance or dissimilarity between clusters.

Divisive (Top-Down) Clustering

- Starts with all data points in a single cluster.
- Iteratively splits clusters into smaller clusters until each data point is a single cluster.
- This method is less common due to its computational complexity.

Problems Hierarchical Clustering Is Good for

- Discovering hierarchical relationships: When the data has an inherent hierarchical structure, such as taxonomies or organizational structures.

- Exploratory data analysis: To understand the natural grouping of data without predefining the number of clusters.
- Small- to medium-sized data sets: Works well with data sets where the number of data points is not excessively large due to its computational complexity.

Problems Hierarchical Clustering Is not Ideal for

- Large data sets: Hierarchical clustering can be computationally intensive and slow for large data sets.
- Flat clustering: When the data is best represented by a fixed number of clusters, methods like k-Means may be more efficient.

Although the process of creating Dendrogram can be tedious for a high-dimensional data set, sklearn has provided an easy interface for the implementation: →C14NB 14.2.2a

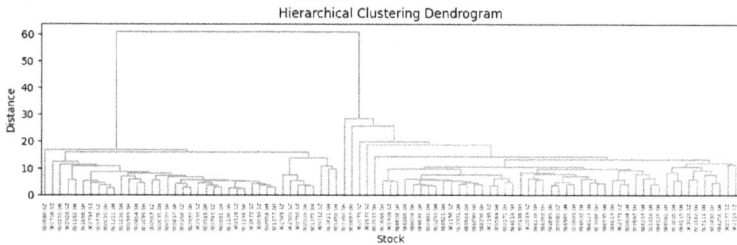

Figure 14.4 Jupyter Notebook screenshot of code and result for generating a dendrogram based on the chapter data

Explanation: In this section, we use the linkage method from scipy. The method performs agglomerative clustering following a specific iteration algorithm, which is specified by the parameter called "method." The 'ward' method minimizes the variance within clusters and is suitable for many financial applications, especially when clusters are expected to be of similar size. The WPGMA method (entered as "weighted") is another ideal choice for financial applications as it calculates the average distance between all pairs of points in two clusters. It forms clusters by linking the two clusters with the smallest average distance.

The linkage method returns a linkage matrix representing the hierarchical relationships between clusters as they are merged. It is an essential structure used to construct a dendrogram, which visually depicts the clustering process. The linkage matrix is then passed to the dendrogram method to create the Hierarchical Clustering Dendrogram.

A dendrogram is a tree-like diagram that records the sequences of merges or splits in hierarchical clustering. For our stock data set, the dendrogram in Figure 14.4 visually represents how stocks are grouped into clusters based on their percentage changes in price and volume over time. Stocks that are merged at low levels are likely to exhibit co-movement in percentage changes in price and volume. For example, "002926.SZ" and "601162.SH" are found to be in the same cluster at the bottom level. As we get into the details of these two stocks, we learn they are two securities companies with a similar range in the industry.

14.3 Dimensionality Reduction

Dimensionality reduction is a crucial preprocessing step in machine learning, especially when dealing with high-dimensional data sets (Bishop 2006). By reducing the number of features while preserving the essential information, dimensionality reduction techniques can improve model performance, reduce overfitting, and make the data more interpretable.

Data Preparation

We will use a new data set called "Nasdaq100 Ratios" to demonstrate the dimensionality reduction techniques. The following code cell operation loads the data from the file and performs a series of preliminary examinations.* →C14NB 14.3a

Explanation: The data set has 283 columns, including stock symbols, company names, sectors, subsectors, and various financial metrics such as asset turnover and year-over-year revenue growth for different years,

---

* The original copy of the data set: www.kaggle.com/datasets/ifuurh/nasdaq100-fundamental-data. Full credit for the original data set goes to the respective owner(s).

and 102 rows, with each row representing one stock. The majority of the columns are numerical metrics describing the financial aspects of the stocks, and there are two categorical variables with meaningful variation—namely, sector and subsector.

This data set has too many features compared to the sample size, making it incompatible with many models, especially parametric models whose validity is established by asymptotic principles. Dimensionality reduction techniques allow us to reduce this large collection of features into a smaller set while retaining the information contributed by each feature.

The outputs also suggest that there are missing values within the data set and that the original data contains variables with differential scales. Additionally, the categorical variables need to be encoded as a series of dummies to be used as inputs for our ML models. The following code cell implements these data preprocessing and cleaning operations. →C14NB 14.3b

Explanation: In line five, a combination of transpose and dropna methods is used to drop any columns (instead of rows) that have all missing values (dropna(how='all')). The result is then transposed back to its original orientation.

A SimpleImputer is then used to fill in missing values in the numerical columns. The strategy is set to *mean*, so missing values are replaced with the mean of each column. Other strategies, such as *median* and *most_frequent*, are also available. The fit_transform method is applied to perform the imputation and return the imputed data.

The data set contains various financial metrics that need to be standardized across all features. Therefore, we use the StandardScaler to standardize the numerical features by removing the mean and scaling to unit variance.

The OneHotEncoder is used to convert the 'sector' categorical variable into a one-hot encoded format. The resulting encoded data is then converted to a DataFrame with the original indices and the unique sector names as columns. Since there are seven unique classes within the sector variable, the original categorical variable is replaced by seven dummy variables in the final prepared data set.

After all the operations are completed, we combine all the features, including the numerical and dummy columns, into one DataFrame.

14.3.1 Principal Component Analysis (PCA)

PCA is a statistical technique used for dimensionality reduction while preserving as much variability as possible in the data set (Jolliffe 2002). It transforms the original features into a new set of uncorrelated features called principal components. These principal components are ordered by the amount of variance they capture from the data. The first principal component captures the most variance, the second principal component captures the second most variance, and so on. This way, PCA can significantly reduce the dimensionality of the data set while retaining most of the original information.

In finance, PCA is commonly used for:

- Risk management: Reducing the number of risk factors that need to be managed.
- Portfolio optimization: Simplifying the correlation matrix of asset returns to identify the primary sources of risk.
- Market analysis: Identifying common movements in stock prices and other financial instruments.
- Feature extraction: Enhancing the performance of machine learning models by reducing the number of input variables.

Before getting into the practical implementation, it is important to explain a few terms we will see in the outputs:

- Principal components: These are the new features created by PCA. Each principal component is a linear combination of the original features and captures a specific amount of variance in the data.
- Explained variance: This measures the amount of variance captured by each principal component. The explained variance ratio indicates the proportion of the data set's total variance that is captured by each principal component.

- Cumulative explained variance: This is the cumulative sum of explained variance ratios. It helps determine the number of principal components needed to retain a desired amount of variance.
- Eigenvalues and eigenvectors: In the context of PCA, eigenvalues represent the variance captured by each principal component, and eigenvectors represent the directions of these components in the original feature space.

The following code block performs PCA on the features from the Nasdaq100 Ratios data set.→C14NB 14.3.1a

When creating a PCA instance, we can specify the number of principal components (p) utilized in the algorithm. The default setting uses the maximum number of components allowed, which is determined by **min(number of samples, number of features)**. Therefore, for our project, the maximum p equals 101.

After fitting the data to the PCA instance, we can access the results through the instance's attributes and interfaces. It is important to check the quality of the PCA by looking into the explained variance associated with each principal component. Scikit-learn provides an easy method for visualizing this result.

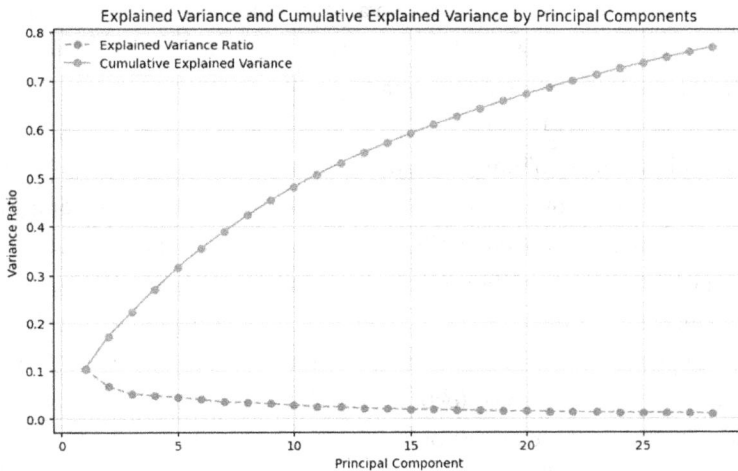

Figure 14.5 Jupyter Notebook screenshot of output displaying the Scree plot based on Nasdaq100 ratios data set

In this plot (also referred to as the Scree plot), the descending blue line represents the explained variance (the eigenvalues) associated with the principal components, ranked in descending order of explanatory power. The orange line represents the cumulative explained variance, calculated as the combined explained variance for all the principal components indicated on the x-axis. By design, the orange line should be concave downward, reflecting the decreasing explained variance for additional principal components.

The first principal component listed on the plot is the one that explains the most variance among the feature variables. It is shown to explain about 10 percent of the variance. This low percentage value indicates that the linear correlation between the feature variables is weak. The plot shows that we can reduce the number of features to 10 percent of the original number by using PCA, and the resulting new features will retain 77 percent of the variance of the original features. Whether this is an acceptable trade-off between dimensionality reduction and information loss depends on the business scenario behind the data set.

Feature Loadings

After fitting a PCA model, we obtain the feature loadings, which indicate the contribution of each original feature to the principal components. These loadings help us understand how the original variables relate to the new principal component axes. High absolute values of loadings suggest a strong relationship between the feature and the principal component. The following code cell generates the loading table containing all the original features. →C14NB 14.2.1b

Explanation: Each column displays the feature loadings for a principal component. Based on the numbers (check chapter notebook for complete data), principal component 1 (PC1) primarily captures the variance associated with financial stability and efficiency in asset utilization. Companies with efficient asset turnover, higher liquidity (cash ratio), and strong equity bases (equity to assets ratio) positively influence PC1. In contrast, companies with higher leverage (debt to assets) and focus on share buybacks tend to have a negative impact on this principal component. This interpretation suggests that PC1 distinguishes between financially stable and efficient companies versus those with higher debt levels and shareholder return strategies through buybacks. It highlights the importance of operational efficiency and financial health in driving the primary trend in the data set.

PCA-Based Clustering

High-dimensional data often contains redundant information and noise, which can obscure the true structure of the data. Clustering algorithms such as k-Means or Hierarchical Clustering can struggle with high-dimensional data sets due to the "curse of dimensionality." PCA addresses this issue by transforming the original features into a smaller set of orthogonal components that capture the most variance in the data. This transformation not only reduces computational complexity but also enhances the performance and interpretability of clustering algorithms.

For our Nasdaq100 metrics ratios data set, we start by applying PCA to reduce the number of dimensions. The data set originally had 283 columns, including various financial metrics and categorical variables encoded as dummies. After preprocessing and standardizing the data, we applied PCA to extract the principal components and reduced the number of features down to 28. We can use them as features for clustering. The following code cell put this idea into code: →C14NB 14.3.1c

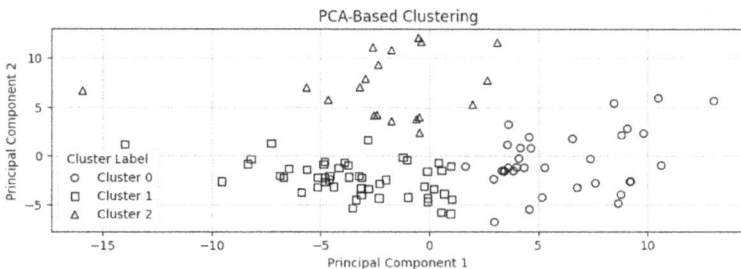

Figure 14.6 Jupyter Notebook screenshot of cluster scatter plot output after performing PCA-based clustering

Explanation: The scatter plot presented in Figure 14.6 using the first and second most significant principal components for the x–y coordinates reveals how stocks group together based on their financial metrics. This PCA-based clustering plot provides a visual representation of the similarities and differences among the stocks in a reduced dimensional space.

By visualizing the clusters in the reduced PCA space, we can gain insights into the underlying patterns and relationships within the data. For instance, stocks within the same cluster might share similar financial characteristics such as liquidity, leverage, and profitability ratios. These similarities could be indicative of similar operational efficiencies, financial health, or capital structure strategies.

Moreover, stocks that cluster together might belong to the same industry sector or be influenced by similar market factors. Identifying these clusters can help in understanding the broader financial landscape, sectoral trends, and can even assist in portfolio diversification by high-lighting stocks with different financial profiles.

Biplot

A biplot is a graphical representation that displays both the scores of the observations (readings of the new reduced features) and the feature loadings. It combines the projection of the data points (usually as points) and the projection of the feature loadings (usually as vectors) on the same plot. This dual representation helps in understanding the relationships between the observations and the original features and distinguishing extraordinary observations.

To make our presentation clearer, we reduced the number of original features to 6 and performed PCA with the number of components set to 2. This scenario allows a 2D plot to encompass all the information regarding the relationship between the original features, the principal components, and the observations in a biplot, as shown in Figure 14.7: →C14NB 14.3.1d

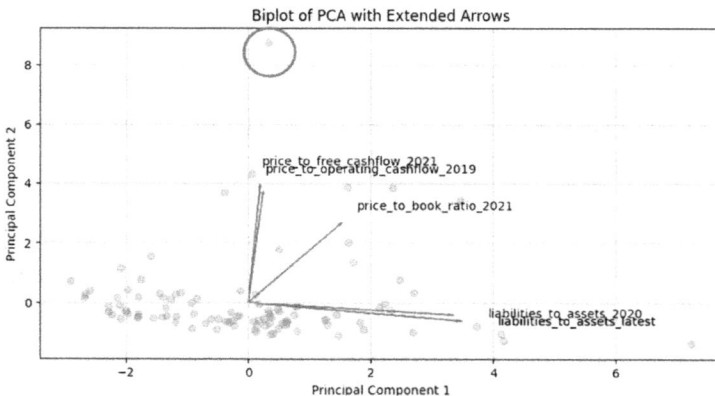

Figure 14.7 Jupyter Notebook screenshot of output that displays biplot

Explanation: The code for generating the plot is available in the chapter notebook. Here, we focus on the interpretation of the plot. The coordinates in the plot represent the scores for the stock observations. The red arrows indicate the loadings for each original feature, with the direction of the arrow showing the sign of the loading value.

For example, the price_to_book_ratio_2021 has positive loadings in both principal components. From this plot, we can see that a small portion of stocks have extreme scores on principal component 2 due to high readings in price-to-cashflow ratios.

14.3.2 t-SNE (t-Distributed Stochastic Neighbor Embedding)

t-SNE is a powerful machine learning algorithm for visualizing high-dimensional data (Maaten and Hinton, 2008). Unlike PCA, which performs a linear transformation of the data, t-SNE is a nonlinear technique that is particularly effective at preserving the local structure of the data in a lower-dimensional space. This makes t-SNE ideal for visualizing clusters or groups of similar observations in data sets with many variables.

Understanding t-SNE

The core idea behind t-SNE is to model each high-dimensional object by a two- or three-dimensional point in such a way that similar objects are modeled by nearby points and dissimilar objects are modeled by distant points. It accomplishes this by:

1. Converting the pairwise Euclidean distances between points in the high-dimensional space into conditional probabilities that represent similarities.
2. Defining similar probabilities for the low-dimensional map.
3. Minimizing the Kullback–Leibler divergence between these two distributions with respect to the locations of the points in the map.

The technical principles behind t-SNE are beyond the scope of this book. To explain the technique simply, t-SNE is particularly useful when we have observations with high-dimensional features (like our Nasdaq100

Ratios data set) and we want to examine the relationships between observations and features by reducing the dimensionality. We have learned to perform such a task using PCA, but PCA can only uncover linear relationships among the features and reduces dimensionality by maximizing the explained variance among the original features. t-SNE serves as an alternative to PCA when the relationships among the original features are nonlinear and when we want to focus on preserving the pairwise relationships rather than explaining the variance of the original features.

The implementation of t-SNE can be handled by scikit-learn. The following partial screenshot of the code cell uses an instance of the TSNE class to reduce the original features of the Nasdaq100 Ratios data set into two t-SNE components and then plot all the data points on a scatter plot using their component scores. The data point markers represent the subsectors (number coded) of the stocks. The complete code for generating the plot is available in the chapter notebook. →C14NB 14.3.2a

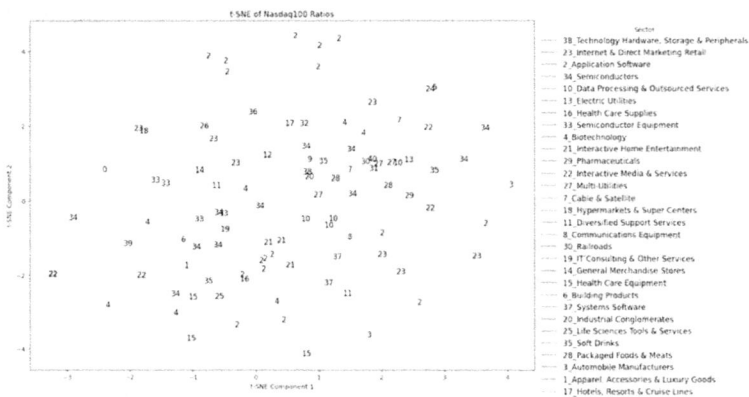

Figure 14.8 Jupyter Notebook screenshot of scatter plot using t-SNE component scores

Explanation: The t-SNE plot, presented in Figure 14.8, offers a different view of the stock clusters. Since the subsector information was not included in the training algorithm, we can use it as a reference to understand the clusters better. Unlike the PCA biplot, where points might be closer together, t-SNE plots often show more dispersed data points because t-SNE focuses on preserving local relationships and clustering patterns within the data.

Interpreting t-SNE components is more complex than PCA because t-SNE is a nonlinear technique that doesn't provide explicit component axes based on original features. Instead, the clusters in the t-SNE plot reflect the similarity of stocks in the original high-dimensional feature space.

By comparing with subsector information, we observe that the cluster at the top center of the plot consists of stocks from the Application Software sector. This suggests that stocks from this subsector exhibit similarity in their financial metrics. For other subsectors that appear randomly distributed, the t-SNE components may not effectively explain the financial metrics behind these subsectors, indicating lack of similarity in financial metrics for stocks within these subsectors.

Conclusion

In this chapter, we explored the significant role of unsupervised learning in finance, highlighting how it differs from supervised learning by identifying patterns in data without labeled outputs. Unsupervised learning techniques are invaluable in various financial applications, such as market segmentation, portfolio diversification, anomaly detection, risk management, customer retention, trend analysis, and sentiment analysis. For instance, clustering methods enable financial institutions to segment customers, tailor services, and identify potential churn, while dimensionality reduction techniques like PCA help manage risk and optimize portfolios by revealing key factors driving asset returns. We delved into clustering techniques, including k-Means and hierarchical clustering, and discussed methods for evaluating clustering quality, such as the Elbow Method, Silhouette Score, and DBI. Dimensionality reduction through PCA was emphasized for its ability to transform high-dimensional data into manageable components, enhancing model performance and interpretability. We also introduced t-SNE for visualizing high-dimensional data by preserving local structures. Overall, these unsupervised learning techniques enable finance professionals to extract valuable insights from complex data sets, facilitating better decision making and strategic planning.

The topics covered in this chapter lay foundation for advanced reading, in deep learning and reinforcement learning applications in finance.

Exercise

1. Use the data from stock_clustering.csv file and daily percentage changes in close price and volume as the original features. Load the data from the file and perform preprocessing and data cleaning. Restructure the original data so that it is ready for machine learning applications. Ensure each row represents one sample, features are listed as columns, features are standardized and properly scaled, and no missing values are allowed.

2. Describe the dimensions of features and the sample sizes of the data set resulting from the previous question.

3. Perform PCA to reduce the features into just two principal components. Before checking the result, what would the two principal components represent? (Hint: The principal components are linear combinations of features, and the features are daily percentage changes of close price and volume)

4. Repeat question 3 using the t-SNE algorithm. Create two scatter plots of component scores, one based on the PCA scores and one based on the t-SNE scores. What are the differences and their implications?

5. Run a k-Means clustering on the reduced features resulting from PCA and t-SNE, and find the best K based on one of the clustering quality evaluation criteria. Provide an interpretation regarding the meaning of the clusters.

6. Produce two Dendrograms based on the new two-dimensional features resulting from PCA and t-SNE, respectively. Describe the difference and the possible cause.

Appendix

How to Install External Python Packages/Libraries

In Python programming, working within a Python environment is a foundational concept. An environment is essentially a self-contained directory that contains a specific version of Python along with a set of installed packages. This allows you to manage different projects independently, ensuring that changes in one environment do not affect another.

What Is a Python Environment?

A Python environment is a workspace that includes the Python interpreter and a collection of installed packages. These environments allow you to manage dependencies for various projects, ensuring that each project has access to the correct versions of packages it needs to function correctly. For instance, you might be working on one project that requires pandas version 1.3.0 and another that needs version 1.2.3. By using different environments, you can isolate these dependencies, avoiding conflicts and ensuring stability in your projects. Note: See Chapter 1 for a demonstration of how to create and manage a Python environment through Anaconda.

Where Are Packages Saved After Installation?

When you install a package, it is saved in a specific directory associated with your Python environment. The location of this directory depends on whether you are using a global environment (system-wide) or a virtual environment (project-specific).

- **Global environment**: If you install a package globally, it is stored in the Python installation directory, typically under site-packages. This installation affects all Python projects using the same interpreter.

- **Virtual environment**: If you use a virtual environment, packages are stored within the environment's directory, typically under env_name/lib/pythonX.Y/site-packages (where X.Y is your Python version). This keeps the installation isolated to that environment.

Different Ways to Install Packages

There are several ways to install Python packages depending on your workflow and the tools you are using. Below, we'll explore installation via command-line, Anaconda, and Jupyter Notebook.

Installing Packages via Command-Line

The command-line interface is the most common method for installing Python packages, especially when using pip, Python's default package manager. Note: See Chapter 2.3.2 to learn how to open a command-line.

To install a package globally or in an active virtual environment, you use the following command:

```
pip install package_name
```

for example, to install the package numpy:

```
pip install package_name
```

You can also specify versions, upgrade packages, or uninstall them using additional pip commands:

- pip install pandas==1.3.0 # Install a specific version
- pip install --upgrade pandas # Upgrade to the latest version
- pip uninstall pandas # Uninstall a package

Installing Packages With Anaconda

You can use Anaconda's conda to install packages. Conda is a package, dependency, and environment management tool that handles packages for multiple languages and external dependencies, making it more versatile but sometimes heavier than pip. Note that conda may upgrade or downgrade your existing packages to manage dependencies and avoid conflicts. The command is similar to pip:

conda install package_name

Installing Packages in Jupyter Notebook

If you're working within a Jupyter Notebook, you can install packages directly from a notebook cell. This is convenient for quick installations without leaving the notebook environment.

There are two main ways to install packages in a Jupyter Notebook:

- **Using ! operator**: This runs a shell command from within a notebook code cell, for example.
  !pip install package_name
- **Using % operator**: This will ensure the installation is applied to the current Python environment, for example.
  %pip install package_name

External Python Libraries/Packages Used in This book

arch

Official web: https://arch.readthedocs.io/.
The arch package is used for modeling and forecasting volatility, particularly in financial time series data, such as GARCH models. It is commonly used in econometrics and finance for risk management and analysis.

Imblearn

Official web: https://imbalanced-learn.org/.
imblearn is designed to handle imbalanced data sets, which is a common issue in classification problems. Imbalanced data sets occur when one class has significantly more samples than the others, leading to biased machine learning models.

matplotlib

Official web: https://matplotlib.org/.
matplotlib is a versatile plotting library in Python, allowing you to create static, animated, and interactive visualizations. It is the backbone for many other visualization libraries and is widely used for generating plots, histograms, scatter plots, and more.

mplfinance

Official web: https://github.com/matplotlib/mplfinance.
The mplfinance package is designed specifically for plotting financial data, such as candlestick charts and moving averages, built on top of matplotlib. It simplifies the process of visualizing financial time series data.

numpy

Official web: https://numpy.org/.
numpy is a fundamental package for numerical computing in Python, providing support for arrays, matrices, and a large collection of mathematical functions. It is essential for performing efficient operations on large data sets.

numpy_financial

Official web: https://pypi.org/project/numpy-financial/.
numpy_financial is an extension of NumPy, providing functions for financial calculations, such as computing net present value, internal rate

of return, and payment schedules. It is particularly useful for finance professionals and students working on time value of money problems.

pandas

Official web: https://pandas.pydata.org/.
pandas is a powerful data manipulation and analysis library that provides data structures like DataFrames for handling structured data. It is widely used in data science for tasks such as data cleaning, exploration, and transformation.

plotly

Official web: https://plotly.com/.
plotly is an interactive graphing library that makes it easy to create complex visualizations like interactive plots, dashboards, and graphs that can be embedded in web applications. It supports a wide range of chart types and is highly customizable.

scipy

Official web: https://scipy.org/.
scipy is a library used for scientific and technical computing, building on NumPy to provide advanced functions for optimization, integration, interpolation, eigenvalue problems, and other mathematical tasks. It is essential for scientific research and engineering.

seaborn

Official web: https://seaborn.pydata.org/.
seaborn is a data visualization library based on matplotlib, offering a higher-level interface for drawing attractive and informative statistical graphics. It simplifies the creation of complex plots such as heatmaps, violin plots, and pair plots.

sklearn

Official web: https://scikit-learn.org/.
scikit-learn (often abbreviated as sklearn) is a popular machine learning library that provides simple and efficient tools for data mining and data analysis, including classification, regression, clustering, and dimensionality reduction. It is widely used in both academia and industry.

statsmodels

Official web: www.statsmodels.org/.
statsmodels is a library for statistical modeling and econometrics, providing classes and functions for estimating and testing models like linear regression, time series analysis, and survival analysis. It is a go-to package for performing statistical tests and data exploration in Python.

yfinance

Official web: https://pypi.org/project/yfinance/.
yfinance is a Python package that allows users to download historical market data from Yahoo Finance. It simplifies accessing financial data for stocks, indices, and other assets for analysis and modeling.

References

Aghabozorgi, S., and Y.H. Teh. 2014. "Stock Market Co-Movement Assessment Using a Three-Phase Clustering Method." *Expert Systems With Applications* 41 (4): 1301–14.

Aha, D.W., D. Kibler, and M.K. Albert. 1991. "Instance-Based Learning Algorithms." *Machine learning* 6: 37–66.

Alpaydin, E. 2020. *Introduction to Machine Learning*, 4th ed. MIT Press.

Bessis, J. 2015. *Risk Management in Banking*. Wiley.

Bergstra, J., and Y. Bengio. 2012. "Random Search for Hyper-Parameter Optimization." *Journal of Machine Learning Research* 13: 281–305.

Bengio, Y., A. Courville, and P. Vincent. 2013. "Representation Learning: A Review and New Perspectives." *IEEE Transactions on Pattern Analysis and Machine Intelligence* 35 (8): 1798–1828. https://doi.org/10.1109/TPAMI.2013.50.

Bezdek, J.C., S.K. Chuah, and D. Leep. 1986. "Generalized k-Nearest Neighbor Rules." *Fuzzy Sets and Systems* 18(3): 237–56.

Bhattacharyya, S., S. Jha, P. Tharakunnel, and J. Westland. 2011. "Data Mining for Credit Card Fraud: A Comparative Study." *Decision Support Systems* 50 (3): 602–613.

Bishop, C. M. 2006. *Pattern Recognition and Machine Learning*. Springer.

Bollerslev, T. 1986. "Generalized Autoregressive Conditional Heteroskedasticity." *Journal of Econometrics* 31 (3): 307–327.

Box, G.E.P., G.M. Jenkins, and G.C. Reinsel. 2015. *Time Series Analysis: Forecasting and Control*. Wiley.

Breiman, L. 1996. "Bagging Predictors." *Machine Learning* 24 (2): 123–140.

Breiman, L. 2001. "Random Forests." *Machine Learning* 45 (1): 5–32. https://doi.org/10.1023/A:1010933404324.

Breiman, L., J.H. Friedman, R.A. Olshen, and C.J. Stone. 1986. *Classification and Regression Trees*. Wadsworth and Brooks.

Brownlee, J. 2019. *XGBoost With Python: Gradient Boosted Trees*. Machine Learning Mastery.

Chan, Ernie. 2013. *Algorithmic Trading: Winning Strategies and Their Rationale*. John Wiley & Sons.

Chatfield, C. 2004. *The Analysis of Time Series: An Introduction*. CRC Press.

Chawla, N.V., K.W. Bowyer, L.O. Hall, and W.P. Kegelmeyer. 2002. "SMOTE: Synthetic Minority Over-Sampling Technique." *Journal of Artificial Intelligence Research* 16: 321–357. https://doi.org/10.1613/jair.953.

Chen, H., 2025. *Machine learning and modeling techniques in financial data science*. IGI Global. https://doi.org/10.4018/979-8-3693-8186-1

Chen, T., and C. Guestrin. 2016. "XGBoost: A Scalable Tree Boosting System." *Proceedings of the 22nd ACM SIGKDD International Conference on Knowledge Discovery and Data Mining*: 785–794. https://doi.org/10.1145/2939672.2939785.

Choudhry, M. 2010. *Fixed-Income Securities and Derivatives Handbook: Analysis and Valuation* , 95 vols. John Wiley & Sons.

Conover, W.J. 1999. *Practical Nonparametric Statistics*. John Wiley & Sons.

Cortes, C., and V. Vapnik. 1995. "Support-Vector Networks." *Machine Learning* 20 (3): 273–297. https://doi.org/10.1007/BF00994018.

Cover, T., and P. Hart. 1967. "Nearest Neighbor Pattern Classification." *IEEE Transactions on Information Theory* 13(1): 21–7.

Davis, J., and M. Goadrich. 2006. "The Relationship Between Precision-Recall and ROC Curves." *Proceedings of the 23rd International Conference on Machine Learning (ICML)*: 233–240. https://doi.org/10.1145/1143844.1143874.

Danielsson, J. 2011. *Financial Risk Forecasting: The Theory and Practice of Forecasting Market Risk, Value-at-Risk and Extreme Returns*. Wiley.

Day, M.Y., T.K. Cheng, and J.G. Li. 2018. "AI Robo-Advisor With Big Data Analytics for Financial Services." In *2018 IEEE/ACM International Conference on Advances in Social Networks Analysis and Mining (ASONAM)* , 1027–1031, August. IEEE.

Dong, H., R. Liu, and A.W. Tham. 2024. "Accuracy Comparison Between Five Machine Learning Algorithms for Financial Risk Evaluation." *Journal of Risk and Financial Management* 17 (2): 50. https://doi.org./10.3390/jrfm17020050.

Downey, A. 2015. *Think Python: How to Think Like a Computer Scientist*. O'Reilly Media.

Engle, R.F. 1982. "Autoregressive Conditional Heteroskedasticity With Estimates of the Variance of United Kingdom Inflation." *Econometrica* 50 (4): 987–1007.

Engle, R.F. 2001. "GARCH 101: The Use of ARCH/GARCH Models in Applied Econometrics." *Journal of Economic Perspectives* 15 (4): 157–168.

Fader, P.S., B.G. Hardie, and J. Shang. 2010. "Customer-Base Analysis in a Discrete-Time Noncontractual Setting." *Marketing Science* 29 (6).

Freund, Y., and R.E. Schapire. 1997. "A Decision-Theoretic Generalization of On-Line Learning and an Application to Boosting." *Journal of Computer and System Sciences* 55 (1): 119–139. https://doi.org/10.1006/jcss.1997.1504.

Grus, J. 2019. *Data Science From Scratch: First Principles With Python*. O'Reilly Media.

Greene, W.H. 2018. *Econometric Analysis*, 8th ed. Pearson.

Hair, J.F., W.C. Black, B.J. Babin, and R.E. Anderson. 2009. *Multivariate Data Analysis*, 7th ed. Pearson.

Hamilton, J.D. 1994. *Time Series Analysis*. Princeton University Press.

Hastie, T., R. Tibshirani, and J. Friedman. 2009. *The Elements of Statistical Learning: Data Mining, Inference, and Prediction*, 2nd ed. Springer. https://doi.org/10.1007/978-0-387-84858-7.

He, H., and Y. Ma. 2013. *Imbalanced Learning: Foundations, Algorithms, and Applications*. Wiley.

Hilpisch, Y. 2014. *Python for Finance: Analyze Big Financial Data*. O'Reilly Media.

Hilpisch, Yves. 2020. *Python for Algorithmic Trading: From Idea to Cloud Deployment*. O'Reilly Media.

Hoerl, A.E., and R.W. Kennard. 1970. "Ridge Regression: Biased Estimation for Nonorthogonal Problems." *Technometrics* 12 (1): 55–67. https://doi.org/10.1080/00401706.1970.10488634.

Hollander, M., and D.A. Wolfe. 1999. *Nonparametric Statistical Methods*. Wiley.

Hunter, J.D. 2007. "Matplotlib: A 2D Graphics Environment." *Computing in Science & Engineering* 9 (3): 90–95. https://doi.org/10.1109/MCSE.2007.55.

James, G., D. Witten, T. Hastie, and R. Tibshirani. 2013. *An Introduction to Statistical Learning: With Applications*. R. Springer. https://doi.org/10.1007/978-1-4614-7138-7.

Jansen, S. 2020. *Machine Learning for Algorithmic Trading: Predictive Models to Extract Signals From Market and Alternative Data for Systematic Trading Strategies With Python*. Packt Publishing Ltd.

Japkowicz, N. 2000. "The Class Imbalance Problem: Significance and Strategies." *Proceedings of the International Conference on Artificial Intelligence*.

Lewis, C., and S. Young. 2019. "Fad or Future? Automated Analysis of Financial Text and Its Implications for Corporate Reporting." *Accounting and Business Research* 49 (5): 587–615.

Johansen, S. 1991. "Estimation and Hypothesis Testing of Cointegration Vectors in Gaussian Vector Autoregressive Models." *Econometrica* 59 (6): 1551–1580.

Jolliffe, I.T. 2002. *Principal Component Analysis for Special Types of Data*, 338–72. Springer New York.

Kotsiantis, S.B., D. Kanellopoulos, and P.E. Pintelas. 2006. "Handling Imbalanced Datasets: A Review." *GESTS International Transactions on Computer Science and Engineering* 30 (1): 25–36.

Lutz, M. 2013. *Learning Python: Powerful Object-Oriented Programming*. O'Reilly Media.

MacKinnon, J.G. 1991. "Critical Values for Cointegration Tests." In *Long-run Economic Relationships: Readings in Cointegration*, edited by R.F. Engle and C.W.J. Granger, 267–276. Oxford University Press.

MacQueen, J. 1967. "Some Methods for Classification and Analysis of Multivariate Observations." In *Proceedings of the Fifth Berkeley Symposium on Mathematical Statistics and Probability*, 1 vol, 281–297. University of California Press.

Maniraj, S.P., A. Saini, S. Ahmed, and S. Sarkar. 2019. "Credit Card Fraud Detection Using Machine Learning and Data Science." *International Journal of Engineering Research* 8 (9): 110–115.

Martelli, A., A. Ravenscroft, and S. Holden. 2017. *Python in a Nutshell: A Desktop Quick Reference*. O'Reilly Media, Inc.".

Maddumala, V.R., H. Chaikam, J.S. Velanati, R. Ponnaganti, and B. Enuguri. June 2022. "Customer Segmentation Using Machine Learning in Python." In *2022 7th International Conference on Communication and Electronics Systems (ICCES)*, 1268–1273, IEEE.

Matplotlib Documentation. 2023. https://matplotlib.org/stable/contents.html.

McKinney, W. 2018. *Python for Data Analysis: Data Wrangling With Pandas, NumPy, and IPython*. O'Reilly Media.

McLeay, S., and A. Omar. 2000. "The Sensitivity of Prediction Models to the Non-Normality of Bounded and Unbounded Financial Ratios." *The British Accounting Review* 32 (2): 213–230.

Molnar, C. 2020. *Interpretable Machine Learning: A Guide for Making Black Box Models Explainable*. Leanpub.

Murphy, K.P. 2012. *Machine Learning: A Probabilistic Perspective*. MIT Press.

Murtagh, F., and P. Legendre. 2014. "Ward's Hierarchical Agglomerative Clustering Method: Which Algorithms Implement Ward's Criterion?" *Journal of Classification* 31 (3): 274–295.

Noriega, J.P., L.A. Rivera, and J.A. Herrera. 2023. "Machine Learning for Credit Risk Prediction: A Systematic Literature Review." *Data* 8 (11): 169. https://doi.org/10.3390/data8110169.

Pandas Documentation. 2023. *Pandas Documentation*. https://pandas.pydata.org/docs/.

Plotly. 2023. *Plotly Graphing Library Documentation*. https://plotly.com/python/.

Powell, N., S.Y. Foo, and M. Weatherspoon. 2008. "Supervised and Unsupervised Methods for Stock Trend Forecasting." In *2008 40th Southeastern Symposium on System Theory (SSST)*, 203–205, June. IEEE.

Python Software Foundation. 2023. "Memory Management in Python." https://docs.python.org/3/c-api/memory.html.

Python Software Foundation. n.d. *The Python 3 Method Resolution Order (MRO)*. Accessed December 24, 2024. https://docs.python.org/3/howto/mro.html.

Ramalho, Luciano. 2015. *Fluent Python: Clear, Concise, and Effective Programming*. O'Reilly Media, Inc.

R Core Team. 2021. *R: A Language and Environment for Statistical Computing*. R Foundation for Statistical Computing.

Ridgeway, G. 2006. "Generalized Boosted Models: A Guide to the Gbm Package." *Documentation for the R package gbm*. https://cran.r-project.org/web/packages/gbm/vignettes/gbm.pdf.

Shumway, R.H., and D.S. Stoffer. 2017. *Time Series Analysis and Its Applications: With R Examples*. Springer.

Tibshirani, R. 1996. "Regression Shrinkage and Selection via the Lasso." *Journal of the Royal Statistical Society: Series B (Statistical Methodology)* 58 (1): 267–288.

Tsay, R.S. 2005. *Analysis of Financial Time Series,* 2nd ed. Wiley.

Thomas, L.C. 2000. "A Survey of Credit and Behavioural Scoring: Forecasting Financial Risk of Lending to Consumers." *International Journal of Forecasting* 16 (2): 149–172.

Vapnik, V. N. 1999. An overview of statistical learning theory. *IEEE transactions on neural networks, 10*(5), 988-999.

Van der Maaten, L., and G. Hinton. 2008. "Visualizing Data Using t-SNE." *Journal of Machine Learning Research* 9 (11).

Wang, C., X.P. Tan, S.B. Tor, and C.S. Lim. 2020. "Machine Learning in Additive Manufacturing: State-of-the-Art and Perspectives." *Additive Manufacturing* 36: 101538.

White, H. 1980. "A Heteroskedasticity-Consistent Covariance Matrix Estimator and a Direct Test for Heteroskedasticity." *Econometrica* 48(4): 817–38. https://doi.org/10.2307/1912934.

Yves, H. 2019. *Python for Finance: Mastering Data-Driven Finance*. O'Reilly Publishing.

About the Author

Haojun Chen holds a doctorate in business administration from the University of Manchester Alliance Business School and an MSc in statistics from Colorado State University. His publications include research articles in reputable financial journals and multiple textbooks on financial data science. Dr. Chen has also served as a reviewer and book editor for top-tier international academic journals and publishers. With extensive experience in hedge funds and the securities industries, Dr. Chen is currently an associate professor of finance at Guangzhou Huali College International School.

Index

www.ingramcontent.com/pod-product-compliance
Lightning Source LLC
Chambersburg PA
CBHW061144220326
41599CB00025B/4347